STATES AND FIRMS

States and Firms is a study in the political economy of the multinational enterprise. It looks at the internationalisation in the 1980s of the twelve leading French- and German-owned multinational enterprises in chemicals and electronics, which form part of a 'European Challenge' in international competition in technology-intensive sectors.

The book examines how and why the internationalisation of these MNEs has interacted with their 'embeddedness' in the domestic structures of their home countries, France and Germany, particularly in terms of their power relationships with home governments and financial institutions. The primary themes are the MNEs' roles as political actors; domestic government policy *vis-à-vis* the MNEs; MNE financial relations with banks in France and Germany; MNE political activity at the level of the European Community, especially evident in technology policy.

Research in political economy has tended to overlook the role of the firm just as managerial approaches have tended to exogenise the political economy environment enveloping MNEs. The primary contribution of this book is an inclusion of a firm-level approach to put the spotlight on fundamental questions of political economy and international business.

Dr Razeen Sally is a lecturer in International Political Economy at the London School of Economics.

ROUTLEDGE STUDIES IN INTERNATIONAL BUSINESS AND THE WORLD ECONOMY

H14
F

STATES AND FIRMS

Multinational enterprises in institutional competition

Razeen Sally

London and New York

First published 1995
by Routledge
11 New Fetter Lane, London EC4P 4EE

Simultaneously published in the USA and Canada
by Routledge
29 West 35th Street, New York, NY 10001

Typeset in Palatino by
Ponting–Green Publishing Services, Chesham, Bucks
Printed and bound in Great Britain by
TJ Press (Padstow) Ltd., Padstow, Cornwall

British Library Cataloguing in Publication Data
A catalogue record for this book is available from
the British Library

Library of Congress Cataloguing in Publication Data
A catalogue record for this book is available from the Library
of Congress

ISBN 0–415–10379–7
ISSN 1349–7906

To my parents

CONTENTS

FIGURES

TABLES

ACKNOWLEDGEMENTS

This book is a revision of my PhD thesis, completed at the London School of Economics in 1992. In common with a number of students of international political economy at the London School of Economics, my interest in the subject was sparked and nurtured by Susan Strange. For her encouragement and guidance throughout the years of PhD research, I owe Professor Strange a great debt of gratitude.

The study has made liberal use of quotes from interviews carried out on field research in France and Germany during 1989 and 1990. My thanks go to all the interviewees who gave so freely of their time to respond at length to my long list of questions. Research in France and Germany was also facilitated by the aid of a number of others. I should particularly like to thank the following: M. Michel R. Drancourt, the Délégué Général of the Institut de l'Entreprise in Paris, for using his good offices to enable me to conduct interviews with civil servants and corporate executives in the French electronics industry; Professor Jean-Claude Casanova of the Institut d'Etudes Politiques, Paris; Tobias Piller of the *Frankfurter Allgemeine Zeitung*; Professor Dr Josef Esser, who arranged for me to be a Visiting Researcher at the Johann Wolfgang Goethe-Universität, Frankfurt am Main, in 1989–90; and Professor Dr Lothar Hack, of Osnabruck University, for numerous and highly fruitful discussions on German companies and technology-related matters.

I should like to express my thanks to my supervisors at the LSE, Professor Gordon Smith and Dr Howard Machin. My special thanks go to my co-supervisor (now colleague), Dr Michael Hodges of the International Relations Department at the LSE, for giving so much of his time to carefully reading and re-reading the thesis. For his advice and criticism I am truly appreciative. Finally, I am grateful to my PhD examiners, Professors John Stopford of the London Business School and William E. Paterson of Birmingham University, for their wide-ranging comments on the end product.

Any sins of omission and commission in the research and writing of this thesis are, of course, mine alone.

1

INTRODUCTION: POLITICAL ECONOMY AND THE MULTINATIONAL ENTERPRISE

This study has as its primary actor the multinational enterprise (MNE), which can be defined as an economic unit that operates across national boundaries, producing in at least one other foreign country as well as in its home market. International production, the value-adding activity (research, development, design, engineering, manufacturing, distribution, sales) owned, controlled and organised by a firm outside its national boundaries, is thus the essence of multinationality.[1] The MNE can be studied from many different angles and perspectives, each with roots in one or a number of academic disciplines in the social sciences. Chief among them are international economics, management organisation, economic and business history, law and, last but not least, political science. The approach utilised here has its roots in the field of institutional political economy, much influenced by the concepts and tools of political science, and it is with such distinctive political economy lenses that the multinational enterprise is constantly viewed.

Political economy is intrinsically interdisciplinary, in so far as it represents a fusion of political science and economics. According to Robert Gilpin it is 'the reciprocal and dynamic interaction between the realm of wealth and the realm of power'. Both Gilpin and Susan Strange see it as the interaction of the 'state' and the 'market'. In Charles Lindblom's influential work *Politics and Markets*, it is the interplay between 'authority' and 'market'.[2]

At all events such political economy scholarship has continually focused on the role of government, that is, the 'state', in both domestic nation-state and international economic affairs. For analysts in the burgeoning field of international political economy, 'what governments do' is studied in terms of their roles in the

1

international economic arena, that is, using the international system as the level of analysis. For political economists more concerned with the role of government within the nation-state, the focus is on the 'state's' activity in the domestic economy. In the many corporatist, neo-corporatist and institutional writings within political economy the government's relationships and linkages with other national aggregate units, such as industrial associations, trades unions and economic sectors (for example, steel, cars, electronics, chemicals), are analysed.

What all these approaches share in common is at worst a disregard, and at best a glaring underemphasis, of the *individual* firm; and in the context of international competition and global markets, of the MNE. Modern neoclassical economics also suffers from an analytic weakness with regard to firms: they are treated as atomistic actors judged on the basis of efficiency gains, without taking sufficient account of their institutional and policy settings which subsume, for example, bargaining relationships with governments over the *distribution*, as well as the generation, of wealth *and power* – the latter variable being largely disregarded in contemporary economic analysis.[3] As Cawson *et al.* put it: 'Firms are themselves systems of power, with constituent groups, challenging each other's power, that to an important extent firms are involved in intermediating between society and state.' Firms as social institutions are involved in power relationships in the domestic nation-state as well as in the international political economy; they shape the market in addition to being shaped by it.[4]

It is of course the function of management organisation studies, subsuming the 'business school' literature, to concentrate on the firm, but the imperative of intra-organisational analysis downgrades the need to observe the firm in its outer political economic environment, notably its power relationships with governments and other actors.

This study thus starts from the premise that it is of vital importance to study the firm as a political economic actor in the external environments in which it finds itself and in which it is *embedded*[5] in a series of power relationships. Given that the frame of reference is of market and firm-level internationalisation, it is the MNE that assumes pride of place for the purposes of analysis. The global strategies of individual MNEs play an ever more crucial role in economic development, in shaping the world economy and in significantly influencing the direction, content and outcome of public policy choices.[6] By constructing an inter-disciplinary theoretical framework and subsequently conducting an empirical investigation into a selection of MNEs as political economic actors, one primary objective is at all times present: to contribute to the accumulation and enhancement of knowledge in 'micro' political economy in a key and timely area of research, at the level of the firm, in which the 'state of the art' is weak and insufficient.

THE EMPIRICAL FOCUS

The literature on institutional political economy in advanced industrial states focuses on the structural make-up and inter-connections on economic policy issues within national political economies, and especially the linkages between the domains of the 'state', 'industry' and 'finance'. A number of these studies specifically view national political economies in terms of their insertion in the international economy. The distinctive contribu-tion of this study is the investigation of the process of economic internationalisation and its relation to the modern evolution of political economic structures and linkages in two advanced indus-trial states in Western Europe, France and Germany, during the 1980s. These countries have the two largest Gross National Products in Europe and are the third and fourth largest economies in the 'First World' OECD (Organisation of Economic Cooperation and Development) BLOC of advanced industrial states.

The MNE lies at the heart of an interaction between the process of internationalisation – the expansion of cross-border production activities for global market coverage – and the structure and workings of national political economies. It is the MNE which engages in foreign direct investment (FDI), which grew four times as fast as international trade between 1983 and 1988 at a rate of 20 per cent growth annually; and has outpaced the growth in world output in this period. The worldwide stock of FDI has tripled during the 1980s to approximately $1500 billion, more than 80 per cent of capital flows being within the US–EC–Japan 'Triad'. The five leading FDI source countries, the US, UK, Japan, Germany and France, account for 75 per cent of FDI, and over 90 per cent of technology agreements are made between firms with Triad home bases. MNEs' share of world production and trade is far greater than that suggested even by their significant equity bases and shares of capital transfers. MNEs control over a quarter of the world's economic activity outside their home countries. Over a half of international trade in manufactured goods, and a greater share of the growing trade in services, takes place intrafirm, that is, between different national subsidiaries of the same MNEs.[7]

On the other hand the MNE itself is deeply embedded in its country of origin, where it retains its headquarters as well as the core of its research, development, design, engineering, manufacturing, sales and distribution activities. It is in its home market that the MNE, as an institution in its own right, is linked in a myriad of historically conditioned power relationships with external actors such as local, regional and national governments, financial institutions, trades unions, small and medium-sized firms, and industrial associations. Once an MNE expands its production networks abroad, it puts down roots in foreign markets and begins to build up a series of similar linkages in those host markets, with suppliers, customers, governments, and labour and financial institutions. But it is in the home market that the MNE has its history – its initial inception, expansion and consolidation – before beginning to cross over its national boundaries. It is there that the MNE is most strongly anchored, both in its commercial coverage of the market and in its relations with other actors. And only on the strength of its position in the home market does the MNE expand abroad in the first place. Indeed the argument in chapter 2 will show that, corresponding with their internationalisation, French and German MNEs are still crucially dependent on their home bases in France and Germany, in so far as these remain quite the most important markets in their cross-border networks of production and sales. Whether it concerns governments, banks or trades unions, the relations MNEs have with external actors are strongest in their home markets. Most political science-based studies of the MNE concentrate on MNE activity and government policy in host countries, but from an institutional perspective the home base is more important in highlighting the *national* characteristics and differences in the conditioning of the firm within its operating environment, as well as the role of the multinational firm in influencing its most proximate public policy setting.

Hence this interaction, between the internationalisation of the MNE on the one hand, and its embeddedness in its home political economy with its government–finance–industry linkages on the other, forms the central connecting thread of this study. For internationalisation does provide a variable of change that impacts on the MNE's pre-existing and historically evolving relations with external actors at home. Conversely it is also argued in this study that the MNE's long-standing linkages with other actors in their home bases do impact on the manner in which the MNEs themselves internationalise.

The concentration on a carefully chosen selection of individual MNEs in addressing a political economy *problematique* thus places this study at a microscopic level of aggregation, with the intention of drawing qualified, middle-range interpretations in a French–German comparative context.

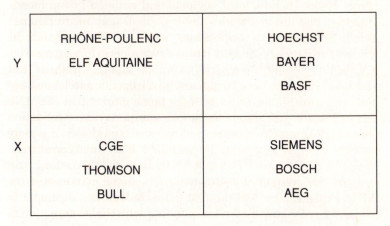

Figure 1.1 Matrix: French and German chemical and electronics MNEs
Note: X = chemical sector; Y = electronics sector.

The empirical focus consists of eleven selected French and German-owned MNEs in the chemical and electronics sectors (see Figure 1.1): their individual strategies and experiences of internationalisation during a specific time-frame, the decade of the 1980s; and their embeddedness in the French and German political economies during that time, particularly configured in terms of their power relationships with external actors such as the home governments and financial institutions. The interaction between internationalisation and the home political economies is reciprocal: MNE internationalisation impacts on the nature of the government–finance–industry relationships in which the MNEs are rooted in the French and German political economies; conversely such MNE embeddedness in French and German domestic structures colours the process of their internationalisation. A key objective throughout is to draw French-German comparisons based on this empirical focus. The particular selection of these firms for analysis has nevertheless to be justified. Four pertinent questions arise.

Why French- and German-owned MNEs?

The MNEs, six of them German (Hoechst, Bayer, BASF, Siemens, Bosch, AEG) and five French (Rhône-Poulenc, Elf Aquitaine, CGE,[8] Thomson, Bull), are headquartered in the third and fourth largest economies in the industrialised world; and furthermore, in national economies that have internationalised their economic structures considerably in recent decades. These MNEs are also leading participants among a number of European-owned MNEs that have internationalised significantly within the last two decades, and have emerged to take their places alongside US and Japanese-owned MNEs as the main commercial actors in international competition. Companies headquartered in the European Community increased their share of total international investment stock to 34 per cent by 1989, roughly equal to that of the US.[9] The *défi americain* (the American Challenge) – the term coined by Jean-Jacques Servan Schreiber to describe the expansion of US MNEs abroad in the 1960s – has been supplemented in subsequent decades not only by a *défi japonais* but also by a *défi européen*.

Furthermore French and German MNEs are belated internationalisers, only expanding and deepening their production networks in quite a major fashion within the last two decades. This stands in contrast, most prominently, to US and British MNEs, who have postwar histories of international presence. Within this context of relatively recent internationalisation, there are distinctive French and German differences: the German MNEs have relied more on exporting, whereas the French ones have been more dependent on home market sales.

In addition the French and German political economies are differently structured, which leads to French–German differences in MNE relations with external actors at home. For example the role of the government and the structure of financial systems differ between the two countries. MNE–government relations are far stronger in France than they are in Germany, whereas MNE–bank relations are much stronger in Germany than they are in France.

Given such French–German differences, internationalisation is a uniting factor among the French and German MNEs which induces certain common effects in MNE relations with external actors in France and Germany, that is, certain common effects in the French and German political economies. Thus the rationale for this French–German comparison: to portray the mix of national similarities and differences on a canvas of continuity and change.

What is distinctive about these MNEs?

These firms are the biggest French and German companies in terms of sales, productive capacity, capital and R&D investment, employment levels and global reach, in their respective sectors of chemicals and electronics, and are among the largest companies in France, Germany and indeed in Europe. The question of how these MNEs became multinational does not loom large, for they are well-established multinationals. Rather it is the extending, deepening and restructuring of pre-existing networks of international production as part of a 1980s internationalisation process that is relevant.

Hence the selection of these companies in order to make up a manageably small sample of individual MNEs. Other French and German MNEs, including some in the chemical and electronics sectors, are excluded because they are smaller and less internationalised. In France the 'second rung' of indigenous chemical and electronics firms are very much smaller than the five French firms chosen here, and have very little international exposure. In Germany there is a backbone of reasonably large companies in these sectors who also have significant international presence (for example, Böhringer-Ingelheim, Merck, Degussa, Hüls and Schering in chemicals, and Mannesmann in electronics). But their size and global reach is still far behind that of the six German companies chosen.

Why chemical and electronics MNEs?

These MNEs are active on a worldwide scale in the chemical and electronics sectors. These sectors account for a large chunk of world output and are deeply integrated in the tissue of the international manufacturing economy: they not only supply end-products to consumers but also provide a whole range of components and intermediate products to other manufacturing sectors as well as to the service economy. Many areas within these sectors in which the selected firms are heavily involved are characterised by technology-intensiveness, increasingly utilising the late twentieth-century core technologies of biotechnology, microelectronics and advanced materials, together with the internationalisation of production to cater for global markets. Therefore broad swathes of these sectors are at the forefront of internationalisation. A later section in this chapter discusses the distinctive technology-intensive-cum-internationalising characteristics of these two sectors.

Why internationalisation during the 1980s?

This study is intended to contribute to scholarship on contemporary issues in micropolitical economy. Hence the importance of tracking the most recent period of internationalisation – which also happens to be the period of greatest international expansion for the MNEs concerned – and relating that to the modern evolution of French and German domestic structures. Nevertheless, it is felt that a certain distance in time is required to aid the analytical process, one step removed from the hurly-burly of the here-and-now in the mid-1990s. A critical and cool perspective on events in the recent past would not, arguably, be aided by taking the narrative up to the present. The period covered is both short enough and recent enough for contemporary relevance; and yet it is sufficiently 'in the past' to allow for marginally greater reflection and consideration without falling into the trap of providing hasty and over-speculative interpretations of current events. It is hoped that the argument developed will have currency for general debates in political economy and international business studies in the 1990s, and serve the additional objective of being a statement on the political economy of the MNE during the chosen period of the 1980s.

These then are the four criteria used to select this particular mixture of firms for analysis during the aforementioned time-scale. The internationalisation of the MNEs is used to put the spotlight on three fundamental aspects of the French and German political economies: the MNEs' roles as political actors in France and Germany, especially pertaining to their relations with the French and German central governments; home government policy *vis-à-vis* these MNEs; and MNE relations with the financial sector in the home political economies. The political economic roles of the MNEs are further analysed in two related arenas that are not limited to the territorial boundaries of France and Germany: at the regional level of European Community policy-making in an integrating market that represents the single most important zone of geographical expansion for these MNEs; and at the functional level of technology policy and firm-level research and development in the core technologies of biotechnology and microelectronics, much of this activity focused on the EC market with relevant policy action increasingly conducted at EC level.

Such an empirical focus used to address the above themes is highly relevant in two respects: it singles out particular firms for examination, the Achilles' heel of the extant political economy literature, which does not 'unpack' the black box of the multi-national firm in globalising markets; and it puts the spotlight on the firm in its outer nation-state political economic environments, the Achilles' heel of the extant literature in the field of business organisation.

Thus this study seeks to gain the attention of two different audiences on the common ground of the multinational firm: the political science/political economy community and the business school community. The requirement for and inevitability of specialisation in the social sciences is by no means contested here. But true interdisciplinary enquiry is exigent precisely because 'gaps' need to be filled in, and 'hidden agendas' revealed, in necessarily correcting the sins of commission and omission that follow in the wake of disciplinary specialisation and exclusivity.

Having presented the empirical focus it is now necessary to clarify and expand on two crucial facets of the study: inter-nationalisation and (French and German) domestic structures.

INTERNATIONALISATION

The cross-border expansion of production networks among MNEs is one of the major features of the increasing interdependence of the international economy. Modern economic theorising on MNEs can be traced back to Stephen Hymer's path-breaking PhD thesis that extended the theory of industrial organisation to the international market place. It attaches certain conditions which must be fulfilled if a firm is to engage in foreign investment. First, it must have specific advantages over other firms both at home and abroad. Second, these advantages must be transferable abroad such that the expected gains outweigh the expected costs. And third, the resulting profits should be more 'profitable' than alternative forms of investment. Then follow three related economic explanations of international production that have been encapsulated and advanced by economists such as John Dunning and Richard Caves.[10]

The ability and incentive to engage in foreign investment is derived from a firm's market power position in imperfect markets at home and abroad. Under such conditions of monopolistic competition, the firm erects 'barriers to entry' which prevent other firms entering into competition. One great market power advantage lies in the exploitation of economies of scale: concentrated, integrated and large-scale production can reduce unit costs which release funds for required and increasing capital and R&D investment. Another advantage lies in the exploitation of economies of scope: a global perspective, for example in applying a technological innovation across a number of product areas, allows the firm to spot opportunities faster than others or to build networks of supply that combine the strengths of various locations.

The second explanation, extended from the market failure literature first propounded by Ronald Coase and developed later by Oliver Williamson,[11] lies in the ability of the firm to create an 'internal' market across borders to protect against or exploit market failure – 'minimising transaction costs' in the economic vernacular. Creating an internal market, by expanding abroad through internal growth or acquisition for instance, allows the firm to control its cross-border transactions and potentially operate more profitably and with greater stability than it would do if it had to rely on transactions in the external market (for example, through trade or licensing). Replacing external markets as transactional modes by internalising them is considered especially important when the firm wants to have control of technology transferred between the parent and its subsidiaries.

The final major explanation concerns the locational advantages of foreign markets for value-adding activity, combining local factor inputs with the other advantages the firm has at its disposal.

Such economic explanations set a framework which provides a

way in to the more detailed managerial explanations of internationalisation, opening up the 'black box' of the firm and
pointing to organisational factors that are difficult to capture
solely by means of economic analysis – most importantly, the fact
that global competition takes place between different systems of
cross-border management that vary not only between firms but
also quite frequently within different parts of the same firm. Each
firm has its own unique evolution behind it that inevitably
separates it from other firms. The structure and dynamics of the
management of sectors and sub-sectors vary, within and between
firms. It is these intra- and interfirm organisational variables that
help, alongside economic analysis, to pinpoint the main motives
of internationalisation: to take advantage of technological ad-
vances in and reduced costs of communications and transporta-
tion; to overcome trade barriers; to serve local markets; to gain
access to raw materials; to access relative cost advantages; to
engage in risk-hedging, particularly with regard to exchange rate
fluctuations; to strengthen existing businesses by integrating
foreign investments with established operations; to adapt to
structural changes in the industry worldwide; and to diversify
into new businesses. Most recently deregulation in areas such as
telecommunications and financial services has encouraged companies to enter foreign markets that were previously closed to
them. An increasingly important motivation among firms is to
establish integrated local presence and sound 'corporate citizenship' credentials in their core foreign markets: such 'global local-
isation', by for example building up solid links with local suppliers and customers, helps gain access to otherwise inaccessible
markets, especially in the public sector (for example, local public
procurement and R&D subsidies).[12]

Such motivations are set against the backdrop of a shift in the
agenda of international competition in many industries and
among a number of firms: the old agenda of serving domestic and
foreign markets separately is moving to one in which competitive
advantage is derived from managing a global unit, forging links
between established units worldwide. According to Michael
Porter, a global industry is one 'in which a firm's competitive
position in one country is significantly affected by its position in
other countries or vice versa'.[13] Firms in these industries hold
dominant market shares by dint of their global reach, although
that does not mean that everything they do is global.

11

For the French and German MNEs analysed here the primary focus of internationalisation is the European Community. The Common Market in the Community, with its removal of internal tariff barriers to trade and the establishment of the unified customs union with respect to non-EC countries, has since its inception been a powerful 'push' factor for the 'outward-boundness' of French and German firms: it has encouraged them to serve the markets of other EC members, first through exports and subsequently through foreign investment as well. The accelerated progress of the EC in moving towards the integration of the Internal Market, especially in the second half of the 1980s, has provided another spur to the 'Europeanisation' of French and German firms.

This second *rélance* (relaunching) of the EC coincided with the incorporation of the Single European Act (SEA) as an amendment to the EC's constitutional document, the Treaty of Rome. The objective embodied in the SEA, as expressed in the detailed proposals of the *White Paper on the Completion of the Internal Market*, was to complete the economic integration of the EC by the end of 1992 through the progressive removal of barriers to the free flow of goods, services, people and capital in the Community. '1992' is in essence a combination of market-led and policy-led forces: market-led in the sense that the internationalisation of business pressures regional integration in the EC; policy-led in so far as market impediments to integration have brought on a mixture of national-level deregulation, the harmonisation of national regulatory regimes, as well as reregulation at the 'supranational' EC level.[14]

The renewed attention and strategy reorientation devoted by corporate planners in MNEs to the EC market has three main aspects to it: entry and/or expansion in other EC member markets in sectors that were previously highly protected (for example, public procurement, telecommunications equipment); the rationalisation of production and sales strategies among existing networks throughout the EC in order to cater for a more integrated pan-EC market; and the use of the large EC 'home market' as a springboard for competition on the global stage.

Technology and the chemical and electronics sectors

The developments highlighted above mean that in a number of industries companies have to compete across the globe, whereas previously competition was more restricted to the national or continental level. A driving force of such internationalisation has been a 'technological imperative' occurring especially in the core, cutting-edge clusters of microelectronics, biotechnology and advanced materials, which have applications across a broad range of sectors. Such technologically driven industries include pharmaceuticals, much of the chemical sector, a good part of electronics, as well as aerospace and automobiles.

Technological innovation and application – basic and applied research, product development, design and engineering, the incorporation of product and process technology into the manufacturing process and its diffusion down the value chain through to the commercialisation of products – is a dynamo of change. The MNEs studied here, in large swathes of their business areas, are 'science-based' inasmuch as they are dependent on the innovation and diffusion of technology. They have to cope with escalating R&D costs, shortening lead times and product life-cycles, and the mastery of different technologies at the same time. Hence the necessity to spend vast sums continually on R&D; in areas such as pharmaceuticals and microelectronics R&D can account for 20 per cent and above of total sales. That in itself is a formidable barrier to entry for smaller firms, unable to enter or stay in the competitive race due to these unaffordable upstream costs. And increasingly firms can only amortise such massive investments through growing worldwide sales, national or regional markets being simply too small as revenue bases to recoup costs. These market-imperfection phenomena mean that internationalisation in some parts of technologically driven industries goes hand in hand with dominant global market shares becoming concentrated in a few relatively large MNEs.[15]

The link between technology-intensiveness and internationalisation is very evident in the chemical and electronics sectors, which are most directly affected by and dependent on the revolutionary innovations in microelectronics and biotechnology.

The chemical industry, with world sales in 1989 of $1000 billion, is one of the most interlocked and integrated in the world economy, providing inputs to sectors such as electronics and engineering. The sector spans petrochemicals, plastics, bulk inorganic chemicals, speciality chemicals (paints, agrochemicals, industrial chemicals and engineering materials) and pharmaceuticals. Scale economies are required for petrochemical and bulk chemical production. Surplus capacity and sensitivity to economic cycles in these products, signified by wide price fluctuations in the 1970s and early 1980s, provoked the major chemical MNEs to concentrate more on the higher value-added and differentiated markets in speciality chemicals and pharmaceuticals, which are more resistant to price swings and variable economic conditions. They are, however, more research-intensive and require global scale and scope to depreciate necessary investments. Hence the incidence in the international chemical industry of a small number of MNEs headquartered for the most part in the US and Western Europe.

The industry leaders have historically had international presence, but largely limited to regional spheres of influence: the British ICI in the Commonwealth, the American Du Pont in North America, and the German IG Farben cartel on the European continent. In the postwar period competition between these players has increased worldwide as they have extended their global reach. Much of the increase of international trade in chemicals is due to intrafirm trade between subsidiaries of the same parent company and between subsidiaries and the parent company.

Biotechnology is the application of scientific and engineering principles to the processing of materials by biological agents to provide goods and services; particularly the so-called third generation of biotechnology embodied in genetic engineering has most relevance to the life-science-based pharmaceutical industry. Biotechnological applications are also important in speciality areas such as agrochemicals. It is in this core technology that chemical MNEs are most research-intensive.[16]

The electronics industry, with sales of $814 billion worldwide in 1989, is among the fastest growing in the world economy with a real annual rate of growth of 6 per cent. This represents twice the rate of growth of the world economy.[17] Like chemicals, it is dominated by relatively few MNEs based in the US, the EC and Japan. The sector comprises the areas of telecommunications equipment, computers and office equipment, consumer electronics, professional and defence electronics, industrial automation, optical and medical instruments, passive components and semiconductors. Technological innovation is key in each of these areas, catalysed in the modern era by the digitalisation process in microelectronics. The semiconductor chip is the central building-block of the industry, forming direct and strategic inputs for all other electronics products. A large number of components are integrated on to a single chip; the sixth generation Very Large Scale Integration (VLSI) chip has more than 100,000 components on it and requires massive R&D expenditures (more than 25 per cent of sales in the 1980s). The cost of developing and tooling up to make Dynamic Random Access Memories (DRAMs), the most widely used chips, is over \$2 bn and doubles with each new product generation. Hence the concentration of the semiconductor industry in a few firms able to afford these costs.

Telecommunications equipment provides another example of market concentration as a result of brutal economic forces at work. Twenty years ago an electrical switching system cost 15–20 million ECU to develop and lasted 20–30 years. A digital switching system now costs upwards of 1 bn ECU with a life-cycle of no more than ten years, and then only with the continuous updating of software. Manufacturers need 8 per cent of world market share each to break even, but the largest national market within the EC represents less than 6 per cent, and the EC market as a whole only a quarter, of the world market. The EC can thus support two or three manufacturers in the future compared to the eight existing in the 1980s. Technological imperatives, growth in demand and the opening up of previously segmented national markets in broad tracts of the electronics sector have forced the pace of internationalisation and concentration through waves of restructuring, mergers and alliances.[18]

DOMESTIC STRUCTURES

The internationalisation process which envelops the French and German MNEs is one facet of this study; their implantation in the 'domestic structures' of the French and German political economies is the other. The MNEs themselves are institutional structures which have evolved over a long period of time. In their home bases in France and Germany they have relationships with other institutions, both governmental and non-governmental. As the political economist Peter Hall points out, these institutions are structural inasmuch as they set the parameters for the day-to-day processes that go on within them. Individuals and groups have their range of 'decisional manoeuvre' constrained by these institutions, which themselves shape their outer operating environments just as much as they are shaped by the latter. Between

15

historical 'turning points' institutions display a dynamic consisting of a blend of continuity and incremental change. The dynamic of internationalisation is one such inducing element of change, existing hand in glove with recognisable and distinctive patterns of policy-making.[19]

The MNE does not exist in isolation. There are issues that affect it, quite apart from direct and indirect commercial relations within the firm, and between it and its external suppliers and customers, that provoke relations with external actors. Given that MNEs appeared and evolved first in their home market one can expect their implantation to be strongest, and their relations with external actors to be most developed, in these home markets of France and Germany; and therefore to be less strong with external actors in the 'newer' host country markets in which they operate. One of the most important of the relevant external actors with which MNEs have relations is the home government, whose economic, industrial and social policies affect the MNEs on a variety of issues – expansion, retrenchment, location, products, technology, health and safety, environmental protection, and so on.

Relations between actors are purposeful in so far as they are geared to specific short-, medium- and long-term objectives which are linked to the self-interests of the key players. In seeking to influence eventual outcomes, actors interact. It is the evolving distribution and control of power, and the nature of bargaining agendas over time in these relations between the MNEs and external actors, that is of central concern from a political economy perspective. As will be argued in the subsequent empirical chapters, these relations are based on mutual dependence, but such interdependence is often asymmetrical as bargaining power is frequently distributed unevenly between actors endowed with differing resources and capacities.

The interactions between the MNEs and external actors are not uniform: they may take place formally or informally, on a bilateral basis (for example, one firm with one government department) or a plurilateral one (for example, a collection of firms grouped in an industry association with many government departments, as well as with trade unions and other groups, on the same issue); interactions may be highly structured and institutionalised, or much more loosely so. In other words there are myriad and varied relations that may criss-cross and overlap with each other.[20]

These relations in which the MNEs are anchored are enveloped

in 'policy networks', which according to Wilks and Wright 'constitute a complex of organisations connected to each other by
resource dependencies and distinguished from other complexes
by breaks in the structure of resource dependencies'. A network
has within it policy processes that function on specific issues or
groups of related issues. Within a policy network are numbers of
tighter and more homogenous 'policy communities' which, according to the same authors, 'encompass all those who own,
manage, finance and work in industrial units, together with those
whose interests are affected by the activities of those units,
customers and clients, for example, and those individuals whose
organisations have a direct interest in, or responsibility for, the
activities of those units and their customers and clients – governments and quasi-governmental organisations at national, supranational and subnational levels'. These communities form dis-
aggregated sub-systems, too discrete to operate at national or
sectoral level, with a reasonably cohesive membership defined by
commonality of products, services, technologies and markets. Put
another way, communities exist to deal with a specific policy
focus. It is a linking process of dependent relations between actors
that group related policy communities in larger and looser policy
networks.[21]

For the vast majority of authors in political economy, policy
communities and networks obtain at national, sectoral and
sub-sectoral levels, having distinctive characteristics that differ
between nations, sectors and sub-sectors. For some authors, the
'strength' or 'weakness' of the government is key in such considerations; for others writing in the corporatist/neo-corporatist
tradition, it is contingent on a continuous bargaining and co-
ordinating process in which the government is invariably involved.

This study, with the MNE as the central focus of analysis, adopts
a different approach. First, the 'strong state/weak state' (that is,
government) distinction is misleading in the French and German
contexts: as will be argued in following chapters the German
government sits uncomfortably in this schema; and the French
government is not nearly as unified and coherent as it has been
portrayed in a number of studies. Second, corporatist applications
can be unhelpful as many of the MNEs and associated non-
governmental actors in the networks and communities examined
in this study enjoy wide autonomy from the government to pursue

their own solutions, which are not the outcome of coordination with the government.[22]

Most importantly, however, it is argued here that MNEs are at the vortex of distinctive policy networks and communities in their home political economies in which they are prominent actors. Disaggregation therefore is taken down to the level of the firm rather than maintained at purely national, sectoral and sub-sectoral levels, as is usual in political economy studies. National, sectoral and sub-sectoral variables are deliberately viewed from the vantage point of the MNE, not *vice versa*. Such MNE-centred networks and communities are distinguishable from others precisely due to the uniqueness of these firms as increasingly important internationalising commercial actors in structures of global competition, quite distinct from other firms and sectors/sub-sectors that do not have such extraterritorial reach. There are public policy foci that concern business activity in general, both domestic and international, for example on questions of infrastructure that have economy-wide effects. But there are issues at the heart of MNE–government negotiations that are distinctive, with MNEs seeking to factor national infrastructures and knowledge bases, heavily influenced by public policy, into global strategies, and governments competing to access the extraterritorial resources and capabilities of MNEs, such as technology transfers and financial flows, for improved national income, skill levels, employment, and so on. These bargaining relations take place on multiple agendas of interaction and are processed through policy channels that differ between nations, sectors and regions.[23]

In interactions with external actors MNEs have distinctive *political* identities, which are not insignificant elements of their overall capacities to improve competitive advantages in international competition. A number of international business studies have investigated the political nature of the MNE in terms of its relations with governments and the leveraging of public policy both to improve market access and opportunities, and to 'close' markets in order to facilitate rent-seeking activity through public subsidies, protection against foreign competitors, erecting entry and mobility barriers against competitors, and so on. MNEs have greater expertise, intelligence on non-market environments, access to political elites, and skills in the exercise of influence and negotiation, compared to smaller national firms without international production networks.[24]

These are prominent features of politics and power in actor relations, but they have to be viewed in an enveloping *institutional* context. The MNE is at the vortex of relationships with a range of external actors, such as banks, industry associations, suppliers and clients, trade unions, research institutes and universities, as well as with different tiers of government. Such linkages define the overall *embeddedness* of the MNE in nations and regions, both sub- and supranational, and there are marked differences manifested in such linkages between nations and regions. MNE–government relations cannot be looked at in isolation, for relations with other actors can have a major bearing on the core of MNE–government interactions.

Finally, the MNE is not viewed as a unified actor. Just as the government has to be 'unpacked' for analysis, so must the MNE. Each MNE's organisation is distinctive and spills over into its external environment, which implies that there are interfirm differences in the action and interaction of MNEs in policy networks and communities. Moreover there are intrafirm differences that hinge on the internal organisation of the firm – its distribution of expertise, competitive positioning, management calibre, horizontal and vertical channels of communication, and so on. Different parts of the same MNE may be involved in different communities within the same policy network, or even in different networks. The degree of discord or agreement of constituent groups of the same MNE in these outer fora depends on the levels of integration and coherence within the MNE.

THE INTERACTION OF INTERNATIONALISATION WITH DOMESTIC STRUCTURES

The MNE has thus far been presented in two contexts: that of internationalisation, and in French and German domestic structures. It is the task of this study to identify and explicate the interaction between the internationalisation of the MNEs and their embeddedness in domestic structures. One important qualification must be made at this stage: the emphasis is more on the impact of internationalisation on the political economy of the MNE within nation-states (France and Germany in this case), and less on the influence of domestic embeddedness on intrafirm organisation and firm-level internationalisation. The latter two aspects would require separate comprehensive studies beyond the manageable scope of this book.

The internationalisation of national firms has worked back to modify the sets of relationships that MNEs have with external actors in their home bases, fashioning new constraints and opportunities for public policy choices and altering the nature of MNE–government relations. The following chapters seek to answer a number of pertinent questions related to this interaction between internationalisation and domestic structures. As a result of controlling international production networks and associated technological capacity, are MNEs in greater positions of power *vis-à-vis* home governments and other external actors in the domestic base? Do they have greater autonomy in keeping government attempts at interference in their corporate affairs at bay? Do they have a greater role in the formulation and implementation of public policy? What is the nature of their public policy action? Is it market-opening or market-closing, or both? Are MNEs asymmetrically concentrated, politically as well as economically, in their home bases and, if so, are they still national, that is, home state, actors rather than global actors? Does the 'nationality' of MNEs really matter in political and economic terms? Can MNE political action be used at different levels of government at the same time on the same policy issues? The last question is particularly relevant in the integration process of the European Community since the mid-1980s. The initiative and development of the plan to complete the Single Market by the end of 1992 has set in train a wave of lobbying and other political action by MNEs at the supranational level in Brussels in, for example, liaising with the European Commission and participating in the work of pan-European industry associations on EC legislation. Corporate activity is especially evident in emerging EC policy communities that deal with collaborative R&D programmes in information technology.

One overarching question that is threaded through the study is this: does internationalisation as a common factor serve to reduce the differences between differently constituted national political economies, or are structural national differences in actor relations (for example between MNEs, governments, banks, unions, and so on) and styles of policy action (the role of the government in the economy, of organised interest groups such as industry associations) seemingly entrenched? The French–German comparison is pertinent and should shed much light on this question. What is at least partially at issue here are national differences in economic institutions and capitalist operation which coexist with the internationalisation of business.[25]

THE IMPACT OF GERMAN REUNIFICATION[26] AND EASTERN EUROPE POST-1989

The period covered by this study is the decade of the 1980s. It was only at the very end of the decade that momentous events began to unfold in Europe – the fall of the Honecker regime in East Germany in October 1989, the opening of the Berlin Wall on 9 November, the series of revolutions that led to the overthrow of Communist governments throughout Eastern Europe. It was only during the course of 1990 that many of these events were consolidated, most notably the forced pace leading to economic, monetary and social union between the two Germanies on 1 July, and political reunification on 3 October. The end of the Cold War era was sealed by the break-up of the Soviet Union into a number of newly independent states.

This study does not take these events – German reunification, and the political and economic opening of the Eastern European countries as well as the ex-Soviet Union – into account, precisely because they largely took place after the period covered here. It is nevertheless worthwhile noting that these changes do not in any serious way affect the analysis and conclusions of this 1980s study.

The first point to make is that German reunification and the opening of Eastern Europe have not fundamentally reorientated the internationalisation strategies of the French and German MNEs studied here. The German MNEs in particular are catering for a bigger German home market and all the MNEs concerned are looking to expand in Eastern Europe. But these are 'second-order' strategies compared to their focus on core markets in Western Europe, North America and South East Asia. A poll of large firms conducted by the *Frankfurter Allgemeine Zeitung* found that there was no significant rethinking of core strategies.[27]

The second point concerns the evolution of the German political economy in light of reunification. Considerable changes are underway, not only in the economic transformation of the new east German states into a market economy fully integrated with that of west Germany, but also in the structure and workings of west Germany's political economy. These mutations, however, are not tantamount to an overhaul. There remains much continuity in the process of change engendered by reunification. Indeed rules, norms, institutions and procedures not only remain intact in the old West Germany; they – the legal and political systems, unions, industry organisations, chambers of commerce, vocational training, workplace organisation, political consensus management, neocorporatist concertation arrangements in the economy, and so on – are being extended to cover east Germany in what amounts to an *Anschluss* (takeover of east Germany by west Germany) as well as a *Wiedervereinigung* (reunification).[28]

THE STRUCTURE OF THE STUDY

The focus of chapter 2 is on the eleven MNEs selected for analysis and their individual strategies and experiences of internationalisation in the 1980s. A general, broad-brush presentation of the companies, with their national and sectoral differences, is accompanied by an attempt to track their methods, location and timing of international production expansion. Chapter 3, in contrast, looks at the very different constitutions of French and German domestic structures in which the MNEs are embedded in networks of relations with external actors such as governments, banks, industry associations and trade unions.

The argument goes on to test the interaction of internationalisation with two central sets of relationships the MNEs have in their home political economies, with government and with banks. Chapter 4 looks first at home (central) government policy orientations on selected issue-areas that are of vital concern to the MNEs and form the bargaining agendas on which MNE–government interaction takes place. The second part of the chapter examines the MNEs' roles as political actors in relations with their home governments. At issue is not only the extent to which national governments take the international dimension of MNE operations on board when making public policy, but also, from the MNEs' perspective, two factors: first, the *autonomy* of the enterprise in defending its range of action from government intervention; and second, the *power* of MNEs in influencing public policy formulation and implementation.

Chapter 5 focuses on the financial function of the MNEs with respect to their financial relations with the home governments and with banks, once again testing power relationships in the wake of internationalisation. Arising from this analysis are arguments which question the validity and explanatory power of certain influential political economy models which, on the one hand, point to the power of the German universal banks in the large German firms, and on the other hand, emphasise both the primacy of the government in the French financial system and the closeness of bank–industry relations in France.

The argument then goes on to deal with the European Community and technology, the subjects of chapter 6. Internationalisation, and particularly EC activity, in the core technologies of biotechnology and microelectronics are picked out for examination. Close attention is devoted to the political roles of MNEs in emerging EC technology policy communities, with an attempt to gauge the extent of corporate influence in public policy at the supranational level. EC information technology policy is a good testing ground to analyse whether and how successfully European-owned MNEs have pursued political strategies of market closure – subsidised promotion in the EC market and protection against foreign competitors.

The Conclusion draws the threads of the argument together by summarising the core of the empirical argument, pointing out implications relevant to the 1990s, and drawing out the theoretical and empirical implications of this approach to the micropolitical economy of the firm for future interdisciplinary research agendas.

The theoretical framework for this study on the political economy of French and German MNEs has now been laid and the empirical focus outlined. This study has also made use of an extensive series of wide-ranging interviews, conducted in various fora in France and Germany between mid-1989 and the end of 1990: in the strategic planning and other departments of each of the MNEs concerned; the chemical and electronics divisions of the Federal Ministry of Economics in Germany and the Ministry of Industry in France; and the respective chemical and electronics industry associations in France and Germany. An assortment of other people with relevant expertise – bankers, journalists, industry analysts – were also interviewed.

One point of qualification is exigent at this stage. The deliberately 'micro' nature of this exposition – the political economy of a handful of firms in two industrial sectors originating from two countries – inevitably results in the exclusion, or at least cursory attention devoted to, other important issues, themes and actors.

There are other French and German MNEs in other sectors, for example in automobiles, food and drinks, banking and insurance, to name a few, who are also at the vortex of interaction between internationalisation and domestic structures. There are foreign-owned MNEs in chemicals and electronics who are significant players in the French and German economies, for instance IBM and Digital Equipment in electronics, Du Pont, Monsanto, ICI and the Swiss majors in chemicals; not to mention a number of Japanese electronics firms who have been increasing their presence in the EC. The focus on French and German-owned MNEs has of necessity excluded these foreign-owned firms from the analysis.

With respect to the embeddedness of the MNEs in domestic structures this book, to reiterate, concentrates on two sets of relationships the firms have, with the home governments and with banks. These linkages are judged as being of most importance for the purposes of this study. Unfortunately this leaves little room to analyse in detail the links between the firms and other actors, notably trade unions and secondary tiers of government (*Land* governments in Germany, regional and departmental councils in France). In both cases there are important 'political economy' trends in the 1980s to be analysed and explicated, with revealing French–German comparisons. Factors concerning firm-level strategy and organisation, and relations with unions and sub-national governments, for example, are brought up and dealt with as background context when necessary in the following chapters. But in trying to shape a clear, microscopic empirical focus, a reasonably robust and heuristic theoretical framework, and a manageably discrete and operational *problematique*, these and other facets of the political economy of the firm, important though they are, are not explored in greater detail here.

As was suggested at the outset, a prime intention is to use this descriptive analysis to show the power and importance of a firm-level approach in political economy scholarship. Whereas the business organisation scholar would focus attention on structures and dynamics within the firm, the political economy searchlight used here is aimed at the behaviour of the MNE in its outer environment, especially in its power relationships with external actors in the home base. As MNEs themselves become more important individual actors in a more interdependent international economy, their administrative capacities – in seeking corporate alliances, negotiating with governments, and so on –

must be taken into account as ever more vital determinants of economic and political outcomes in a changing world order. It is the task of political economists to home in on the skills of managerial technocracies, varying between and within firms, that condition variables of power and outcome in the international political economy. It is the political economy of the firm that is at issue, with the company as the central unit of analysis; and this book aims to make its contribution to this relatively new and much-needed area of research.

2

THE
INTERNATIONALISATION
OF FRENCH AND
GERMAN MNEs

This chapter first examines the internationalisation of French and German economic structures and provides an overview of how this process has accelerated in recent decades. This sets the backdrop to the internationalisation strategies and experiences, during the 1980s, of the eleven selected MNEs in chemicals and electronics. The final section incorporates the evidence gleaned from the above in order to draw some broad generalisations, especially in attempting to distinguish between French and German firm-level experiences, but also in pointing out sectoral and sub-sectoral characteristics.

ECONOMIC STRUCTURE: FRENCH AND GERMAN ECONOMIES AND OUTWARD FOREIGN DIRECT INVESTMENT

This section deals with a brief economic analysis of the internationalisation of the French and German economies, with the chemical and electronics sectors particularly in mind. Although internationalisation of national economies concerns both the entry of foreign-owned MNEs into the local market as well as the expansion of indigenous MNEs abroad, it is to the latter aspect that attention is devoted.

The hallmark of international production is the modality of foreign direct investment (FDI).[1] International production encompasses FDI as well as *de facto*, non-equity control of production through, for example, product licensing and management contracts; but FDI indicators are used here to illustrate the expansion of French and German MNEs abroad.

After the Second World War right up to the beginning of the 1970s, FDI was overwhelmingly dominated by US MNEs. The 1970s and 1980s, however, have witnessed a major change in the composition of world FDI stock. Although the US remains the largest FDI exporter, still accounting for about two-fifths of all OECD flows, its proportion of total stock has declined. At the same time, the proportions for a number of source countries in Western Europe, as well as Japan, have increased and many of them have become major FDI exporters. On the basis of FDI indicators alone, the internationalisation process is no longer purely an American phenomenon, but has also become a European and Japanese one, as Table 2.1 shows.

Table 2.1 Group of Five foreign direct investment

Country	Stock (1988) $ billion	Real growth in flows (1983–8) % p. a.	Total flows (1980–8) $ billion
US	324	20	157
UK	184	16	133
Japan	114	37	96
W. Germany	78	15	52
France	57	32	43

Source: Julius (1990)

Table 2.1 also shows West Germany and France accumulating increasing shares of outward FDI stock, and with the fourth and fifth positions respectively in the international rankings by 1988. By end 1989, outward German FDI had reached a level of DM184 billion stock, up from DM100 billion in 1980; in 1989 alone there was a record outflow of DM20 billion. The French outward flow for 1989 was FFr115.3 billion, up 51.6 per cent on the 1988 figure and nearly six times the 1985 figure of FFr20 billion.[2] Hence the most significant increases of French outward FDI have occurred in the late 1980s.

Figure 2.1 illustrates the importance of the USA and Western Europe as the two major recipients of French and German FDI. FDI in Western Europe was overwhelmingly concentrated in the EC. As Figure 2.2 makes clear, the late 1980s evince a much greater concentration on the EC in French and German FDI flows. In general, there has been a relative de-emphasis of investment by

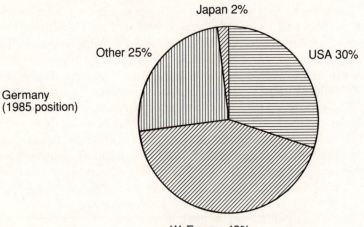

Germany
(1985 position)

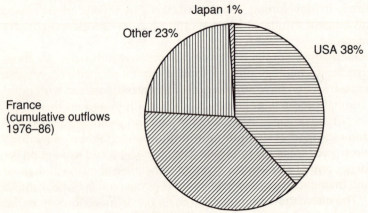

France
(cumulative outflows
1976–86)

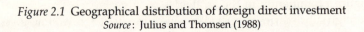

Figure 2.1 Geographical distribution of foreign direct investment
Source: Julius and Thomsen (1988)

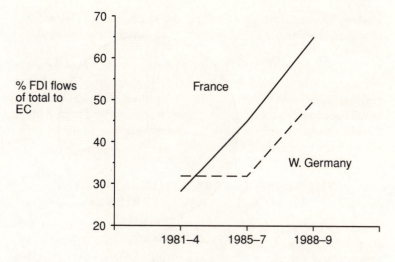

Figure 2.2 Flows of foreign direct investment to the EC as % of total flows
Source: OECD (1990)

firms in developing country markets in favour of increased investment in other high per capita income developed country markets.

Germany's strongest exported-orientated industries are those that are technology and/or human capital-intensive: it is these industries that have supplemented export-orientation with international production, going abroad initially based on their firm-specific advantages, especially in skills and technology, as well as domestic market strength. Chemicals and electrical engineering/ electronics are at the forefront. The chemical sector accounted for 16 per cent of all outward investment by 1990, the largest share of any manufacturing sector; electronics accounted for 7 per cent.[3]

The internationalisation of large French firms follows from the period of industrial concentration of 1965–74 with its ensuing financial and industrial diversification. Before that, FDI did not figure prominently in the strategies of large French firms; what foreign subsidiaries they did have were rarely integrated into their domestic structures and business strategies. These were concentrated in the former North African colonies, from which the share of French FDI drastically fell, from 29 per cent of the total in 1968 to less than 5 per cent in 1980. By the early 1980s, foreign production had become an integral part of the strategies of the

leading French firms. By this time, the chemical and electronics/
electrical engineering companies were among the most internationalised.[4]

In conclusion to this section, the FDI figures show that there has
been some convergence in the internationalisation of French and
German economic structures, including their chemical and electronics sectors. Such expansion has been commonly directed at the
North American and West European markets, and above all at the
increasingly integrated EC market.

THE MNEs: INTERNATIONALISATION STRATEGIES AND EXPERIENCES

This section descends from the national/sectoral level of analysis
in the previous section to that of the individual firm. As was
emphasised in chapter 1, it is firm-specific analysis that is lacking
in the extant political economy literature, which rarely descends
into the black box of the firm from national and sectoral levels of
analyses. In this section it will be abundantly evident that national
and sectoral variables are at play, but they are studied in the
context of the experiences of individual firms. The eleven French
and German chemical and electronics MNEs are examined in turn,
with the focus on their internationalisation in the 1980s.

The German chemical MNEs: Hoechst, Bayer, BASF

On the basis of turnover, these are the three largest chemical
companies in the world and are historically the most extensively
internationalised MNEs in the selection studied here. A long
record of multinational investment this century has been punc-
tured by forced divestment during both World Wars. The IG
Farben cartel was formed between Hoechst, Bayer and BASF in
the interwar years, only to be broken up into its original con-
stituents post-1945. Reconstruction followed in the 1950s together
with the development of an export base. International expansion
of production started gathering pace from the mid to late-1950s.[5]

Hoechst and Bayer are focused more on speciality chemicals
and pharmaceuticals, whereas BASF, the so-called *Rohstoffladen*
(raw materials store), is heavily involved in bulk chemicals and is
integrated upstream into raw materials and energy. The differences between the three should not, however, be exaggerated:

all are represented across the spectrum of chemical activities, from speciality through intermediate to bulk chemicals; and each one has a proven record of using capital intensity and science-based innovation to diffuse specialisation and value-added to the whole range of its portfolios.

All three firms have expanded steadily since the early 1960s in their main regional market, the European Community, through internal growth, acquisitions and joint ventures, many of which have been subsequently fully taken over. By the end of the 1980s, Western Europe accounted for 60–65 per cent of total sales, with the EC alone accounting for 50–60 per cent of total sales. Such strong European implantation positions them well to pursue integrated, rationalised production and sales strategies for a Single Market. Substantial expansion in North America is very much a phenomenon of the 1970s and 1980s, although presence was initially re-established, after Second World War divestment, in the 1950s and 1960s. Bayer was the first to make major acquisitions in the US in the 1970s, the most prominent of them being Miles Laboratories and Cutter Laboratories, speciality companies active in pharmaceuticals and genetic engineering. Hoechst made the biggest industrial acquisition abroad by a German company with its $3 billion agreed takeover of the Celanese Corporation in 1987, integrating it with its much smaller American Hoechst subsidiary. BASF's most notable acquisition was that of the Inmont Corporation in the mid-1980s. North America accounted for 18–23 per cent of total sales for Hoechst, Bayer and BASF by the end of the 1980s. All now have critical mass in the US – they are all among the ten leading chemical firms there – to pursue internally generated growth as opposed to relying on further acquisitions. The three are targeting expansion in Japan and the Far East, where markets are growing faster than anywhere else. Relying on joint ventures and licensing, they are still at the early stages of embedding themselves in new and difficult markets.

For Hoechst and Bayer, 75–80 per cent of sales were abroad; for a less internationally exposed BASF it was about 66 per cent. Each had annual sales in the DM40–45 billion range for 1988. BASF had one-third of total sales accounted for by its overseas production; Bayer was the most internationalised, with 60 per cent of global sales derived from non-German production; Hoechst was in an intermediate position (40 per cent).[6]

The German electronics MNEs: Siemens, Bosch, AEG

Like the above three chemical firms, the electronics MNEs in the sample have a history of multinational presence interrupted by divestment during the World Wars. Reconstruction in the FRG in the 1950s was followed by re-internationalisation from the mid-1950s onwards.[7]

Siemens is the second-largest German company, with 1988 sales of DM60 billion, and is spread throughout the engineering and electronics sectors: nuclear energy, power and mechanical engineering, transport systems, automotive electronics, medical electronics, microelectronics, factory automation, telecommunications and data processing. With its acquisition of Nixdorf in Germany in 1989–90, it has become the second-largest European computer manufacturer behind IBM.[8]

Robert Bosch is half the size of Siemens, with sales of DM28 billion in 1988, and is the world leader in automotive components, of which electronics takes up an ever-increasing proportion. In the 1980s it has diversified significantly into telecommunications, catalysed by its acquisition of AEG's activities in this area. Such a strategy of diversification was judged necessary to cover the company from increasing foreign and domestic competition in its core auto electronics business.[9]

AEG has had much trouble over the last two decades, partly brought about by its domestic and foreign diversifications. Two major attempts at restructuring, subsidiary-shedding and withdrawing from existing joint ventures did not pull the company out of what seemed an intractable crisis – until AEG was taken over by the Daimler Benz concern in 1986. This represented the first major step in Daimler's conversion from an automobile and truck manufacturer into an internationally active technology concern. AEG's sales of DM13 billion in 1988 represented only a fraction of those of Germany's largest concern: Daimler's overall sales were 75 per cent accounted for by its motor vehicle and trucks arm, Mercedes. Despite extensive post-1986 restructuring, AEG continued to make substantial losses and was a drain on Daimler's financial resources. The bulk of the firm's losses were accounted for by its office-equipment and white-goods subsidiaries, for which AEG was seeking joint venture partners and/or buyers.[10]

Internationalisation strategies and experiences are much more differentiated between Siemens, Bosch and AEG compared to the three chemical majors. For Siemens internationalisation has occurred across the range of its product lines but, due to its diversified nature, is highly differentiated within the company: it is more internationally active in its medical electronics business than in its more 'national champion' areas of telecommunications equipment, data processing and nuclear plant construction, in which dependence on the home market is still strong. Bosch has responded to a worldwide trend in automotive components: following its customers, the car companies, abroad as they internationalise, and establishing production presence close to suppliers and customers abroad. Acquiring AEG's foreign telecommunications equipment network, especially in France, provided another spur. In AEG's case, it has decided post-1986 to concentrate its energies on its targeted core areas of microelectronics, transport systems and automation: it came to the conclusion that in these areas it was too dependent on production in the FRG and needed to expand abroad in order to be internationally competitive. This it has begun to do, as a result of its own strategy and with the financial backing of Daimler Benz. The latter acts first and foremost as a portfolio shareholder, designating broad strategic and operational authority to its constituent groups.[11]

All are more dependent on the home market than the chemical Big Three: Siemens and Bosch had only 50 per cent of total sales abroad and AEG even less (40 per cent). Proportions of total sales derived from foreign production were also lower: Siemens 25 per cent, Bosch 18 per cent and AEG 10 per cent.[12]

Presence in the European Community has become strong. Western Europe accounted for 70–80 per cent of total sales by the end of the 1980s. In areas of weakness, however, significant acquisitions have been made recently, notably Siemens's joint acquisition with GEC of the British Plessey group in 1989. Expansion in North America has been particularly evident in the 1980s and has largely been pursued through acquisitions. Siemens has been most prominent, buying Rolm from IBM in telecommunications and Bendix in auto electronics. AEG has acquired three small microelectronics companies since 1987. North America accounted for 10–15 per cent of total sales, a figure noticeably below that for the German chemical majors. All three firms are weak in Japan and the Far East, although Bosch has strong local name recognition in Japan where its products are licensed by local companies.[13]

The French MNEs

Unlike their German counterparts, the French firms did not have to suffer the wrench of divestment during the World Wars. Nevertheless, they manifest more inconsistency and change in their postwar internationalisation in comparison to the relatively steady progress of the German firms. Until the early 1970s, the focus of overseas production was largely limited to the franco-phone colonial and ex-colonial markets; only within the last two decades has international expansion been primarily pursued in North America and Western Europe. Common among these French MNEs was a reliance on growth at home from the late 1950s onwards through diversification of business areas and concentration of firm size, facilitated by mergers, acquisitions and alliances with other firms. Such concentration and diversification was frequently engendered and promoted by governments of the day, with the aim of building up selected 'national champions' able to compete internationally.

The French chemical MNEs: Rhône-Poulenc, Elf Aquitaine (Roussel Uclaf)

Rhône-Poulenc is the flagship of the French chemical/pharma-ceutical sector and the eighth largest chemical firm in the world, with 1988 sales of FFr65 billion. Foreign production accounted for 48 per cent of total sales. Growth in previous decades has been heavily dependent on two factors: the acquisition of a number of smaller companies; and government-promoted mergers and alliances with other large French firms. Nationalised in 1982 and privatised by the Balladur government in 1993, Rhône-Poulenc has made strenuous efforts to radically restructure its product lines, focusing on speciality chemicals, agrochemicals and phar-maceuticals, while at the same time withdrawing from its previous loss-making operations in dyes and slimming down its heavy chemical activities.

Elf Aquitaine is primarily a petroleum company that has expanded steadily in chemicals and pharmaceuticals only over the last two decades. State-owned since 1946 and partially privatised in 1993, it has grown with the aid of important acquisitions. The petroleum operations accounted for about 60 per cent of sales in 1989. Elf's chemical subsidiary is Atochem, formerly a joint venture with the other major French petroleum company, Total, but since 1982 fully owned by Elf. Atochem has expanded considerably in the 1980s in heavy and speciality chemicals, and was ranked 17 in the world chemicals league by the end of the 1980s. In 1989 it acquired some parts of the French chemical firm Orkem, which was split up between Elf and Total. Elf's activities in pharmaceuticals go back to its acquisition of Sanofi in 1973, which has expanded since then to be ranked 37 in the international pharmaceuticals league and number 2 in France behind Rhône-Poulenc/Rorer (1989). It is also active in biotechnology and cosmetic products. Elf gives wide strategic and operational leeway to Atochem and Sanofi, concentrating on its financial-holding function.[14] Given the concentration of this study on firms active in the chemical and electronics sectors, it is Elf as a chemical/pharmaceutical firm, in so far as it is the parent of Atochem and Sanofi, that is of relevance. Elf as an oil company has no direct relevance here.

Rhône-Poulenc has the reputation of the internationaliser *par excellence* among the large French MNEs and has at great speed pursued a corporate strategy of achieving critical mass in its core foreign markets for its main-line product areas. This global strategy – acquisitions where close synergies exist with Rhône-Poulenc, together with sizeable divestment in non-core areas – has been widely commended for its ambition, analytical clarity and effectiveness in implementation. Acquisitions worth $2.7 billion were made in 1989 alone; 35 companies were bought between 1987 and 1990. Atochem and Sanofi have also internationalised in the 1980s, albeit in a more cautious and limited manner.[15] Such rapid internationalisation is borne out by the decreasing dependence on the home market during the 1980s. In 1984 Rhône-Poulenc relied on the French market for 50–60 per cent of sales; in 1990 France accounted for less than 25 per cent of global sales. This represents quite a remarkable feat of expansion in the space of such a short period. Atochem and Sanofi are more dependent on the home market, which accounted for 50–55 per cent of total sales for each group by 1989.

The main focus of such internationalisation has been the European Community. The highlight of such European expansion remains Rhône-Poulenc's acquisition of the British RTZ's speciality chemical activities in 1989, adding to its already strong presence in the UK market. West Europe as a whole accounted for over 60 per cent of total sales for all the groups concerned here. North America accounted for over 20 per cent of Rhône-Poulenc's total sales at the end of the 1980s, up from 12 per cent in 1988 and 3 per cent in 1985. Such growth has been mostly purchased by the 19 acquisitions the company has made in the US, the most notable ones being the agrochemical activities of Union Carbide, Stauffer Chemicals in basic chemicals, GAF-SCC in speciality chemicals, and above all the takeover of the drugs concern Rorer to form the sixth-largest pharmaceutical firm worldwide. The acquisition of Connaught BioSciences in Canada in 1989–90 enabled Rhône-Poulenc's subsidiary, Institut Merieux, to become the largest vaccines producer in the world. Atochem and Sanofi are much weaker in the US, which accounted for little over 10 per cent of total sales by 1989. Acquisitions have nevertheless been made, notably of Pennwalt, active in heavy chemicals, by Elf in 1989. All three groups are weak in Japan and the Far East, although Rhône-Poulenc has been laying the basis for targeted expansion in Japan and South Korea through a series of joint ventures.[16]

Finally, the pharmaceutical/agrochemical MNE Roussel Uclaf merits consideration. It is not, in its own right, one of the MNEs selected for the study, for it is smaller than the other companies by some measure and, unlike the others, is owned by a foreign parent. The fact that the parent is one of the German MNEs studied here – Hoechst – justifies some mention of it.

In brief, Roussel is France's third largest pharmaceutical firm with international production that is especially strong in Japan, Italy, North Africa and Latin America. Since Hoechst acquired a majority share in the company in 1974, Roussel has enjoyed substantial and exceptional autonomy within the Hoechst network, guaranteed by a series of legal agreements between Hoechst and the French government. After protracted negotiations with Hoechst, the new Socialist–Communist government took a large minority stake in Roussel in 1982, which it ceded to Rhône-Poulenc in 1989. Throughout the decade, the distinctive Hoechst–Roussel relationship continued, both in France and in joint ventures and undertakings abroad.[17] The evolution of this quite exceptional Hoechst–Roussel–French government relationship in the 1980s is taken up in the chapter on government policy and government–MNE relations (chapter 4).

The French electronics MNEs: CGE, Thomson, Bull

Thomson is France's largest consumer and professional electronics concern, with 1988 sales of FFr75 billion. Its history is dotted with a gamut of diversifications in electronics and energy, many of them subsequently reversed. Following its nationalisation in 1982, it has specialised in two main areas: professional electronics in the form of Thomson CSF, which is heavily dependent on the defence market and accounted for 43 per cent of group sales by 1989; and consumer electronics in the form of Thomson Consumer Electronics (TCE), formerly Thomson-Brandt, which accounted for 45 per cent of group sales. Under the umbrella of Thomson CSF, a semiconductor manufacturing capability has been developed, culminating in the formation of SGS-Thomson in 1987, 50 per cent owned by Thomson and 50 per cent by the Italian STET group. The latter constitutes the second biggest European-owned semiconductor manufacturer.

The Compagnie Générale d'Électricité (renamed Alcatel-Alsthom in 1990) is France's second largest company next to Elf and is the French flagship in telecommunications equipment and mechanical/power engineering, accounting for FFr128 billion of sales in 1988. It has had a history of diversification, but since nationalisation in 1982 has concentrated on two main poles of activity: telecommunications equipment manufacture in Alcatel, the world leader, with sales of FFr78 billion; and power engineering/transport systems in GEC-Alsthom, with sales of FFr28 billion. CGE was privatised by the Chirac government in 1987. The constituent companies enjoy large management autonomy under the CGE roof.

Groupe Bull is France's leading indigenous data processing company with 1988 sales of FFr43 billion, and has been the chosen vehicle to spearhead the French government's computers and information technology drive since the late 1960s. This led to the participation in Bull of Honeywell of the US and NEC of Japan; and, for a limited period in the 1970s, Bull was owned by CGE. Bull was also nationalised in 1982 and has continued to specialise in computer hardware manufacture. Both Thomson and Bull are still in majority state ownership at the time of writing (early 1995), but the Balladur government has plans to privatise them in due course.[18]

Internationalisation has proceeded rapidly in the 1980s for all three firms as they have tried to break out of home market dependence in these globalising areas of the electronics sector. They have relied heavily on foreign acquisitions to attain critical mass in North America and West Europe, and most of all in the European Community. Of the three, CGE remains in the healthiest financial state with the best prospects in international competition. Thomson and Bull have ended the 1980s in deep financial trouble and struggling from positions of weakness to face American and Japanese competitors in global markets.

Thomson's sales abroad represented 70 per cent of the total by the end of the 1980s, having been half that proportion in the mid-1980s. This transformation is mostly accounted for by the international acquisitions programme of TCE that doubled its size between 1987 and 1988 to become the fourth largest consumer electronics group worldwide with 90 per cent of its sales outside France. It must be borne in mind that the former Thomson-Brandt had little exposure outside the French market in the early 1980s. The reversal of this introvertedness is indicated by the fact that TCE's sales in Germany, at 14 per cent of total sales, exceeded sales in the French home market by 1989 (11 per cent). CGE's sales abroad have mounted to 60 per cent of the total due to the internationalisation of both its telecommunications and power engineering poles. This is particularly the case with Alcatel, which between 1986 and 1987 doubled its turnover through acquisitions. Bull's international expansion has been such that in the seven years up to 1989 foreign sales had doubled, as a percentage of total sales, to 60 per cent of the total. Between 1987 and 1988, sales increased 75 per cent due to the acquisition of majority stakes in existing joint ventures.

Acquisition activity in the European Community has been most evident. Thomson CSF has a strategy of gaining a bigger share of a declining defence market through acquisitions and joint ventures. TCE acquired Telefunken from AEG in Germany as well as Ferguson in the UK. Thomson-SGS has rationalised its production between its French and Italian plants and made the major acquisition of Inmos in the UK. Alcatel built on its consolidation in the French market by taking over ITT's European telecommunications operations, including the jewel in ITT's crown, its German SEL subsidiary. GEC-Alsthom was formed in 1988, with equal ownership shared between CGE and the British GEC, although management control resides preponderantly with CGE's Alsthom in Paris.

In 1990 CGE concluded a swap operation with Fiat in Italy in which it acquired Fiat's telecommunications and transport system operations. Expansion in North America is mainly evident with TCE and Bull. Thomson-CSF and CGE remain weak in the American market. Most notably, TCE arranged a global swap with General Electric of the US, in which it ceded its medical electronics activities to the latter in exchange for the television manufacturer RCA: this alone made the US TCE's largest market, with 50 per cent of total sales there. Bull's microelectronics activities were substantially built up by the acquisition of Zenith, the second largest laptop manufacturer worldwide. Bull also took majority control of the Honeywell Bull operation in the US (renamed Bull HN), Honeywell reducing its stake. Japan and the Far East, the fastest-growing electronics markets in the world, remain regions of acute weakness for all three groups. TCE and Thomson-SGS, however, have established important production facilities in Singapore.[19]

Tables 2.2 and 2.3 capture some of the most pertinent statistics regarding the internationalisation of the MNEs as analysed above in this sub-section. Table 2.2 shows the geographical spread of their sales at the end of the 1980s; and Table 2.3 their global sales and employment levels at this time.

Table 2.2 Geographical spread of MNEs' sales by 1988 (% of total sales by region)

MNE	Europe	N. America	Asia	Other
Hoechst	59	22	14	
Bayer	67	18	7	
BASF	62	21	7	
AEG	86[b]	8[c]	4	
Bosch	82.5	11.7[c]	5.8	
Siemens[a]	75	11	6	
Rhône-Poulenc	61[b]	12	5	(8.9% in Brazil)
Thomson	51	27[c]		(14% in Mid-East)
CGE	76			
Bull[a]	76	18		

Source: Annual Reports
Notes
% of overall sales in the EC: Hoechst (50%); BASF (58%); AEG (77%)
[a] figures for 1989
[b] for West Europe
[c] for North and South America.

Table 2.3 MNEs' global turnover and employment, 1988

MNE	Sales	% of which abroad	% of employees abroad
German	(DM bn)		
Hoechst	40.964	76	47
Bayer	40.468	84	62
BASF	43.868	67	34
AEG	13.380	41	22
Bosch	27.700	51	32
Siemens	59.374	48	37
French	(FFr bn)		
Rhône-Poulenc[a]	65.334	74	52
Elf[a]	126.100		
(Atochem)	(31.200) [b]	(50)	(40)
(Sanofi)	(14.569) [c]	(55)	(41)
Thomson	75.100	72	48
CGE	128.000	57	46
Bull[a]	31.547	63	56

Source: *Annual Reports*
Notes
[a] figures for 1989
[b] 26.1% of Elf sales
[c] 11.6% of Elf sales.

Internationalisation of MNE organisational structures

Accompanying the internationalisation of production have been wholesale changes in the MNEs' management organisations. As the business historian Alfred Chandler and others have pointed out, the matrix structure – divisionalisation into product lines and geographical regions – has been extended abroad. Some functional areas have been characterised by recentralisation of control at headquarters level and in the home market, for example in aspects of finance, personnel, basic research and logistics. But the dominant trend has been one of international decentralisation to devolve more responsibility down the line to more discrete, narrowly defined worldwide product divisions as well as to overseas national/regional market divisions.[20]

The German MNEs underwent major organisational changes in the 1980s. Between 1986 and 1990 AEG had expanded to ten product divisions. Siemens has shown the most radical change with a five-year overhaul of its hierarchical and highly centralised management structure, expanding to 16 product divisions and devolving more autonomy to its foreign regional divisions. The French MNEs have proceeded further down this road due to the wholesale domestic restructuring of product portfolios and because foreign acquisitions have had to be integrated into existing inter-national intra-firm networks. For many of these MNEs, regional responsibility has been transferred from central headquarters to a regional HQ base, especially in the US and increasingly so in the Far East. In certain instances, worldwide product responsibility has been shifted to a foreign location, for example to Hoechst-Celanese in the US for fibres; and Zenith has responsibility in the US for Bull's microelectronics operations worldwide.

These changes, accompanied by the progressive international-isation of management personnel, are quite remarkable for com-panies with long records of organisational centralism. Never-theless, problems of integrating newly acquired foreign opera-tions and personnel with those in the firms' home bases, and with their international networks, persist. For the German MNEs, overcoming these difficulties is no small task; but it is all the more daunting for the French MNEs. Unlike the former, they have not been able to expand internationally relatively steadily, relying on a judicious mixture of internal growth and acquisition; rather their internationalisation has been preponderantly dependent on acquisitions, posing significantly greater challenges of restruc-turing and organisational integration. In the cases of Bull and TCE, serious difficulties of integrating their US acquisitions have not yet been overcome.[21]

French and German MNEs: world/European rankings

Table 2.4 ranks the MNEs in the European and world company leagues for 1988, using indicators of turnover (sales), not market capitalisation. Indicators of market capitalisation tend to under-estimate the size of comparatively undercapitalised French and German MNEs, given that French and German capital markets are underdeveloped in comparison to those of the US and the UK.[22] Furthermore, they do not account for the state ownership of the French MNEs, which has restricted their access to share listings on the major financial exchanges. From Table 2.4 it is clear that the German MNEs tend to be significantly larger than their French counterparts. Using 1987 figures on the basis of sales, there were eight German and three French companies in the largest 50 industrial groupings in the world. Figures 2.3 and 2.4 give some idea of the relative sizes of the MNEs according to sales and employment levels.

Table 2.4 World and European rankings for MNEs, 1988

	World ranking Sales (1987)	Eur. ranking Sales	Eur. ranking Employment
Daimler Benz	20	4	1
Siemens	31	6	2
BASF	44	16	6
CGE	47	21	3
Elf	48	22	
Bayer	49	20	4
Hoechst	50	18	5
Bosch		30	
Thomson		40	
Rhône-Poulenc		54[a]	
Bull		164[a]	

Source: 'European Top 500', *The Financial Times*, 19 December 1989; 11 January 1991; *The Times 1000* (1988)
Note: [a] In 1989.

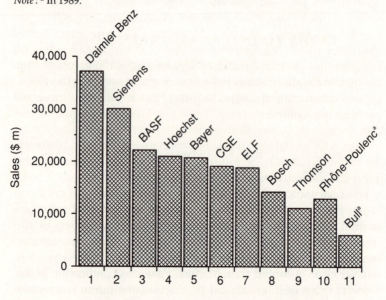

Figure 2.3 Sales levels of MNEs, 1988
Source: 'European Top 500', *The Financial Times*, 19 December 1989, 11 January 1991
Note: [a] Sales for 1989.

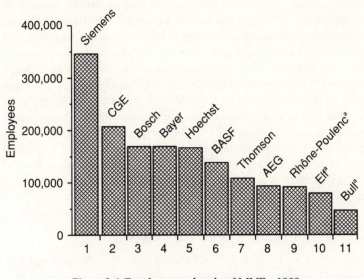

Figure 2.4 Employment levels of MNEs, 1988
Source: Annual reports
Note: Employees in 1989.

PATHS TO INTERNATIONALISATION

The previous section on the MNEs quite clearly displays that internationalisation factors have figured prominently in the 1980s. Such internationalisation has induced French–German firm-level convergence, complementing that at the level of economic structure indicated in the first section of this chapter. Corporate strategies for globalising markets have been implemented through the rapid expansion of production in the key markets of the European Community and North America.

This final section of the chapter draws on the empirical evidence in the previous two sections to make some general and over-arching interpretations of the recent internationalisation of the French and German firms. The comparisons are cross-cutting, homing in on sectoral and national differences, as Figure 2.5 makes visually clear. Adapted from Michael Porter's classification of the different types of international production, the figure is a matrix of the configuration and coordination of production: configuration in terms of the spatial extent of production, 'low' representing concentration in the home market and 'high' representing cross-border dispersion; coordination in terms of managing the different parts of production networks, from strategies geared to treating national markets separately ('low') to strategies geared to global markets ('high'). Combining the two axes, there are four types of international production: (a) home market dependence with not very significant foreign activities; (b) loose-knit federations of affiliated, 'local for local' national units catering for separate national markets; (c) production concentrated in the home market both to serve that market as well as to export globally – the 'export platform' phenomenon; (d) the combination of widely dispersed cross-border production networks with extensive coordination among subsidiaries to cater for both global strategies and local adaptiveness – the 'transnational' phenomenon.

Sectoral differences

First, it has to be pointed out that there are intra-sectoral differences that are played out within and between MNEs (see Figure 2.5). Sub-sectors within the chemical and electronics sectors are differently constituted, with varying dynamics and different paths to internationalisation. Consumer, micro and medical electronics, and speciality chemicals have tended to shift from centralised export-platform production to international production for global market coverage. Telecommunications equipment and data processing have also been moving in this direction, but from a different starting point: production was previously geared to cater almost exclusively for the home market. The starting point for pharmaceuticals and agrochemicals has been internationally diversified production, but of an unintegrated 'local-for-local' nature, catering for separate and discrete national markets.

These intra-sectoral differences within the chemical and electronics sectors point to different paths to internationalisation between the MNEs, for instance between TCE in consumer electronics on the one hand and Siemens, Alcatel and Bull on the other hand in telecommunications and data processing. Furthermore, they highlight different paths to internationalisation within the MNEs, given that all of them are diversified across several sub-sectors within the chemical and electronics sectors. The paragons of such pan-sectoral span are Siemens, Hoechst, Bayer and BASF. For Siemens, internationalisation in its telecommunications and data processing divisions proceeds in a different manner to that

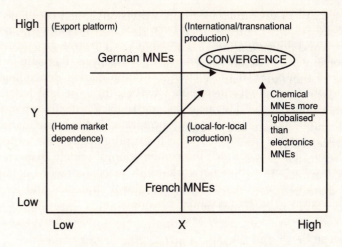

Y axis: Coordination of international production
X axis: Configuration of international production

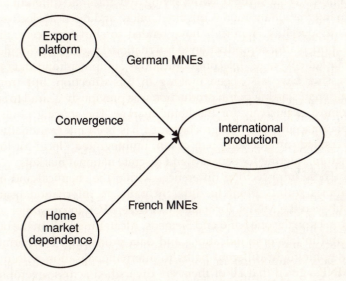

Figure 2.5 Matrix of international production: French, German and sectoral convergence

of its medical and microelectronics divisions. Such differences exist as well for the diversified CGE (between its telecommunications and power engineering activities) and Thomson (between its consumer and defence electronics activities); and are also to be found within the Big Three German chemical concerns in addition to Rhône-Poulenc and Elf, for example between their speciality chemical businesses and pharmaceuticals.

Second, there are inter-sectoral differences that distinguish the chemical MNEs from the electronics MNEs, particularly with respect to the German group of firms (see also Figure 2.5). The three German chemical MNEs are noticeably more internationalised than their electronics counterparts: their presence abroad is deeper and stretches back over a longer period of time in the core markets of the European Community and the US. Whereas Hoechst, Bayer and BASF were at the market entry and development stage in Japan and the Far East by the end of the 1980s, Siemens, Bosch and AEG were not all that far beyond that stage in the US by that time.

A prime cause of this state of affairs of relatively under-developed internationalisation lies in the degree of involvement of home public authorities in the electronics industry. Internationalisation has been retarded by the 'national champion' syndrome: the context of insulated and highly regulated home national markets in Western Europe which has bred the over-dependence of the electronics MNEs on those markets. Government protection and promotion, for example through subsidies, preferential public procurement contracts, and nationally exclusive standards and norms, have been major factors. Nevertheless, this scenario is being rapidly changed by an amalgam of market-led and policy-led forces: the globalisation of markets; the escalating costs of technological innovation and development, which can only be recouped by sales spread over much larger market areas; the shortening of product life-cycles through to commercialisation; and the combination of national public policy deregulation and EC policy harmonisation that bring in their wake greater competition in home markets together with enhanced market opportunities abroad. But the other side of the coin is that these developments have left European-owned and home-market-dependent electronics firms, with acute competitive weaknesses, much more exposed to sharp competition from more efficient and globally active American and Japanese firms. This is the case in computer hardware and data processing, in which firms such as IBM and Digital Equipment are well-established inside the EC as well as in other international markets, with a rising competitive threat from a number of Japanese firms in this area; it is equally true of consumer electronics and semiconductors, global markets which are increasingly dominated by Japanese firms, many of whom are establishing a more integrated presence in the EC. Such weakness on the part of the French and German electronics MNEs studied here sets them apart from their chemical counterparts, who are on firmer ground in competition with non-European competitors.

Siemens provides a useful illustration of retarded internationalisation and home market dependence in some of its product areas. Seventy-five per cent of its System 2000 mainframe computers line was produced for sales in the German market by 1989, with only 20 per cent of sales on the rest of the European market. Siemens-Nixdorf had 60 per cent of its sales in Germany and only 34 per cent for the rest of Western Europe. In data processing, Bull is similarly handicapped by its historic dependence on the French market. In telecommunications equipment and particularly in public switching, Siemens has long-standing and privileged relations as the predominant supplier to the German Bundespost in a market in which prices were 100 per cent above the world average by the mid-1980s. French prices were 50 per cent above the world average, which represented a corresponding source of plentiful revenue for the French national champion in telecommunications, Alcatel.[23]

In these and other areas, government policy has promoted privileged national champions in the pursuit of national solutions for the domestic market, an example of which was the long-standing French government insistence that a minimum of one-third of all public sector contracts for computers be given to Bull. Governments and firms, however, have come to realise that such nationally based solutions contradict the logic of internationalisation. For these competing national policies have bred different and incompatible standards on relatively small national markets within Western Europe, weaning insular national champions unable to reap sufficient economies of scale, lacking product sophistication and slow in technological development. Such a realisation accounts for the inducement of deregulation in France,

Germany and other European Community markets, as well as of EC policy harmonisation, which have especially affected tele-communications and public procurement in the electronics sector. The objective is, at least in part, to pressurise indigenous MNEs such as Siemens and Alcatel to become more efficient.[24] The aspects of 'national champion promotion' and of the shift of focus of public policy from the national to the EC level will be dealt with in detail in chapters 4 and 6.

In contrast, the chemical sector has not been as protected or regulated by governments, with the exception of the pharma-ceutical industry, which is structurally beset with differing national regulatory regimes on health, patent protection and new drug approval. Although regulation on environmental protection is increasing, levels of government intervention in the sector remain lower than they do in electronics. Above all, the sector and the firms within it are not as dependent on national governments for subsidy and public procurement contracts. Gerd Junne and Rob van Tulder put it thus:

> Links between governments and MNEs are especially in-tense in the electronics sector but less important in a sector like the chemical industry. MNEs in electronics are more national in character because they receive the bulk of R&D subsidies and are strongly oriented towards the state market (for example, in defence and telecoms), whereas the chemical industry finances a larger share of its research itself and sells only a small fraction of its products to governments.[25]

The above sectoral phenomena are international in nature and have been very evident in a number of national markets in Western Europe. They do not exclusively apply to France and Germany. But the distinction between the German chemical MNEs and the German electronics MNEs is more marked than the comparable divide between the French chemical and electronics MNEs. What the latter share in common, spanning the chemicals/electronics sectoral divide, is historical protection and promotion as national champions by the French government, resulting in overall overdependence on the home market and retarded inter-nationalisation. This leads on to the most important distinction for the purposes of this study, namely French–German firm-level differences.

National differences: the French and German
models compared
(See Figure 2.5)

The German MNEs have stood out as export platforms, with centralised production at home to serve the German market and export finished capital-intensive goods to the rest of the world. BASF is the outstanding example: production in Germany accounted for two-thirds of total sales, split equally between the domestic market and exports, that is, German-based production for export represented one-third of total sales.

Among the German MNEs, the realisation has grown that the *Exportmodell Deutschland* is no longer viable on its own as a means of serving globalising markets, and that international production is an integral component of overall strategies. Siemens, Bosch and AEG provide an impression of rapid change, internationalising in a 'catch-up' fashion and using the mechanisms of acquisitions and alliances to make up for lost time and weak foreign market positions in areas such as telecommunications, data processing, automation and microelectronics. For Siemens and Bosch, international expansion has occurred throughout the 1980s; for AEG, it has only been possible after the Daimler Benz takeover in 1986. For Hoechst, Bayer and BASF, the emphasis is much more on continuity rather than change, extending and deepening already strong worldwide presence: hence the common parlance within these firms of consolidation in the integrating EC market and in the US, where critical mass is already a reality, as well as targeting expansion in the Far East. Having said this, there is a determination on the part of all these firms to maintain and upgrade their positions in their home bases in Germany, so that export-oriented strategies move in tandem with international production. The evolution undergone by these German MNEs is indicated by the following comments by interviewees:

> I want to differentiate Hoechst as a multinational in the past, having more local-for-local production abroad and value-added concentrated in Germany, with its position as a multinational today, having integrated production in core overseas markets and global strategies.
>
> (Corporate planner, Hoechst)

> Three to four years ago [that is, in the mid-1980s], we realised that we were too dependent on the German market and were

too much a 'German' firm – more so than Bosch and Siemens. Therefore, we made a strategic decision to internationalise, without which we would have been exposed to injury and decline.

(Corporate planner, AEG)

The above 'German model' of internationalisation stands out from its French counterpart. In the past, the French MNEs have not had the characteristic export-orientation of the German MNEs; rather an introverted dependence on the home market together with an array of semi-independent satellites in the old franco-phone colonies of North Africa and in the French 'spheres of influence' in the Middle East. Internationalisation in the 1970s and 1980s has proceeded from this starting point and has reoriented its focus on the North American and West European markets. The most active phase of internationalisation, in the mid to late 1980s, has focused particularly on the EC. The French MNEs have also been acutely aware of their competitive disadvantages *vis-à-vis* their main competitors, comparison with German firms on the other side of the Rhine seeming to be something of a reflex action. Compared to the German MNEs in the context of international competition, especially in the technology-intensive parts of the chemical and electronics sectors, they lacked size as well as international spread. The rush to internationalisation *à grande vitesse* (at high speed) has thus been even more a case of *rattrapage* (catching-up) than with the German electronics MNEs, the point of departure being somewhat further back.

Reliance on a spate of costly acquisitions abroad has therefore been great, in a scramble to buy up market share and knowledge. French acquisitions abroad were valued at FFr76 billion in 1988 and FFr108 billion in 1989. A Bain & Co. survey for the French Ministry of Industry reported that size was the first strategic objective of the larger French firms, especially the 'champions', in the preparation for the Single Market in the EC post-1992. International competitive advantage has thus primarily been figured in terms of competition in the EC, where the French firms have been weaker than their German counterparts. The same Bain report found that acquisitions represented two-thirds of real growth between 1985 and 1988 for its sample of the 300 largest French firms. This figure was expected to rise to three-quarters of real growth in the period 1988–92, 70 per cent of that realised outside France.[26] In addition, an internal Ministry of Trade report on French competitiveness pinpointed the problems French companies have because of insufficient size in world markets in comparison with their main competitors. The French share of the industrialised world's foreign direct investment was a third lower than its share of world exports by the late 1980s. French companies had 1017 subsidiaries in Germany, whereas German companies had twice that number in France. The average turnover of the top 250 German companies was $2.2 billion in 1987; for the top 250 French companies it was only $1.3 billion.[27]

Hence the rationale for foreign acquisitions. But that is only the necessary enabling condition to compete in international markets, for, as an interviewee observed:

> Now that they have sufficiently internationalised by buying up market share, the challenge is to convert that to growth by internal expansion. That will be the litmus test of success or failure [of internationalisation].
>
> (Ex-civil servant, Ministries of Finance and Industry)

Other interviewees summed up the transformation of French corporate attitutes towards global markets in the following terms:

> French MNEs had a history in the colonies and the Middle East until the 1970s, to which much of French foreign policy was directed. Thus the two [business and government] were hand-in-glove [for example, in telecoms, arms, oil]. The real break came with the first and second oil price shocks. It dawned suddenly on introspective French firms that the key markets were in industrialised countries. Hence the quick reorientation of geographical internationalisation and of corresponding product internationalisation. This has little to do with old-style French government support in the colonies; rather with firm-specific advantages in international competition.
>
> (Industry correspondent, *Le Monde*)

> The French remain particularistic, and with that less open and internationalised. They have become more Europeanised but still not internationalised, quite unlike the Germans. This is especially true of companies in sectors that have had a history of state involvement, such as chemicals and electronics.
>
> (Head of a French industry association)

The French and German MNEs thus present two distinct paths to internationalisation, as the starting points were so far apart. But these paths are converging, as Figure 2.5 shows. Comparing the positions of the MNEs at the end of the 1980s, it is fair to assert that the French MNEs have done much catching up relative to the German MNEs in terms of international size and spread. Indeed, if global sales figures for the firms are split up by geographical region (see Table 2.2), the French electronics MNEs have become *more* internationalised than their German counterparts in the space of a few years. By 1988 Thomson and Bull had 70 per cent and CGE 60 per cent of total sales realised abroad due to their acquisitions; whereas Siemens and Bosch had only 50 per cent and AEG 40 per cent of total sales recouped outside Germany. If particular areas are selected – for instance, Alcatel in telecommunications, TCE in consumer electronics or Bull in microcomputers – the extent of internationalisation is considerably greater. In the chemical sector, Rhône-Poulenc is on the way to achieving the geographical spread, concentrating on North America, West Europe and the Far East (that is, the 'Triad' markets), already attained by Hoechst, Bayer and BASF. Elf's activities in chemicals and pharmaceuticals remain on a smaller scale and less internationalised.

Despite such catching-up by the French MNEs, in absolute terms they remain less internationally active than the German MNEs because the latter are still bigger in overall terms (see Table 2.4 and Figures 2.3 and 2.4).

CONCLUSION

French and German economic structures have become more interlinked with the international economy, both through inward and outward investment. Moving from the nation/sector level of analysis to that of the individual firm, each of the MNEs in the sample of firms was analysed, particularly in terms of strategies and experiences of international expansion in the 1980s.

From the above empirical examination, certain qualified generalisations were made regarding firm-level paths to internationalisation. First, there were sectoral differences: intra-sectoral differences played out within and between MNEs diversified across the spectrum of the chemical and electronics sectors respectively; and differences between chemical MNEs as opposed to electronics

MNEs. The chemical MNEs are more internationalised than their electronics counterparts because the latter have been subject to more government intervention and weaned on protected domestic markets.

Second, there were national comparisons. French–German convergence has been manifested at two levels of examination: at the level of economic structure, as the national economies and the chemical and electronics sectors within them have internationalised; and at the level of the the firm, for the French and German MNEs have internationalised along converging paths, with similar goals in mind. Nevertheless, these paths are not one and the same; they are different: the German MNEs have added international production strategies to continuing strategies based on export-oriented production in Germany; the French MNEs have jumped to the international production stage from that of home market dependence and insulation, and have primarily used the mechanism of acquisitions to facilitate this transformation.

Having analysed the phenomenon of internationalisation in the 1980s of a selected number of firms, the stage is now set to link internationalisation to the manner in which the MNEs are embedded in the French and German political economies. This link between firm-level internationalisation and the French and German political economies forms the meat of this study and will be explored from a number of different angles. In order to focus on particular aspects of this linkage, however, an analysis of the make-up of French and German domestic structures, and the MNEs' embeddedness within them, is required. This forms the subject of the following chapter. Then we can be in the position to analyse the interaction between internationalisation and domestic structures: with respect to government policy and MNE–government relations (chapter 4), MNE financial relations with banks and the government (chapter 5), and at the level of the European Community (chapter 6).

3

MNEs IN DOMESTIC STRUCTURES

This chapter deals with French and German economic structures, as well as the relationships between the domains of government, finance, industry and labour. Just as the MNE was the central focus of the treatment on internationalisation, so it remains in this analysis of domestic structures. The essential purpose is to examine the way in which these MNEs are embedded in their home bases in the French and German political economies and how they relate to external actors – the government, banks, unions, industry associations, smaller companies – within them. As was discussed in chapter 1, it is in their home bases, as opposed to host-country markets, that the MNEs are most strongly implanted and in which they are most firmly linked in long-standing relationships with external actors.

A first cut is taken by looking at the economic structures of France and Germany in the 1980s; and the manner in which the competitiveness of the home base, particularly in the relevant sectors of chemicals and electronics, factors into the competitive advantages of the MNEs. For them the home base is one market among many to be served and is only one element, albeit the most important one, in the MNEs' international production networks. Second, a political economy approach is taken by examining the linkages that join the MNEs to external actors in the French and German political economies, something which it is argued relates to national competitiveness and MNE competitive advantages in international competition.

In his book *The Competitive Advantage of Nations*, Michael Porter looks at the role of the nation as a home base for successful, internationally competitive firms with global strategies. He poses the question of why industrial leaders, who sustain competitive advantages over the long term in specialised areas, are concentrated in a few nations. He answers that question by arguing that this is a process which involves differences in national economic structures, values, cultures and institutions. In the context of international competition, the home nation's role is as important as ever, the base from which indigenous MNEs conduct global strategies through mechanisms such as trade and FDI. The firm no longer operates exclusively in the home nation, as in the days predating global competition, but uses it as a base of ever-expanding international networks; and in the process changes the character of the nation. As Porter puts it:

> A firm's home nation shapes where and how it is likely to succeed in global competition ... As competition becomes more knowledge-intensive, the influence of the national environment becomes even more vital. It shapes the way opportunities are perceived, and how specialised skills and resources are developed.

Porter defines a nation's competitive advantage – what is referred to in this study as competitiveness – by its track record in improving national productivity, defined as output per unit of labour or capital, which is the main determinant of standards of living and per capita income.[1]

Porter's argumentation is not contested here, but his terminology is. Henceforth, competitive advantage is referred to only in so far as it affects firms, not nations; and for nations the term competitiveness is utilised so as not to confuse it with firm-specific competitive advantages. The two remain conceptually distinct. National competitiveness is in effect another term for the long-run and dynamic comparative advantage of countries in an international economy integrated by flows of trade, direct investment, technology transfers, *inter alia*.[2]

THE FRENCH AND GERMAN ECONOMIES AND THEIR CHEMICAL AND ELECTRONICS SECTORS

In the aftermath of the Second World War the West German industrial structure, once the reconstruction process was under way, was well suited to the needs of postwar competition without having to undergo major structural change. The organisation of the German economy was geared to industrial-based, export-led growth. France, on the other hand, had to undergo an industrial transformation following postwar reconstruction: to consolidate France in the European Economic Community; and to adjust to the modern world economy. This rationale was used for justifying a leading role for the government in economic planning as well as in channelling capital in a concentrated fashion through financial markets to targeted sectors; for jolting French firms into competition on the EC market; for consolidating medium-sized firms into large corporations in a process of government-led concentration; and for inflationary growth as a means of relatively redistributing an enlarged cake of national resources in favour of industry and at the expense of agriculture.[3]

The French and German economies have thus undergone different paths of development in the postwar era, but have converged in their structural make-up and macroeconomic outlook by the end of the 1980s. Table 3.1 presents some of the most pertinent macroeconomic indicators.

Table 3.1 Macroeconomic indicators, end 1980s

	Share of total OECD GDP (% 1987)	Inflation (% 1989)	Current Account balance ($ bn 1989)
Germany	8.9	2.6	55.4
France	7.1	3.4	−3.8

Source: OECD, *Economic Outlook*, December 1990 (Paris: OECD)

Germany and France represent the third and fourth largest economies in the OECD (the US had a 36 per cent share of OECD GDP and Japan 19 per cent by 1990). French rates of inflation have converged downwards in a German direction: the low inflation differential at the end of the 1980s contrasted with an average annual rate between 1978 and 1987 in Germany of 3.4 per cent and in France of 8.6 per cent. The current account balances of the two countries remained structurally different at the end of the decade: a persistent French deficit, mainly in industrially traded goods, contrasted with a sizeable German surplus, the second-largest in the world, considerably contributed to by Germany's position, along with the US, as one of the two greatest exporting nations in the world. This surplus has shrunk in the 1990s as funds get redirected to finance the restructuring of the East German economy in the wake of German reunification.[4]

There are some notable aspects of French–German convergence. The interest rate differential between the two countries was reduced to less than one percentage point by the end of 1990. A joint Banque de France–Bundesbank study found that the financial performance of French companies had converged somewhat to German levels since 1984. French direct investment in Germany had multiplied sevenfold in 1988–9 to DM4.2 billion, doubling the accumulated stock of French direct investment there – to such an extent that it arrived at a position of rough equality with German direct investment in France, standing at DM8.2 billion French DI stock between 1975 and 1989 in Germany compared to DM9 billion German stock DI in France. The ex-French minister for external trade, Jean-Marie Rausch, interprets these figures as 'a new dynamic that is part of a general tendency of convergence of performance between the economies of Germany and France'.[5]

Table 3.2 French and German chemical sectors compared, 1988

	France	Germany
% of world sales in chemicals	4.8	7
Employment	266,000	575,000
Investment (DM bn)	5,101	10,500
% of world exports in chemicals	8.2	17.9
% of world imports in chemicals	6.6	9.5

Source: *Chemiewirtschaft in Zahlen, 1989* (Frankfurt am Main: Verband der Chemischen Industrie)

The figures in Table 3.2 show that the German chemical industry was roughly twice the size of its French equivalent by 1988. The former was the fourth-largest chemical industry in the world, with sales of DM150.9 billion in 1988, nearly 10 per cent of all sales in Germany; and it was the leading world exporter of chemicals, worth DM80 billion, with a trade surplus of DM35 billion. Germany represented 27.5 per cent of sales and 29.9 per cent of employment in the EC – the largest market within it by far. Research spending in 1989 was DM11 billion, DM3 billion of which was on environmental protection. Investment abroad by the German chemical industry was DM6 billion in 1988, compared to DM10 billion investment at home.

The French chemical industry was the sixth-largest in the world and third-largest in the EC, with sales of $53 billion in 1989, R&D spending of $2.8 billion, and a trade surplus of $3.5 billion. It has made strides in gaining size in the 1980s through overseas expansion and foreign acquisitions, worth $3 billion in the 1986–8 period. Forty per cent of production of indigenous companies was located abroad by 1989, compared to 29 per cent in 1980. The average size of the top eight French chemical companies remained less than half that of the German top eight and median by world standards.[6]

Table 3.3 French and German electronics sectors compared, 1988

	France	Germany
Sales	FFr166.3 bn	DM76.4 bn
Employment	215,000	487,000
Trade balance	FFr–11.8 bn	DM+1.3 bn

Sources: *The French Electronics Industry 1988 Report* (Paris: Groupement des Industries Électroniques);
Zukunftskonzept Informationstechnik (Bonn: Bundesministerium für Wirtschaft/ Bundesministerium für Forschung und Technologie, August 1989)

As Table 3.3 shows, the French electronics industry was two-thirds the size of its German counterpart by 1988; the latter was half the size of the German chemical industry. Germany had roughly a balance of trade in electronics whereas in France there was a sizeable deficit, worsening from a surplus of FFr8.4 billion in 1983.[7]

ECONOMIC STRUCTURE

As an MNE becomes more interlinked across borders within its production networks, it is better able to compare the relative merits of production in different national economies and, on relative cost and other grounds, is more capable of transferring important parts of the production chain across borders to suit its advantage. Cross-border linkages in the value-adding chain intertwine the home market with foreign markets, which is not the case when multinational production is 'local-for-local' orientated, subsidiaries catering separately for a series of discrete national markets. Integrated cross-border production represents a double-edged sword for the home economy, which can be either positively or negatively affected. The negatives manifest themselves when production and employment are effectively exported from the home market due to its comparative disadvantages. This could lead to indigenous firms relocating to a developing country in search of, for example, a labour cost advantage. The net result is a 'hollowing out' of the home production base as key capital, labour and/or technology-intensive manufacturing operations are transferred abroad by the firm. There is some evidence of such occurrences in industrial sectors in the US, UK and Sweden. The other side of the coin is when the home economy's competitiveness is actually upgraded as a result of the internationalisation of home MNEs: by exporting intermediate goods intra-firm, such as technology and components, to newly set-up operations in foreign countries; using foreign presence as a catalyst to the export of finished goods from the home base, once the brand names and reputations of the companies' products become established in those foreign markets; using skills and know-how abroad, especially in technology, as an input to improved production at home; and repatriating profits, fees and royalties from foreign operations.[8]

Within this context and with reference to the French and German economies, there is little evidence to suggest that the home markets had suffered from this process of internationalisation by the end of the 1980s; on the contrary, available economic data suggest that they improved competitiveness as a result. This argument also applies specifically to the sectors of concern here, being at the forefront of internationalisation. 'The two forms of access to foreign markets [exports and FDI] would seem to be complimentary with rather than competitive to each other', write Charles-Albert Michalet and Thérèse Chevallier on the experience of French MNEs. Paulgeorg Juhl comments that international investment positions are most marked among the German MNEs that are clustered in industries which lead in the trade of goods and technology as well as in R&D intensity.[9]

How are the MNEs affected by the competitiveness of their home production bases in so far as it relates to their international competitive advantages? What are the main public policy issues involved? And what French–German comparisons can be drawn?

Standort Deutschland[10]

As the OECD has pointed out, many of the weaknesses of Germany as a location for production (*Standort*) are found on the supply side in microeconomic structural market rigidities that impede economic growth. The persistence of these problems is attributed to the lack of positive structural adjustment policies to enhance the working of markets and that should accompany macroeconomic stability in the form of a reasonable fiscal and monetary policy mix.[11]

There is a common complaint of a high corporate tax burden, of up to 70 per cent of profits, that is set to remain the highest in the industrialised world. There are, however, significant tax breaks in a number of areas, for example, on capital and R&D expenditure. Direct and non-direct wage costs have come to be the highest in the EC, at DM33/working hour in 1988 compared to DM25 in the US. Only Switzerland had a higher figure. Germans also had the lowest working hours in the world at 1633 hours per head per annum, 280 fewer hours than the US and 500 fewer hours than Japan. There is also a plethora of stringent regulations governing production, employment, finance, taxation, social policy, the environment and wages. Telecommunications and transport costs are in addition very high.[12]

The main *Standort* problem specific to the electronics industry in the 1980s was the pressure, particularly from the powerful IG Metall trade union, for shorter working time and rigidly fixed working hours at a time when technological developments and East Asian competition called for more flexible production. For example, in memory chip production there is a need for factories that have multi-shift, round-the-clock production throughout the week. Siemens introduced this at its Regensburg plant, overcoming IG Metall opposition by gaining the agreement of its Works Council at the factory.[13] In the chemical sector the main problems related to the escalating costs and hurdles posed by increasingly stringent German environmental regulations, as well as specific problems relating to biotechnology and genetic engineering (dealt with in chapter 6). Regarding the former, the bureaucratic procedures involved in getting approval of chemical production are among the most testing and long-drawn-out in the world, taking an average of two years per application, much higher than in the US. There were in 1989 some 33 laws on environmental protection in the process of amendment, creating a climate of uncertainty for companies, which have to plan long-term.[14]

In pharmaceuticals, profits at home have been much depressed by cost-cutting measures taken by the federal government, particularly through the Health Reform Act of 1989, which tightened the cap on public contributions to the cost of drugs prescribed by doctors. This legislative measure was estimated to cost the German pharmaceutical industry DM200 million in lost profits in 1990.[15]

These problems are especially acute for medium and small-sized firms, and for foreign firms considering entry into the German market. Although the 'manageability' of such disadvantages is somewhat easier for well-established 'Big Business' in Germany, there are signs that these negative factors of the *Standort* have worsened in the early 1990s, with a number of large firms, including the chemical majors, Daimler Benz and Volkswagen, seriously considering transferring lower value-adding and more labour-intensive parts of the production process to other countries which have lower wage and non-wage costs of production. The *Standort* debate in the last few years has thus been even sharper than in its previous incarnation in the early and mid-1980s, exacerbated by the problems of unification, a deep recession and a changing international division of labour that seemingly favours more flexible and lower-cost production in other countries, particularly in South-East Asia and the Pacific Rim.

Having dealt with these negative factors, it is time to consider the advantages of the *Standort*. First, a decade (the 1980s) that witnessed solid and continued growth, following the recession of the late 1970s and early 1980s. Between 1982 and 1988 average per annum growth in GDP was 2.4 per cent, among the highest in the OECD area. The need to completely restructure the East German economy in the wake of German reunification imposed severe burdens on and upset the balance of macropolicy in 1990 and 1991: to finance the huge transfers from west to east Germany, taxes have been raised and bond markets tapped for funds; the federal budget thus suddenly dived into substantial deficit, putting upward pressure on interest rates and lowering confidence in the Deutschmark. Accompanying the public sector deficit has been an emerging current account deficit.[16]

Second, Germany has an advanced and integrated infrastructure in transport and communications in the most important European national market. The infrastructural base in technology is also among the most developed in the world, given the web of interlocking links on R&D that unites large firms with universities, semi-autonomous research institutes and medium-sized firms.

Furthermore, the DIN German product standards are noted for their toughness on quality criteria and are considered to be effective in maintaining competitiveness and diffusing innovation in the economy.[17]

Third, Germany has a level of vocational skills that contributes much to its high levels of productivity and is tailored to the production of high value-added, capital-intensive and differentiated goods. The system of training through apprenticeship is as rigorous as it is specialised. Its dual character encompasses theoretical instruction combined with practical on-the-job experience, and is geared to the accumulation of detailed knowledge of products and processes in manufacturing. Overall the level of skills in the FRG is, along with those in Japan and Switzerland, among the highest in the world. Germany and Switzerland have a combined annual intake of apprentices nearly as great as that in the remainder of the OECD area. Germany and Sweden have higher levels of mobility at all levels of training than is the case in France and the UK.[18]

The capital- and technology-intensive MNEs studied here tend to need higher-than-average job skills; hence the increasing real sums devoted to training and retraining. For this Siemens spent DM770 million, Bayer DM215 million and Hoechst DM136 million in 1989. Bayer's training/retraining programmes involve a third of its employees and cover areas such as environmental protection, occupational safety, foreign languages, management and communication. The Robert Bosch Kolleg has acquired much prestige as an institute of continuing education for graduate employees at Bosch.[19]

For all these reasons, the German *Standort* is a world leader in terms of skills, accumulated human capital, company-funded research, patents registered, and is the leader in the trade of goods of a high skill content, representing 20 per cent of world trade by the end of the 1980s. France's share was 7 per cent, with 15 per cent for the US and 17 per cent for Japan.[20]

French economic structure

The negative aspects of the French economy for MNEs located there include deficiencies in skill levels and in the system of training both of qualified engineers and in vocational education. The quality and quantity of qualified chemical and electronic engineers is not so much the problem; rather it is that their theoretical training, as is the case with the vocational education of apprentices, is not particularly well orientated to industrial applications. This is in contrast to the German dual system of training. Indeed in a wide-ranging study on French companies, Jacques Lesourne comments that, 'for many managers, the German system of apprenticeship appears to be worthy of examination [in order to improve the workings of the French system]'.[21]

In France there has been considerable price regulation and control by government in product, financial and labour markets. Government regulations are numerous on social and employment policy matters. In addition to the existence of a statutory minimum wage, there are regulations requiring government approval for the layoff of employees. Many of the controls in product and financial markets, however, have been removed in the 1980s, a considerable part of them in compliance with EC norms and regulations.[22] An example of continued price control lies in pharmaceuticals. Control of drug prices across the range has resulted in low prices on the French market in comparison with those on other high per capita income markets. This has artificially depressed company profits and thus limited the pool of funds available to plough into R&D. The situation continues to be a competitive handicap for the French pharmaceutical industry in restricting its innovatory capability.[23]

Despite these problems pertaining to supply-side rigidities, the attractiveness of the French economy for the location of production has been enhanced in the 1980s. As in Germany, there was a macroeconomic climate of continued growth from the early 1980s up to the recessionary years of the early 1990s, averaging 1.9 per cent growth per annum between 1982 and 1988; the difference was that this time it occurred in France under conditions of monetary stability, with inflation converging downwards towards the German level. This represents a major departure from past experience of inflationary growth and structurally inbuilt inflation in the macroeconomy. Following the reversal of policy after the failed Keynesian demand-led dash for growth between 1981–3, monetary policy consistently had an anti-inflationary strategy hung on a commitment to a strong franc in the European Monetary System; and fiscal policy has, in the same period, consisted of public expenditure control and a declining budget deficit, down successively each year since 1985 from 3.3 per cent of GDP in that year to 1.6 per cent in 1989.[24] In addition business circles have welcomed the general tendency of the French government towards less intervention and more market orientation in significant areas of microeconomic policy in the 1980s; this contrasts with the *dirigisme* of previous decades. The chapters on government policy/MNE–government relations (chapter 4) and on finance (chapter 5) will discuss these trends in micropolicy more extensively.

As in Germany, the infrastructural level in communications and transport is very favourable in France. The technological base, however, is not as developed as it is in Germany. Although the situation has improved, the R&D links that the large firms have with smaller firms, universities and publicly funded research centres are not as strong as they are in Germany. Research work in the latter has not been 'applied' enough for the commercial needs of the large firms; and the cultural gap between public and private arenas of research has remained large due to the low numbers of personnel moving across this institutional divide.[25]

The French MNEs, like their German counterparts, have to spend considerable and increasing sums of investment in training and continuing education for their employees. In 1984, CGE spent 2.5 per cent of wages on training, and Bull spent 7 per cent and by 1989 devoted 5 per cent of working hours to training. By 1989 Elf spent FFr75.3 million on training in its chemical activities (3.3 per cent of wages) and FFr93.9 million in pharmaceuticals (4.6 per cent of wages); Rhône-Poulenc spent FFr800 million on training in that year.[26]

Conclusion

On balance, the positive aspects of the home production base for the indigenous MNEs concerned have outweighed the negatives in the 1980s, with more favourable supply-side factors obtaining in Germany than France, for example in human capital and technology diffusion. Hence no significant 'hollowing out' effects were observable in either country. This was shown by buoyant levels of production and investment, fixed capital formation growing by 8.5 per cent in Germany and 6.9 per cent in France in 1989. In the same year GDP grew in Germany by 3.9 per cent and in France by 3.6 per cent. The French, though, continued to have year-on-year aggregate trade deficits; in electronics it was alarmingly large and increasing. Germany's export orientation accounted for its persistent trade surpluses, particularly evident in the chemical sector. By the early 1990s, however, with Western Europe suffering the effects of a German unification-induced recession, business confidence in both France and Germany had declined somewhat.[27]

Finally, long-run convergence of the French and German economies had taken place, reinforced by the similarity of macroeconomic policies followed in the two countries. Such macroeconomic convergence was arrested and reversed by German unification, the financing of which led to budget and current account deficits, as well as higher rates of inflation, in Germany.

POLITICAL ECONOMIC STRUCTURE AND MNE RELATIONS WITH EXTERNAL ACTORS

Following on from the brief economic analysis of the previous two sections, the core of this chapter focuses on a political economy treatment of the embeddedness of the MNEs in national institutional configurations in France and Germany. It is argued that this is an important component of the competitiveness of the national economies as well as of the competitive advantages of the MNEs. The linkages the MNEs have with external actors are significant factors in the overall commitment they (the MNEs) have to the home base and their use of the home base as the foundation and platform of their global strategies. Moreover, it is in examining the institutional make-up of the French and German political economies that sharp French–German differences emerge, something that cannot be sufficiently comprehended from a purely economic perspective, but which necessitates going down to the very roots of institutional political economy. Thus far, the political economy literature has not devoted sufficient attention to the embeddedness of multinational firms in domestic structures, and least of all the embeddedness of MNEs in their home bases. This chapter lays the foundation for such analysis as an integral component of the political economy of the firm. It is therefore appropriate to view the MNE at the vortex of the actor linkages in France and Germany that are to be analysed. Who are the main external actors in the national political economies to which MNEs are linked? What is the nature of these linkages, and are they strong or weak? And how does all of that relate to national competitiveness and MNE competitive advantages? Before addressing these questions, a brief historical review is apposite.

History shows that each country's domestic structures are unique, for they are rooted in certain historical transformations – the end of feudalism, the Industrial Revolution and the building of the 'state', that is, governmental institutions.[28]

Like Japan, Germany shook off its feudal vestiges and industrialised fairly late in the nineteenth century. The centralisation, concentration and organisation of business was propelled by the Prussian aristocracy with its iron/rye coalition. Business centralisation was more clearly organised by the formation of peak organisations and cartels in the late 1800s. Investment banks formed an integrated whole with the industrial sector by providing the brains behind industrialisation strategies. Although the post-Second World War Allied Occupation and partition removed the landowning Junkers from the scene, and despite Allied attempts at decartelisation and deconcentration, it is remarkable how the centralisation and linkage of industry and finance has persisted. The organisation of the government and the power of the bureaucracy in particular were ruptured by the Occupation. The new Basic Law deliberately downgraded the powers of central government and put stringent checks and balances on it, thereby sowing the seeds of a decentralised government.

The Napoleonic reforms at the beginning of the nineteenth century endowed France with a centralised governmental apparatus in which the ethos of government-led action in industrialisation strategies, and economic affairs in general, was cultivated. Bureaucratic activism in a centralised government has been particularly evident in the Fourth and Fifth Republics: it filled a void left by revolving-door governments and an unstable party system in the former; and a Gaullist political superstructure in the Fifth Republic was prepared to leave the initiative to the bureaucracy. French business was traditionalist in outlook and small-scale, and for a long time it failed to overcome its position of economic backwardness in the Industrial Revolution. Its decentralisation and lack of hierarchical structure was further manifested by the traditionally loose contacts between finance and industry. Only in the postwar period has business appreciably modernised with concentration in larger firms, but it remains far less centralised than in Germany.

Thus the forces of history have led to distinctive modern

domestic structures in France and Germany: in the former, a centralised government coexisted with decentralised domains of industry and finance; in the latter the reverse held: a decentralised government coexisting with centralised domains of industry and finance.

Germany

The German MNEs find themselves deeply rooted in a national political economy of relatively stable institutional structures, in the government, financial, industrial and labour domains, with strong, historically conditioned linkages to external actors. This system has been described as one of 'organised capitalism' by Andrew Shonfield.

The checks and balances on executive power in a decentralised German government include: the horizontal, administrative federal system in which the functions of implementing federal policy reside largely with the *Länder* bureaucracies; stringent judicial review upheld by the Federal Constitutional Court; a powerful Upper House of the federal legislature, the *Bundesrat*, with powers to block bills passed by the Lower House, the *Bundestag*; and many semi-autonomous federal regulatory agencies. There are numerous 'consensus-enforcing' mechanisms that impart some structure and coherence to the government, with cooperative and relatively closed relations between a few 'insider' groups – the senior federal civil service, its *Länder* counterparts, and hierarchically structured *Bundesrat* and *Bundestag* committees.[29]

Economic policy networks have prominent roles for the Ministry of Economics, the Ministry of Finance and the Bundesbank. They all have a commitment to a liberal ideology on international economic matters: export-orientated growth through trade in an open international economy together with an open door to foreign direct investment. The Bundesbank, with its legally binding independence from government, dominates monetary policy and uses policy instruments such as money-supply targets, the control of benchmark interest rates and the lender-of-last-resort function to maintain price stability and ward off inflationary pressures.

The philosophy and postwar practice of the *Modell soziale Marktwirtschaft* (the social market economy model) does not allow government an interventionist microeconomic role in the affairs of sectors and individual firms. By and large there has been little strategic and operational intervention in the chemical and electronic sectors, *Sektorpolitik* being restricted more to crisis-ridden, declining sectors such as coal, steel and shipbuilding.[30] The social market economy concept allows the government an *Ordnungspolitik* function (the policy of order) in the first instance to provide macroeconomic stability through anti-inflationary monetary policies and fiscal conservatism, and second, to maintain the regulatory and supply-side environment for the efficient operation of market forces in which business should be left free to compete. *Ordnungspolitik* empowers the government and/or autonomous regulatory authorities to undertake the necessary measures to provide the public goods most needed by industry. These are the removal of market impediments to competition, prominent among which is the enforcement of a rigorous competition policy; and the assurance of a healthy environment for demand (without necessarily entailing a Keynesian counter-cyclical policy), so that inter-firm competition proves a breeding ground for innovation and a springboard for global strategies. There are other aspects of public policy which have had strong emphasis in Germany: the maintenance of a tough regime on standards and norms in the certification of goods and services in order to ensure quality and innovation; the provision of taxation and financial policies, for example, tax credits, to encourage savings as well as capital and R&D investment; the creation of a suitable environment for low-cost capital allocated efficiently through the banking system; and the establishment of mechanisms to pool information and diffuse it throughout the market economy. The objective of such policy orientations is not only to breed efficient firms operating in a competitive home market, but also to encourage firms to have an international outlook by serving foreign markets through exports, FDI, alliances and technological transfers.

Decentralisation is another facet of the German political economy that impacts on competitiveness. Decentralisation is not only manifested by the federal political and administrative system, but also in the economy. The major German chemical and electronics firms, for example, are headquartered in different parts of west Germany, for example, Siemens in the Munich area, Bosch around Stuttgart, Hoechst in Frankfurt, Bayer in Leverkusen, BASF in Ludwigshafen, the world's largest chemical complex. This has allowed them to build up close working relationships with their *Land* governments: Siemens in Bavaria, Bosch in Baden-Württemberg, BASF in Rhineland Palatinate, Hoechst in Hesse, Bayer in North Rhine Westphalia. Such decentralisation combined with geographic concentration of production is conducive to Länder policies playing a part in factor creation. Indeed, in Michael Porter's view, regional-level policies can in certain cases be more important for competitiveness than national ones. Hence, as he sees it, the advantages of German (and Swiss) federalism over Anglo-Saxon and French centralism.[31]

The German MNEs have privileged links with the large universal banks. These links take the form of equity stakes by a centralised financial sector – the pillars of which are the 'Big Three' universal banks, headed by the Deutsche Bank – in industry, proxy voting rights on shares deposited with the banks, seats for the banks on the supervisory boards of companies, and the pooling of information and expertise between banks and firms. In the past the banks have had much influence in industrial restructuring as well as in the channelling of long-term credit to different sectors. Chapter 5, on finance, expands on bank–firm relations and puts forward the proposition that these links militate against the pressures of 'short-termism' that plague American and British companies – pressure from shareholders to maximise dividends by concentrating on quarterly results and short-range return on investment variables, the threat of hostile bids and takeover – and serve to provide a more secure environment in which to pursue long-term orientations geared towards increasing market share and sales. But at the same time these very links, with occasional cartel-like overtones, threaten to impose barriers of entry and mobility in competition, sitting somewhat uncomfortably with the free market objectives of *Ordnungspolitik* and undermining the efficacy of its instruments, such as anti-trust enforcement.[32]

Trade unions in the FRG form a centralised labour movement representing 35–40 per cent of all workers: they are organised industry-wide in 16 major unions, which unite to form the *Deutsche Gewerkschaftsbund* (DGB), with nearly 8 million members in 1987. The most important single constituent is the IG Metall, which has a membership of 2.6 million and represents workers in the electronics as well as metal-working sectors. The IG Chemie, the third-largest union, with a membership of 650,000, represents those in the chemical industry.[33] The unions have an important role to play in the fields of labour and social policy. The legally enforced *Mitbestimmung* (co-determination law) institutionalises worker participation, especially of union members, in the supervisory boards of all medium-sized and large firms. The unions' main preserve is on collective wage bargaining; shopfloor and plant-level affairs are mainly dealt with by the *Betriebsräte* (works councils), which have about 80 per cent union membership but are semi-independent of the unions.

There are well-established and institutionalised management–labour forms of cooperation and information exchange in the large firms, whether it be on supervisory boards or at a more decentralised level with the works councils. A better understanding on the part of labour of corporate decision-making, especially on investment and technology matters, brings the unions in behind overall corporate strategies geared to product and process innovation and international competitive advantage. This consensus orientation is particularly evident in the chemical sector: Hoechst, Bayer and BASF have excellent and intimate relations with the IG Chemie, which has the reputation of being the most conservative of the German unions. On the other hand, it is often argued that the power of the German trade unions leads to uncompetitive cost structures and contributes in general to the inflexibility of labour markets, which places an unequal burden on the shoulders of medium and small-sized firms.

One of the particular advantages of many large German firms is the close relations they enjoy with a solid and widespread base of medium-sized *Mittelstand* companies on whom they rely as intimate sub-contractors and suppliers to their own production processes, for example, between Siemens and a cluster of companies around Munich; between the chemical Big Three and the German printing ink industry. Bosch in its own right acts as the most privileged supplier of components to Daimler Benz. Such a long-standing German interlock between large and medium-sized firms is all the more advantageous given that contemporary industrial trends propel big manufacturing MNEs to concentrate core activities in-house and farm out as much of their non-core production as possible. Ongoing coordination with specialised home-based suppliers can be a key competitive advantage in terms of innovation and upgrading for global strategies.[34]

Finally, the links between the MNEs and the sectoral industry associations deserve consideration. The large German firms have a history, dating back to the Nazi era, of coordinating and channelling much of their 'public affairs' work that have economic and sector-wide implications through established industry associations. The peak associations with national authority are key players in the consultative process of public policy formulation, something legitimated by the German constitution.[35] Sector-wide associations are grouped in the Federation of German Industries (*Bundesverband der Deutschen Industrie* – BDI); there are also sectoral and national employers' associations which deal with collective bargaining matters; and the *Deutsche Industrie und Handelstag* (DIHT), which groups local chambers of commerce and of which membership is compulsory. Overall, industry associations represent 80–90 per cent of all German firms; in the chemical industry, it is 90–95 per cent.[36]

The *Verband der Chemischen Industrie* (VCI) is the industry association for chemicals; the main association in electronics is the *Zentralverband der Elektrotechnischen und Elektronischen Industrie* (ZVEI). Foreign-owned firms in the German electronics industry are grouped in the other main industry association for the sector, the *Verband Deutscher Machinenbau* (VDMA). Both the VCI and the ZVEI are powerful and rich in financial resources and in-house expertise, benefiting from the tendency of the large companies to pool resources to serve their collective interests. The industry associations are structured in such a way that it is difficult to discern where the companies end and the industry associations begin: their working committees and those of the product sub-associations which they house are replete with representatives of the large companies; and the chief executives of the large companies usually rotate as head of the industry association as well. For example in 1990 Hermann Strenger, the chief executive of Bayer, was also the head of the VCI; and Dr Karlheinz Kaske was in that year both the head of Siemens and of the ZVEI. The VCI has an established policy of alternating its leadership from year to year between one of the chief executives of the Big Three and that of a smaller company.[37] These characteristics of firm-level backing for industry associations are especially evident in the VCI, which the Big Three go to great lengths to support and which they unquestionably dominate: together they account for 35 per cent of sales in the German chemical market. Siemens has a preponderant influence in the ZVEI. Both the ZVEI and the VCI play an important intermediary role between government and industry.

The perception by management in the German MNEs of these institutional linkages and their places in them is, by and large, positive. There is a common purpose among different actors to maintain and enhance the competitiveness of the German economy; a common purpose that imparts a substantial degree of risk reduction, stability and consensus-orientation to relationships between a number of actors. There is a strong consciousness in the MNEs that such factors are key to making the home base the platform of international success. Michael Porter comments that, of his 13-nation sample, it is the German and Swiss firms who place the most importance on the home base and who are exemplary in contributing to its competitiveness. They avoid the common trap of companies in other countries – he singles out the US and the UK– who tend to see 'public good' areas, for instance vocational training and infrastructures of transport and communication, as preserves of government policy and therefore little to do with them.[38]

Such cooperative mechanisms are seen as an advantage to adapt to changes in the competitive environment, especially changes in the international economy. Adjustment and adaptation have been vital for the German chemical industry, for example, in the face of the rise in raw material input prices after the two oil price shocks, overcapacity in the late 1970s/early 1980s, and sharp price competition from competitors in the newly industrialising countries, the Gulf and the Eastern Bloc.[39]

Plurilateral, multi-actor cooperation in the social fabric is manifested not only at superstructural level in interactions between the most important governmental, financial and industrial actors, but has also become decentralised to apply to a myriad of cooperative links between large and small firms, employers' associations, works councils in firms, the established trade unions, chambers of commerce, the peak industry associations, not to mention research institutes and universities. These linkages cover matters ranging from workplace methods and collective bargaining, through vocational training, to the key aspects of adapting to technological changes and diffusing them throughout the economy.[40]

The six German MNEs examined in this book are all tightly interwoven in these networks, and enjoy prominent positions in them. As such they are national institutions in their own right. These institutional linkages form the political economy component of a German *Verbundwirtschaft* (the interconnected economy), which complements the tight upstream–downstream integration along the production chain, both intra- and inter-firm, that characterises the German economy. The implications of this for the internationalisation of German MNEs are rather pertinent. First, 'German' ways of doing things at home spill over into the firms' international operations, for example, taking a long-term view of establishing and building up market share in core foreign markets, even at the cost of ploughing-in financial resources and tolerating losses;[41] and also paying scrupulous attention to skills and product quality in those foreign operations.

Such potential competitive advantages are frequently associated with the 'industrial vocation' and 'long-termism' of business strategy and planning that is attributed to German MNEs and to which, as has been argued above, the domestic political economic/institutional environment can be conducive.[42] The business historian Alfred Chandler asserts that such long-termism and industrial orientation, with a concentration on technical skills, vocational training, product and process innovations, were the 'first-mover' advantages that gave firms such as Siemens and AEG their grasp on world markets a century ago, and that still help to sustain them in international competition today.[43]

Nevertheless, such a seemingly rosy picture requires substantial qualification. There are structural problems that beset the German political economy and impair competitiveness, and some of these problems relate to the very relationships analysed above. Centralised collective bargaining on wages and conditions, compulsory union membership on the supervisory boards of firms, tight links between large firms and medium-sized suppliers, between industry and finance, and between industry associations and government departments, all may contribute to long-term consensual goal orientation and a commercially rational 'social peace'. But they do have other facets with potentially negative costs. Corporate links with the unions can lead to inflexible labour markets with high wage and non-wage costs of production; just as links between large firms and the universal banks can blunt competition on financial markets and shield established large firms from competition in industrial goods markets. Cosy relations with long-standing suppliers can lead to a complacency that allows the latter generous margins on inputs and weakens overall price competitiveness; just as cosy, neo-corporatist relations between industry associations, unions and government departments can block public policies of deregulation.

These structural problems were less in evidence, and were certainly glossed over, in the high-growth years of the mid and late 1980s; but they have been more evident and much discussed in the recessionary years since unification between the two Germanies. There have been calls to reduce the overall corporate tax burden and levels of public spending on welfare. The incidence of conflict in labour relations has been on the increase, with industry pressing harder, especially in the new east German states, for more decentralised bargaining on wages and conditions. Relations between large firms and their suppliers have become somewhat more strained, with pressure to reduce margins on input prices. More cracks are appearing in the links between large industrial firms and the universal banks. The federal government is placing more emphasis on privatisation (for example, of the PTT and the national airline, Lufthansa) and on deregulation. None the less, the bilateral and plurilateral actor linkages of 'organised capitalism', German-style, remain in force and do not threaten to disappear in the near future, even if they are not as strong as they were at the end of the 1980s.[44]

This political economy argumentation reinforces the economic case argued in the previous section. Internationalisation among the German MNEs in the 1980s has complemented rather than substituted for a continued export platform strategy, the two going hand-in-hand, as was argued at the close of chapter 2. This accounts for record investment by German firms from 1987 up to the 1991–2 recession both at home and abroad. The complementarity between domestic and international production has, perhaps, been less evident in the early 1990s, with some firms transferring labour-intensive production out of Germany to escape the high costs of the German *Standort*. Safeguarding and upgrading the home base and its export orientation, however, the wellspring of their competitive advantages, is part and parcel of expanded international production by the German MNEs. At the core of the MNEs' global strategies stand both the economic advantages of the German *Standort* and their embeddedness in German domestic structures.

France

The French political economy is radically different in structure and linkage in comparison to its German counterpart: it displays neither the stability and resilience of institutional structures nor the strength of linkage between actors that are found in Germany.

Aspects of the centralisation of the French government include a unitary system of government, with an administrative elite that retains control of policy implementation down the line; and a strong executive under the Fifth Republic constitution that co-exists with a trammelled legislature. Policy-making is nevertheless splintered: there is a plethora of institutions involved within the government with overlapping jurisdictions. This detracts from the coherent formation and execution of policy and, more generally, from the 'strong state' argument that is frequently applied in the French context.[45] The government extends its web into society, notably through the *pantouflage* system by which the administrative elite circulates in business and politics (to be discussed in the following chapter on government–MNE relations).[46] Economic policy networks consist of a fair number of governmental institutions: the Ministries of Industry, Foreign Trade, European Affairs, and Finance; the Bank of France which, unlike the Bundesbank, was not independent and came under the control of the Finance Ministry;[47] the Planning Commission; various interministerial committees, as well as a number of parastatal institutions which have responsibility for the channelling of credit to industry.

In the past policy objectives have encouraged exports and selective protection against imports, with a patchy record on outgoing and incoming direct investment. In the 1970s and 1980s shifts in objectives have taken place in line with changing French positions in a more integrated EC and a more interdependent world economy: import protection has been considerably relaxed, as have restrictions on FDI. For a long time monetary policy objectives were geared to maintaining an undervalued exchange rate to help exports. Once again policy shifts have occurred, especially with regard to the franc in the European Exchange Rate Mechanism: pressures to devalue the franc have been outweighed by the imperatives of a strong currency/anti-inflationary strategy. A wide array of sector-specific policy instruments have been used by the government in the postwar period in order to restructure the French economy, including those of credit allocation, loans and grants through a number of parastatal institutions as well as the nationalised sector. Administrative regulation has also been much relied upon.

These then are some of the characteristics that have delineated the role of the government in the French *Économie Mixte*, which combines a private sector and market orientation with a sizeable public sector and a significant, direct role for the government in the microeconomic affairs of sectors and firms.[48] The government has clearly been an active player in industrial affairs, using a set of Napoleonic pre-capitalist institutions within the governmental apparatus to 'sponsor' capitalist development and 'administer' industrialisation. The reliance on a liberal ideology to achieve policy goals has until relatively recently had little currency in the French mercantilist tradition, which has not had much faith in market forces as a mechanism of resource allocation. Hence government intervention through structural policy measures has been seen less as a means of righting market imperfections or compensating for market failures than it has been in Germany; rather it has been justified in terms of protecting national inde-pendence and preserving France's place in the international pecking order.[49]

Indeed, the government–industry linkage issuing from a history of government intervention is the strongest and most direct of all inter-institutional linkages in the French political economy. The government and its evolving industrial policies have had direct impact of great import in shaping and restructuring the affairs of the French MNEs examined here. Sectoral policy in chemicals and electronics has existed in forms that go way beyond any German-type *Ordnungspolitik* function. Such government intervention has changed drastically in the 1980s, owing much to the international-isation of the MNEs and of markets in general, as well as to the speeded-up process of European integration. These themes will be discussed in the following chapters in some detail. This change of government policy towards the MNEs is, moreover, part of a wider 1980s phenomenon: the *dirigiste* consensus has been eroded, not only on the Right but also within business, and in the ranks of the Socialist Party, which governed France for most of the 1980s.

One point worth emphasising is the contrast between German federalism, a central component of the decentralisation that char-acterises the German polity, and the centralised French govern-ment: the prefectoral system extends Parisian central jurisdiction deep into the provinces; local, departmental and regional tiers of government have little power and influence in comparison to the German *Länder*. Nevertheless there has been a decentralising trend in France in the 1980s, giving greater power to departmental and regional tiers of government, that was catalysed by the Deferre legislation of the new Socialist government in 1981. In the longer term it is expected that business, especially the smaller and medium-sized firms, will expand and deepen their relations with the secondary tiers of government.[50]

But apart from the Big Business–central government linkage in France, there are no other important ones that have German-style strength or coherence; indeed the picture is frequently one of a lack of organisation, cooperation and consensus.

To begin with, a solid base of small and medium-sized firms is lacking in France. In a report to the Ministry of Industry in 1990, Gerard Constant concludes that the two million enterprises with fewer than 500 employees are on the whole weak in terms of innovation and R&D intensity, with a dearth of sufficiently qualified personnel. Forty per cent of them do not survive after the first four years of existence. Links between the *petites et moyennes entreprises* (PMEs) and the large MNEs are also not particularly strong, as they are in Germany. This is partly a result of government policy, which for decades has underemphasised the PMEs in favour of the large national champions. Such unstructured PME–large-firm relations are 'a handicap in comparison to Germany or Japan', according to a study for the Institut de l'Entreprise. Big companies simply do not consider themselves responsible for the prosperity of the constellation of enterprises that gravitate to them.[51] Interests and actions can thus have the potential of being in conflict, as interviewees commented:

> The main French weakness is one of the quality of management in the PMEs: they remain badly structured and organised, especially in the context of supplier relations with the larger firms.
>
> (Ex-civil servant, Ministry of Industry)

> The big companies have Europeanised; the small ones have not . . . There are PME–big company cooperative relations on specific projects, but there is no structured, comprehensive and long-term linkage, quite unlike the Germans.
>
> (Executive, French electronics industry association)

There are some exceptions to this rule. Rhône-Poulenc puts its commercial network in 140 countries at the disposal of smaller French firms who have product portfolios related to that of Rhône-Poulenc and who build up solid supplier relations with it. Elf Aquitaine has a special arm, the Sofrea, created in 1978, to develop its links with PME in certain regions in France where it is strongly implanted, for example, in Rhône-Alpes, Sud Est and the Loire, and to build up their R&D and innovation capacity. It had aided 20,000 firms by the end of the 1980s and spent FFr1 billion in 1989.[52]

The French labour movement is, unlike its German counterpart, decentralised, disorganised and badly divided. There are a number of rival trade union confederations engaged in sometimes fratricidal conflict with each other and with a total of only 15 per cent membership, at best, among the workforce. The confederations themselves are loosely and incoherently organised, with deep fissures running within them. Their financial resources and in-house expertise tend to be weak. The largest, the CGT, with a membership of around 1.5 million, is also the most militant and is allied to the Communist Party. It is strong in the chemical sector and has been among the most vocal in voicing its opposition to the internationalisation of French firms, on the grounds that this process threatens the export of jobs and production from France. The other main federations are: the *Confédération française démocratique du travail* (CFDT), with links to the Socialist Party; the *Force ouvrière* (FO), which is independent of political parties; and the *Confédération française des travailleurs chrétiens* (CFTC), a breakaway offshoot of the CFDT.

Given this decentralisation and division within the labour movement, the trade unions have great difficulty in organising the rank and file and in presenting a united front on policy matters to management and the government. Until recently, collective wage bargaining was largely unregulated by law and the unions had limited legal status in the workplace. The anarcho-syndicalist tradition of the union movement has bred in them the tendency to organise mass demonstrations and frequent one-day strikes, but little ability to sustain collective action in industrial disputes. Hence the unions have a weak bargaining power position *vis-à-vis* management and the government. The incoming Socialist–Communist government did legislate in 1982 to strengthen the unions by giving them greater rights in the workplace and as intermediaries with government, but given their structural weak-

Table 3.4 Union representation in the *conseil d'administration* of the SNEA (Société Nationale Elf Aquitaine) in 1989

	per cent of votes	Seats
CGT	30.5	2
CFDT	27.1	2
CFE/CGE	19.1	1
CFTC	8.1	–
FO	15.2	1

Source: Elf Social Report, 1990

nesses it seems to have had little effect.[53] The splintered nature of the unions is reflected in their representation on the administrative councils of the large firms, as Table 3.4 on Elf illustrates.

The upshot of this decentralisation and weakness of labour is that the unions have a track record of incapacity and unwillingness to cooperate in a consensus-orientated fashion with management in the MNEs, for whom labour relations remain a constant irritant. The contrast with the German case is indeed great: in France the unions are by no means deeply enmeshed in common structures with management in furthering training, diffusing technology and resolving conflict; rather they remain excluded from corporate decision-making and, more often than not, show very little understanding of the competitive needs of firms.

Institutionalised relations between industry and finance in France are sparse and much weaker than in the FRG, being at best intermittent but not at all strongly grounded in business culture and the structure of financial markets. The financial sector is not as centralised as it is in Germany, being divided first between parastatal funding institutions, commercial and investment banks, with only the latter having a history of portfolio stakes in industry; and second, between the nationalised and private banks. (The remaining nationalised banks are in the process of being privatised by the Balladur government from 1993 onwards.) In the postwar period the financial sector has been used by the government to channel funds in a targeted manner to sectors of industry.[54] Nevertheless, the structured linkage between big banks and the large firms in common institutional fora, as manifested in Germany, is not evident in a French business culture which has not had a history of such deep involvement of the financial sector in industrial strategies and development. Chapter 5 on finance explores these points further.

French industry associations are also relatively decentralised and weak in comparison to their German counterparts. The umbrella association for French firms is the *Conseil national des patronats français* (CNPF), commonly known as the *Patronat*. It is dominated by the large firms, especially those grouped in the Agref, and has been the accredited spokesman for business since 1969. The *Patronat* itself is divided and disparate, being organised both horizontally by sector and vertically by region; it maintains little control over its 800,000 member firms. Its relations with the umbrella association for small and medium-sized firms, the *Confédération générale des petites et moyennes entreprises* (CGPME), to which it is affiliated, are somewhat strained and difficult.[55]

The sectoral industrial associations in France of relevance to this study are the *Union des Industries Chimiques* (UIC) for the chemical sector and the *Fédération des Industries Électroniques et Électrotechniques* (FIEE) for the electronics sector. They are by no means as powerful as their German counterparts, the VCI and the ZVEI; nor are their relations as symbiotic with their member firms. One reason for this state of affairs relates to the way in which the industry associations themselves are structured – with some pertinent French–German differences. The firms tend to deal directly with the largely autonomous product sub-associations which group in a loose alliance to form the central sectoral associations (UIC and FIEE), so that the firms deal less directly with the latter. Thus an organisational barrier exists that prevents the firms from giving maximum support to the peak industry associations. Such a decentralised structure also weakens the power of the latter in dealing with the product associations, in presenting pan-sector views and in mediating and resolving disputes between the product associations. In Germany, in contrast, the top management of the large firms are directly involved in the central associations (ZVEI and VCI), which exert strong control of their product associations in a centralised, top-down organisational structure; this enables them to speak that much more effectively for the respective sectors and to act as more forceful mediators in inter-product association dealings.

As an interviewee in the FIEE remarked:

Our companies work through us when they divine a pan-sectoral interest and when they see the need for a referee/arbiter in intra-sectoral disputes. But the collaborative spirit among the large firms for us is less evident than it is in the FRG. Unlike the ZVEI, the top management of the main companies do not involve themselves heavily in our affairs ... [On the relationship between the FIEE and its product associations] The key link is the financial one: the firms fund the product associations, who in turn fund us. That puts us in a position of dependence on them; it makes it harder for us to build unified fronts ... we have an organisational tendency to go our separate ways and run into conflict with one another due to a lack of centralising glue ... [On the companies] ... The Big Three [CGE, Thomson, Bull] don't tend to cooperate very much. They focus their activities in the product associations [for example, Alcatel in the one for telecoms, Bull in IT, Thomson in those for consumer electronics and components]: because of their different specialisations, they don't run into one another very much – our organisational structure is not conducive to that.

The other main factor that undermines the sectoral associations is the tendency of the large firms to deal directly and bilaterally with the government, largely bypassing the industry associations. Unlike the German associations, they are not treated as privileged interlocutors with government.

From the same interview:

I do have the impression that the ZVEI is powerful due to its backing by the big firms. It would be difficult to imagine M. Suard [chief executive of CGE] or M. Gomez [chief executive of Thomson] as head of the FIEE [in contrast to Dr Kaske of Siemens being the head of the ZVEI]. The large multinationals have a tendency to deal directly with government on matters of most concern to them, for example, on high definition television, semiconductors, defence electronics, and bypass us altogether.

In conclusion, the ruptures and fissures that run through the institutions and in linkages between actors in the French political economy contrast sharply with the integrated German *Verbundwirtschaft*. Many institutions – in the domains of labour, industry associations, small and medium-sized firms, finance – are decentralised and weak, as are their linkages with the MNEs. There is thus lack of a common purpose and little pooling of effort plurilaterally on certain policy areas which involve factor creation and infrastructural upgrading in order to improve national competitiveness.

Vocational training is a good example. In Germany many educational institutions, the governments at both federal and *Land* level, trade unions, chambers of commerce, industry associations and works councils cooperate with the MNEs in the training system which plays such an integral part in both the competitive advantages of the firms and in German national competitiveness. The disjunctures between institutions in the French system of training, especially the gap between the educational institutes and the companies, prevent the French from attaining German standards. Similarly, strong axes of cooperation on R&D between firms, research institutes and universities in Germany aid the innovation and diffusion of technology throughout the economy, whereas the lack of such cooperation in France prevents it having a technology base as advanced as Germany's. Indeed in France bilateral linkages are far more evident than the German model of plurilateral linkages, especially in government–group relations. Hence the government tends to deal separately with groups, whether they be the companies, the *Patronat* or the unions.

These factors go some way towards explaining differences between French and German MNEs in terms of their commitment to the home base. Although a general commitment among the management of the French MNEs does exist towards maintaining and upgrading French national competitiveness, it is not as strong as in the German MNEs: they simply do not display the same conviction as their German counterparts in the home political economy and their places in its institutional networks. Interviews, exemplified in the following extract, quite vividly brought out these differences:

> We are more Latin and individualist than the Germans, who have more of a group mentality, and are more co-operation and consensus-oriented. We have to gradually learn to be more like that as a multinational in the international market place.
>
> (Corporate planner, Rhône-Poulenc)

CONCLUSION

The commitment of the German MNEs to the German home base is not only a function of the economic advantages of the German

Standort; it runs much deeper than that and is linked to institutional structures and their webs of linkages in the German political economy. There are, however, potentially anti-competitive and sclerotic effects of such neo-corporatist mechanisms that became more evident in the early 1990s. Having said that, the advantages of such cooperative networks are not to be found in France. Institutions in society are decentralised and weak, as are their relationships to the MNEs. There is less capacity to pool efforts into upgrading factors. Hence the lower levels of commitment by the French MNEs to the home base. In addition, quite unlike postwar Germany, France has not had a historical ideological commitment to free markets in an open international economy, although this position has changed somewhatin the 1980s.

From an economic viewpoint, the French economy has converged in some respects to more German-style positions, especially in monetary policy. As *The Economist* observes: 'There is a continual obsession with Germany – a continuous need to treat the performance and structure of the economy across the Rhine as the benchmark of its own success ... Germany is an almost unconscious and not always accessible yardstick many French people use when thinking about their own country.'[56] But convergence is limited and partial due to the manifest differences in French and German domestic structures.

Finally, this chapter provides a window into the following chapters that concentrate on the home political economies in light of the internationalisation of the MNEs. The bases of economic competitiveness in France and Germany have been laid out, as has the manner in which the MNEs are embedded in these political economies. Understanding these institutional relationships in which the firm is anchored, as well as the phenomenon of internationalisation, is key to the comprehension of the subject matter in the following chapters – government–MNE relations, government policy, and finance–industry relations. Also in the chapter on the European dimension and technology (chapter 6), it will be evident that these domestic institutional relationships are played out, and to some extent replicated, at the EC level. There is therefore an undercurrent running right through this study that encapsulates an interplay between internationalisation and domestic structures. Internationalisation as described in chapter 2 provides the dynamic that imparts the shades of change to the canvas of continuity provided by domestic structures.

In concentrating on what are considered, for the purposes of this study, the most pertinent aspects of the role of the MNE in its environment – relations with central government and banks, the EC dimension, technology – other aspects have had, unfortunately, to be relegated to the background if this study is to remain reasonably compact and conceptually and analytically clear. This chapter has noted important French–German differences in the relations of the MNEs with secondary tiers of government, unions, and medium and small-sized enterprises. In Germany these linkages are not insignificant contributory factors of firm-level competitive advantage, and have been evolving in light of both the internationalisation of the MNEs and the process of European integration. Similar linkages in France also changed in the 1980s as a result of these forces, although they remain structurally weaker than is the case in Germany. These are considerations which deserve extensive analysis, something which is not possible in this book. It is hoped that other research efforts and other scholars will rise to the challenge.

4

GOVERNMENT POLICY AND MNE–GOVERNMENT RELATIONS
Multinationals as political actors

This chapter concentrates on one central aspect of the embeddedness of the MNEs in domestic structures – the relationship between the MNEs and the French and German governments. Certain questions arise in using the government–MNE relationship as one focus of the interaction of internationalisation with domestic structures. What are the major lines of public policy that concern the MNEs? How have these policy agendas evolved in light of the internationalisation of the MNEs, that is, to what extent have government authorities and their policy packages acquired an international dimension in becoming more understanding of and sensitised to the internationalisation of indigenous MNEs? And finally, what are the contours of the relationship, or set of relationships, between the MNEs and their home governments in the context of internationalisation? These questions touch on the role of the MNEs as political actors in their outer environments, with quite vital French–German comparisons that shed light on the government–industry linkage in the domestic political economies.

In the first section the very different and historically conditioned conceptions of and approaches to government policy in France and Germany are explored, extending the interpretations in chapter 3 on the role of the government in the German *soziale Marktwirtschaft* and the French *Économie Mixte*. Next, the main public policy areas that have affected the selected chemical and electronics MNEs in the 1980s are identified, as are the main players involved in dealing with these policy agendas within the government apparatus. Throughout, attention is devoted to central government and central government policy. Secondary tiers of government are important to the MNEs, especially in the decentralised German federal system. As was pointed out in chapter 3, the German MNEs have built up strong links with governments in the *Länder* where they are headquartered; and the *Land* governments have significant prerogatives in areas of economic, employment, social and environmental policy, apart from being responsible for the administration of the bulk of federal legislation. Regional and departmental councils in France are far less powerful in the French centralised system, but their powers were gradually increased in the 1980s through measures of local government decentralisation. It can be expected that relations between large firms and local governments in France will assume more importance than has hitherto been the case. For reasons of space and rigour of conceptual design, however, the local government dimension cannot be included within the compass of this study. Rather the focus is on the French and German central governments which, in dealing with domestic and foreign economic policy issues that impact on the MNEs and their internationalisation, are more important for the MNEs than subsidiary tiers of government.

The second half of the chapter then goes on to concentrate on MNE–government relations in a handful of the policy areas identified in the section on government policy. The MNE–government linkage is subsumed in policy networks and communities that address relevant policy agendas and involve players from within the MNEs as well as from within the government apparatus. The structures and make-up of these policy networks/communities are examined, especially in terms of the lines of linkage that connect the MNEs to the government.

HOME GOVERNMENT POLICY WITH RESPECT TO THE MNEs

The focus in this section is on *selected* policy areas in chemicals and electronics in the 1980s that have been of central concern to the MNEs and the home governments, at the same time identifying the main players involved within the government apparatus. Hence the concentration on environmental regulation, telecommunications deregulation and anti-trust policy in the FRG; and on foreign direct investment regulation, sectoral restructuring and state ownership in France.

An international trend throughout the 1970s and 1980s was the increasing intervention of governments in so-called 'sunrise' industries, concentrating promotion on a narrow range of industries and technologies, a number of which come under the headings of chemicals and electronics. But the combined impact of the internationalisation of firms and markets, European integration and the development of new technologies has induced more recent changes – belonging more to the 1980s than the 1970s – in the regulatory framework. Two aspects of regulatory change, in competition policy and telecommunications deregulation, are briefly instanced here in order to illustrate the increasing international and European dimensions to policy agendas.[1]

First, we shall look at the reorientation of competition policy. As national markets internationalise, it becomes less tenable to base a number of anti-trust decisions on the basis of market share in any one national market. Delineating the relevant market also becomes more difficult due to the blurring of sectoral boundaries through the development of new basic technologies. National governments have thus become increasingly worried that competition enforcement, traditionally used to making decisions – regarding mergers, acquisitions, breaking monopolistic and oligopolistic behaviour – on the basis of market shares in the national market rather than in the global market, can disadvantage domestic companies in international competition. Hence the rationale for national competition authorities to take global market shares more into account; and for the transfer of much competition policy competences to the EC level in cases of large and cross-border mergers and acquisitions in the Community. Where relevant markets are judged to be European and/or global in nature, policy-makers in the EC have come to the conclusion that a supranational institution such as the Commission is better able to enforce competition than authorities in the member-states. The experience of EC competition policy competence in the early 1990s has been mixed and there have been many disputes: over its politicisation, that is, the discretionary nature of many decisions taken in the Commission, in contrast to those of a politically independent authority such as the Federal Cartel Office in Germany; over the infiltration of sometimes interventionist and arbitrary industrial policy criteria in competition enforcement, diluting the latter's market-conforming intent; and over the division of authority between national competition authorities and the EC. Having said that, the increasingly cross-border dimensions of competition policy are quite evident.

Second, there has been a competitive race to deregulate among national governments, most evident in the telecommunications sector. As was discussed in chapter 2, long-standing regulations protecting national champions have become counterproductive: they have slowed down technological development and cramped the competitive advantages of the very firms they sought to promote. Ring-fences around national markets might have kept foreign competitors out, but they have also prevented indigenous companies expanding abroad, in effect retarding their inter-nationalisation, as was found with the French and German electronics MNEs studied here. Thus deregulation has been aimed at promoting competition and technological development at home, and at gaining access to foreign markets, expansion abroad being vital to reap a sufficient sales level to finance necessary R&D costs in a technology race between firms wishing to develop and market new products. In France and Germany such deregulation has been pressured in large part by policy made at the EC level. This has been especially evident in measures on public procurement and telecommunications equipment, which have required compliance by the member-states.

In both cases, latter-day international and particularly European dimensions to national government policies have been evident. French and German experiences have corresponded to these trends of convergence and will be analysed in the following sections. Nevertheless, alongside these converging international trends must be juxtaposed the remaining differences in French and German policy approaches that are part and parcel of their very different domestic structures. For instance, government financial support to industry is very differently constituted in the two countries. In Germany there is more reliance on tax concessions, representing 58 per cent of total support in 1989, a policy instrument that does not facilitate strong government intervention in industry. In France tax concessions accounted for only 11 per cent of government support, whereas more directly interventionist means such as equity participation (26 per cent) and soft loans (38 per cent) accounted for the bulk of it.[2]

Germany

There are two landmark pieces of federal legislation in the history of German industrial policy: the 1957 Law on Restrictions on

Competition, which was very much informed by free market *Ordnungspolitik*; and the 1967 Law for the Promotion of Stability and Economic Growth. The latter, which was the brainchild of the then Economics Minister, Professor Dr Karl Schiller, ushered in the era of *Konzertierte Aktion* (concerted action) and what came to be known as *Modell Deutschland*. Aside from an ambitious commitment to countercyclical policy, the guiding principles were those of greater cooperation between the government and the organised social partners in order to reduce conflict, encourage consensus and facilitate structural economic adjustment. Part of the *Modell Deutschland* ideology envisaged a commitment to a *Sektorpolitik* that would promote knowledge-intensive, high-technology industries; its influence in the computer and microelectronics fields can be traced back to 1967. From that time there has been government encouragement of mergers and cooperation between large companies through, for example, tax concessions and preferential public procurement contracts, such as government support for a joint Siemens, Nixdorf and AEG project in computers in 1970, and the creation of the Unidata European computer consortium in 1973.[3]

Many of the more ambitious aims of the *Modell Deutschland* were not achieved in the course of political practice and went out of favour in the 1980s with the return of a CDU–CSU–FDP coalition to power in Bonn. But even in its heyday *Modell Deutschland* did not come close to approximating French-style *dirigisme*. *Sektorpolitik* has largely been confined to declining industries and to parts of the electronics sector. Even in the latter, its track record has been only mildly interventionist in comparison to government intervention in the French electronics sector. There has been comparatively less intervention to speak of in the German chemical sector. And in times of industrial and firm-level crisis, the government has often left the restructuring process to the self-organising capability of industry and finance. The crises that have befallen AEG in the 1970s and 1980s are indicative of these points. When AEG was on the verge of bankruptcy in 1982, with considerable impact on a German economy in recession, the federal government resisted pressures from the trade unions to intervene in favour of 'private-sector' solutions.[4]

The federal government ministry that maintains the closest contacts with the German MNEs studied here and their industry associations is the Ministry of Economics (*Bundesministerium für*

Wirtschaft – BMWI), in particular the divisions within its Industrial Policy section that deal with the chemical and electronics sectors.[5] Given the lines of contact between the civil servants in these divisions and the MNEs/industry associations, it is not surprising that they show the most sensitivity to questions of industrial competitiveness and the need to adapt domestic and foreign economic policy to take account of the internationalisation of markets and the international activities of German MNEs. They realise that purely 'national thinking' – considering the German economy in isolation, focusing exclusively on the old agenda of *Exportmodell Deutschland* without international production – is outdated and that an international dimension must be given priority to prevent home-brewed policy from conflicting with and damaging both the German *Standort* and the firms' competitive advantages. As an interviewee in the BMWI remarked:

> The German *Standort* has undergone structural economic change with the internationalisation of our MNEs. The debate on it has acquired a different meaning and form. Ten years ago, it was taken for granted that German companies were dependent on the home market. Now that is not the case, as the German market has become the most important location among a number of locations for these firms. It is the task of public policy to respond to this change.

At the forefront of such international dimensions to policy-making in the BMWI is 'Europeanisation': the intertwining of national and EC policy in the process of the integration of the Single Market, particularly since the mid-1980s. The major policy debates pertaining to *Standort Deutschland* which have affected the German chemical and electronics MNEs – on competition policy, telecommunications deregulation, environmental regulation and biotechnology – have had considerable ramifications at the EC level: on these issue-areas policy-making in Brussels for the Community as a whole has intensified, and there has been as a result reciprocal interaction between national and EC policy processes and outcomes.

Such an international/European dimension with competitiveness criteria at the forefront is shared by the Ministry of Research and Technology (*Bundesministerium für Forschung und Technologie* – BMFT), which is frequently in alliance with the BMWI on a number of issues against other ministries that downplay competitiveness criteria in favour of others and that are closer to other interest groups.

The public-policy area of main concern to the chemical sector in Germany is regulation of the environment. Public conscious-ness of the environment rose throughout the 1970s and 1980s, finding political expression in local citizens' groups, the Green Party at *Land* and federal levels, and even in the mainstream political parties. Environmental issues have worked their way to the very top of the political agenda. The politicisation of the issue-area has brought much criticism and bad publicity to the German chemical sector because of its environmental record of chemical discharges into the air and rivers, and its treatment of waste, most notably in the wake of a number of chemical spillages by Hoechst, Bayer and BASF into the Rhine during the course of 1986–7.

The regulatory framework has consequently become very much more stringent. The principle of industry self-regulation, main-tained as recently as 1980 in the Chemicals Law to implement the EC's sixth directive on the classification of dangerous substances, has been substantially eroded in recent legislative action: the *Bundesemissionsschutzgesetz* of 1986 imposes strict limits on chemical emissions; measures to approve chemical production processes have also been tightened considerably in long-drawn-out bureau-cratic procedures.[6] From the firms' point of view, there are com-petitive disadvantages involved for them in what they regard as overly rigid rules and regulations: the costs of compliance with new laws are significantly higher in Germany than in practically any other country; and the stringency of the regulatory framework puts greater limits on them than it does on their main competitors that have home bases in other North American and European countries with more flexible regulation. Running in tandem with changes in the German regulatory framework have been legislative measures on the environment at the EC level, to harmonise different national standards as part of the Single Market programme.

Competition policy has been of great concern to the two largest electronics MNEs in Germany, Siemens and Daimler Benz. The regulatory framework for competition enforcement emanates from the 1957 Law on Restrictions on Competition which rules out cartels and empowers the legally independent Federal Cartel Office (*Bund-eskartellamt* – BKA) to act in cases of mergers, abuse of dominant market positions, and horizontal and vertical agreements/alliances that are 'anti-competitive'. The competition policy debate became especially controversial in 1989 when Daimler Benz put forward its plan to take over MBB, a Bavarian-based concern active in aerospace, defence electronics and armaments. The proposed acquisition was blocked by the BKA on the grounds that Daimler would have too large a share of the German aerospace/defence market; it would be in a position of market dominance and thus the proposed link-up was deemed to be anti-competitive. Daimler argued very forcefully that for these business areas the relevant market was not the German one, the criterion used by the BKA, but the international one, in which its market share even with the MBB acquisition would be dwarfed by a number of American competitors. It argued that the BKA decision should be overruled by the Federal Minister of Economics on the grounds of essential national interest, which he in fact ultimately did.

Since this landmark case, there has been some evolution of thinking within the BKA, taking international market shares more into account in key sectors. This was shown when the BKA gave the green light in 1990 to the Siemens acquisition of Nixdorf. Both companies had been active in information systems and together would constitute the largest concern by far in the German market and the second-largest in Europe. But the BKA did allow for the fact that in the relevant business areas of operation, computers and information technology as well as telecommunications, Siemens-Nixdorf would be part of internationalising markets with increasing future competition at home from foreign-owned competitors. Thus no anti-competitive threat was thought to exist.[7]

Although a number of cases of cooperation in the IT sector were not approved by the BKA (for example, a joint optical factory by Siemens, SEL, AEG and others, and the planned Thomson takeover of Grundig), it has not been able to halt the recent wave of large mergers and, at least in the MBB case, lost ground to the BMWI. The latter case was perceived as a defeat for a competition-enforcing *Ordnungspolitik* in favour of industrial policy criteria working in the direction of concentration.[8]

Finally, reference should be made to the deregulation of the German telecommunications equipment market which, although belated and not as radical as deregulation in the US and the UK, has conformed with international trends and moves in parallel with deregulation at EC level as part of the Single Market measures of the 1992 programme. The liberalisation programme in the 1989 *Poststrukturgesetz* provides for complete freedom in the terminal equipment supply market, after it had long been the preserve of the two national champions, Siemens and SEL; furthermore the Deutsche Bundespost was split into three businesses, although the Bundespost monopoly of the telephone trunk network was maintained.[9] The deregulation of telecommunications in Germany, as in other countries, has proceeded apace in the early 1990s, with the intention of partially privatising the Bundespost in the next few years and preparing for the opening of the trunk network to competition in the EC by 1998.

These then are the main public-policy areas in Germany which have been of central concern to the German MNEs studied here in the 1980s, and which have exhibited strong international and European dimensions. The influence of the MNEs in such policy processes and outcomes will be analysed in the second half of the chapter as a gauge of the state of government–MNE relations in Germany.

France

The *étatiste* tradition of government intervention in industry has been evident right throughout the postwar period. Henri Aujac points to successive phases of government policy activism: initiating reconstruction and modernisation through concentrated channelling of funds to selected sectors, together with the development of indicative planning (1946–mid-1960s); focusing on concentration on national champion firms in what were judged as the *industries de pointe* of the future, in which a 'technology gap' was thought to exist (mid-1960s–mid-1970s); and greater reliance on market mechanisms combined with continued intervention, reaching a zenith in the *politique de créneaux* targeted at niche areas of sunrise industries (mid-1970s–early-1980s). To achieve set objectives, the French government has had a plentiful arsenal of policy tools at hand: in addition to the standard array of instruments of tax concessions, public procurement, export, R&D and other subsidies, it has used the myriad of parastatal financial institutions to selectively funnel funds to industry.[10]

Competition policy is highly indicative of French–German differences. The strong German regulatory framework designed to prevent over-concentration and enforce competition contrasts with the very weak regime in France: the French government has acted more as an agent of concentration than a competition enforcer. Only in the late 1980s were competition laws toughened, in line with EC harmonisation measures. Since the 1986 reforms the Competition Commission can initiate inquiries without government permission but, unlike the BKA in Germany, it has not been able to prevent mergers on anti-competitive grounds. That prerogative continued to reside with the Ministry of Industry, although for large mergers and acquisitions above a threshold of ECU5 billion, authority has been transferred to EC level as of September 1990, illustrating that the emerging Community-wide regime on this issue-area is set to bite deeply into previously national policy preserves.[11]

When examining the structure of the French government, the picture is somewhat more complex and unstable in comparison to the relatively neat, streamlined structure with its parcelling of policy authority in the German federal government. The Ministry of Industry in Paris has the most intimate relations with the MNEs from within the government apparatus, especially its semi-independent divisions that deal with the chemical and electronics sectors. The Ministry is widely regarded as being a weak supervisory agency of industry; indeed, it is considered as the lobby for business within government. Its status declined in the 1980s, with the removal of responsibility for foreign trade, research, posts and telecommunications. Responsibility for industrial policy was consequently split between many ministries: apart from the Ministry of Industry, there were the Ministries of European Affairs, Research, Posts and Telecommunications, and Foreign Trade; the increasingly marginalised Planning Commission; the *tutelle* ministries that have intimate relations with the firms in their sectoral purviews (for example, the Ministry of Health for the pharmaceutical sector); not to mention the vast number of parastatal funding organisations. An *état éclatée* (splintered state) has vast potential for confusion and conflict over policy turf, although lower levels of government in the centralised French system do not get involved in policy processes to the same extent as in the decentralised German federal system.

Finally, mention must be made of the most powerful governmental player in French economic policy and even in the specific domain of industrial policy: the Ministry of Finance and especially its 'sanctuary within the temple', the *Trésor* (Treasury), which oversees financial questions relating to state-owned MNEs. It is the Ministry of Finance that is at the very centre of industrial policy, with undisputed dominance over the macroeconomic policy levers and the public budget. It plays a financial co-ordinating role and has the clearest goals of any ministry. The appointment of Edith Cresson as Prime Minister in 1991 to replace Michel Rocard saw a further and unprecedented strengthening of the already formidable position of the Finance Ministry within the government: the gamut of ministries responsible for industrial policy – Industry, Posts and Telecommunications, Research, European Affairs, Foreign Trade – came under its direct super-vision and control for the first time.[12]

Policy on outward (and inward) foreign direct investment has been more controlled in France than in Germany, which has consistently maintained an 'open door' to both incoming and outgoing direct investment. French policy zigzagged during the 1970s and into the early 1980s. The late 1960s and early 1970s witnessed restrictions on the outward flow of investment by French companies, mainly to protect the balance of payments and an artificially overvalued franc. Policy on outward direct invest-ment has undergone profound and dramatic change since the early 1980s in favour of actual encouragement of the international expansion of home MNEs, both public and private.

Correspondingly, restrictions on both outward and inward investment have been progressively removed along with overall liberalisation of capital movements. Removal of capital controls triggered the spurt of investment abroad by French MNEs towards the mid-1980s as a means of releasing pent-up demand that had been accumulating for some time. By 1990 inward investment controls were removed completely from source countries within the EC area.[13] Once again, the European dimension has been important in pressuring domestic deregulation: capital liberal-isation in France has been propelled in large part by the obligation to comply with EC measures to free capital movements within the Community. The door has thus been substantially opened and the French government is no longer the 'gatekeeper' to foreign invest-ment; but it is still not quite an 'open door' in the German sense. There is still some *Trésor* oversight of foreign investment together with some bureaucratic hurdles that MNEs have to overcome before they can go ahead with foreign expansion. For state-owned MNEs, permission must be obtained from the *Trésor* for foreign investments and the financing arrangements must be negotiated between them and the *Trésor*. Furthermore, production abroad has to be justified by firms. For example, Rhône-Poulenc had to fight to justify its policy of maintaining laboratories in the US by arguing that it would not jeopardise jobs at home.[14] But that is not to underestimate the extent of liberalisation. As an interviewee in Alcatel said:

> We have to fill in some forms for the Trésor [when making foreign investments] – a formality. I can't think of a case when they would stop us.

The meat of relevant French industrial policy, and the changes involved in it, are at the sectoral level in the form of the restructuring of the chemical and electronics sectors in the 1980s. The previous decades were marked by successive government-engendered restructurings and concentrations of the firms in question, partly accounting for the fact that many of them have grown within the French market by relying on acquisitions, mainly of smaller companies. It is interesting that this phenomenon was in the 1980s externalised to the international stage as French MNEs went on a buying spree abroad to gain critical mass in international competition. This is a poignant example of how the French path(s) to internationalisation has been coloured by structures and actions within the French political economy.

Previous sectoral and firm-level policy activism by the government can be gleaned from the following examples. It was the government that involved the aluminium-maker Pechiney-Ugine-Kuhlmann and the glass-maker St Gobain-Pont-à-Mousson in the chemical sector, only to encourage them to withdraw from it in the early 1980s; and it was the government that prevented Rhône-Poulenc from shedding capacity in fibres in 1978 because of the threat of job losses. Similarly, the government launched the *Plan Calcul* in data processing in 1967, promoting Bull as the French national champion at the core of this *Grand Projet*.[15]

This then brings us up to the core period under examination, which begins with the election of François Mitterrand as the first Socialist President of the Fifth Republic in 1981, followed soon after by the formation of a Socialist–Communist government with an overwhelming majority in the National Assembly. The President was elected on a manifesto commitment to nationalise leading concerns in finance and industry, which had been a shibboleth of the Union of the Left since 1972.[16] Five industrial concerns were nationalised outright: CGE, Rhône-Poulenc,

Thomson, Pechiney and St Gobain. The government took a majority stake in CII-Honeywell-Bull, forcing Honeywell to decrease its stake from 47 per cent to 20 per cent in the concern and thus below a blocking minority, losing its say in management control. The government entered into negotiations with Hoechst with the intention of acquiring a majority in Roussel Uclaf, the French pharmaceutical concern acquired by Hoechst in 1974. Thus by 1982 30 per cent of all industrial sales in France were by state-owned concerns, which accounted for 50 per cent of investment and over 20 per cent of employment in the French market. Over half of the electronics industry's production and R&D activities came within the government's purview; all the major chemical and pharmaceutical concerns, with the exception of Roussel Uclaf, were now state-owned.[17]

At this time the newly nationalised firms were in the throes of a crisis. The main firms in the chemical sector totted up losses of FFr3 billion in 1981 alone, one and a half times the intervention budget of the Ministry of Industry, a product of recession and overcapacity, but also of defective management organisation, unbalanced product portfolios, a shortage of funds for long-term investment, and inefficient production and sales networks. The scenario in the electronics sector was not much better. The incoming government was determined to pursue an activist policy of industrial intervention: to restructure sectors in accordance with a *politique de filières* (policy of vertical streams) geared to concentrating 'poles of competence' in specialised, vertically integrated state-owned firms; to 'reconquer' the domestic market; and to inject considerable subsidy into the newly nationalised firms in order to aid the restructuring process.[18] This initial period was decisive in preventing these firms going under, being split up or taken over by foreign competitors. The economic rationale of the policies that were followed, on firm-level as well as economy-wide efficiency grounds, was, however, debatable.

Capital contributions by the government to the firms in the initial years were substantial: the total package announced in 1982 amounted to FFr9 billion, a third of which came from the government budget; in 1983 direct government aid to the nationalised industries amounted to FFr12 billion. The *filière électronique* programme was intended to provide the electronics industry with FFr70 billion of support in the period 1982–6 period. In 1982 Rhône-Poulenc and CII-Honeywell Bull, two of the main beneficiaries of public largesse, received FFr1.8 billion and FFr1.55 billion respectively in capital contributions from the government. In addition, 3–5-year planning contracts – crucial instruments of industrial policy – were signed in 1983 between each of the nationalised firms and the Ministry of Industry. These committed the firms to reaching certain medium-term objectives, on investment, profitability, and so on, in return for government approval of their overall strategies and public contributions of financial aid.[19]

The government's *plan de devolution* involved the restructuring of the chemical sector around three poles along with the exit of Pechiney from the sector, splitting its chemical activities and handing them over to Elf and Rhône-Poulenc. The heavy-chemicals pole was concentrated in Elf's Atochem, until then a joint venture with Total but fully acquired by Elf; speciality and agrochemicals in Rhône-Poulenc; organic chemicals and plastics in CDF-Chimie, also state-owned (and later renamed Orkem). The restructuring of the electronics sector, following the recommendations of the Farnoux Report, involved concentrating components production in Matra and Thomson; data processing in CII-Honeywell Bull, which acquired Thomson and CGE's subsidiaries in this area; telecommunications in Thomson, CGE and CGCT (ITT's subsidiary, also nationalised in 1981); consumer electronics in Thomson; and defence electronics in Thomson and Matra. There were plans to restructure the pharmaceutical industry around Roussel Uclaf, Elf's Sanofi and Rhône-Poulenc Santé, but this foundered, to some extent because of the inability of the government to nationalise Roussel and the nature of the special Roussel/Hoechst relationship (of which more in the sections on MNE–government relations, pp. 123–4).[20]

The post-1983 period saw a reinforcement of this trend of concentration and specialisation: the second restructuring of the chemical sector in 1989 when Orkem (the former CDF-Chimie) was split up between Total and Atochem; and the 1983 swap between Thomson and CGE, in which Thomson ceded its wire, cable and telecommunications divisions in return for CGE's components, military and consumer electronics operations.[21] Such concentration and specialisation was subsequently pursued on the international stage as the French firms internationalised through acquisitions. Thus *mondialisation* overlaid *concentration* and *specialisation* in corporate jargon – and in the lexicon of public policy-makers.

From the outset of the 1981 nationalisations, there was the realisation in government circles that the new state-owned concerns were already multinational and that that process could not be reversed without dire competitive consequences for the firms, which would rebound to the detriment of the French economy. The government, in effect, accepted the pre-existing integration of the French economy with the international economy as well as the industrial logic of global strategies for the nationalised MNEs. Both government and management figures went out of their way to stress that it was 'business as usual' for the nationalised firms as regards their foreign operations. If anything the incoming left-wing government was keener to promote the expansion abroad of French MNEs than its right-wing predecessor had been: government policy statements continually reiterated this goal, particularly post-1983; and Elf's acquisition of Texasgulf in the US, the largest to that date by a French company abroad, was given the go-ahead by the government in 1981, whereas its predecessor had vetoed Elf's plan to make a sizeable US acquisition in 1980. As the mid-1980s approached it was clear that a number of MNEs were gearing up to make a clutch of foreign acquisitions, with the full blessing of the government.[22]

But this awareness of internationalisation had to coexist with an ingrained and highly prevalent *attitude hexagonale* among politicians and civil servants that introvertedly focused on the French market and neglected the global dimension of corporate strategies. Sporadic intervention, particularly during Jean-Pierre Chevenement's tenure as Industry Minister, often compromised both management autonomy and strategies for global competition, by, for example, insisting on the preservation of inefficient production and employment levels in France, leading indeed to the resignation of the Rhône-Poulenc chief executive, Jean Gandois. The Chevenement resignation in 1983, and his replacement by the more market-minded Laurent Fabius, heralded the decisive rupture that set the contours for industrial policy for the rest of the decade.[23]

For after that time the government became less interventionist, somewhat more market-reliant in approach to industrial policy, and more emphatic in its appreciation and support of the internationalisation needs of French MNEs. Such a reorientation of thinking and practice was helped by the initial success of the sectoral restructurings: the crisis-ridden MNEs of 1981 were returning to financial health. For example Rhône-Poulenc made a net profit of FFr2026 million in 1984 compared to a loss of FFr787 million in 1982. Levels of subsidy were radically cut, for the additional reason that budgetary restraint was now practised in line with the deflationary macroeconomic U-turn undertaken by the government from 1982–3.[24]

Indeed, as Elie Cohen remarks, it was this rupture of industrial policy orientation post-1983 that signified that the government no longer kept faith with the purely national policy solutions of the 'administered economy'. Attention turned to the EC as the fast-developing framework within which to tackle the competitive problems of French industry.[25] This trend of increasing inter-national and European dimensions to public policy has accelerated unabated throughout governments both of the Left and of the Right, all of which have supported, actively or passively, the inter-nationalisation of French MNEs. As an interviewee commented:

> There has been a distinct evolution of government policy from one of promoting French 'national' champions to one of promoting 'international' champions that are French-owned, particularly evident in the second Socialist adminis-tration [1988–93]. This entails providing the firms with environmental support on the international stage – removing financial constraints, providing subsidies at home and at the EC level, some protection against the Japanese [in elec-tronics] – to allow them to do abroad essentially what they want to do.

Government support for internationalisation was not only evident in policy on foreign direct investment and sectoral re-structuring – concentration, specialisation and internationalisa-tion being the necessary, albeit not sufficient, conditions for these firms to gain scale economies and critical market share to compete in international competition – but also in a number of related policy arenas. It was first and foremost evident in the realm of financial policy (as will be discussed in chapter 5 on finance), and in addition on the issue of privatisation versus public ownership.

Privatisation versus public ownership

The issue of privatisation versus public ownership is not at the forefront of policy agendas in Germany, at least as far as the

German MNEs examined here are concerned: they are all private-sector companies. All the French firms, in contrast, had equity held by the government at some stage in the 1980s; and at the end of the decade all except CGE and Roussel Uclaf were state-owned in the sense that the government held a majority of the equity.

The RPR–UDF Coalition of the Right was elected to office in 1986 on a liberal platform which included the promise to privatise much of state-owned industry, including the batch of companies nationalised in 1981. In the end, however, of the companies examined here only CGE was privatised. A combination of the inability of the Paris equity markets to absorb too many privatisations at any one time, the stock market crash in October 1987 and the re-election of the Socialists in the twin presidential and parliamentary elections of 1988, served to keep the rest in government hands. None the less the privatisation programme was a notable landmark in the evolution of industrial policy in the 1980s. The debate on whether or not to privatise companies gathered pace in the early 1980s while the right-wing parties were in opposition; in the process a markedly liberal ideology suffused political discussion on economic policy. The actual implementation of the privatisation programme between 1986 and 1988 had an immediate impact both in governmental and corporate circles: by many in the government it was seen as a sharp and definitive disjuncture with the *dirigisme* of the past; in many firms it was viewed as the major victory of management autonomy over government interventionism. Such a position was held very strongly by Pierre Suard, the chief executive of CGE, who master-minded the company's path through to eventual privatisation and became closely associated with the government's privatisation programme in general.

Although there were no further outright privatisations during the second period of Socialist government in the late 1980s and early 1990s, the informing liberal principles behind the 1986–8 program of sell-offs – market-reliance, decreased government intervention, increased management autonomy – continued to exercise a major influence in government policy and government–MNE relations, despite the change of government. Indeed this period witnessed a trend of ongoing and partial privatisations of state-owned firms, with an attendant decrease in government intervention and increase in management autonomy.

The new Socialist government in 1988 was committed to an

industrial policy that came to be nicknamed *ni–ni*: neither new privatisations nor any further nationalisations. *Ni–ni* was nominally adhered to in the sense that the government's majority ownership of publicly owned parent companies was not reversed. Certainly, at the level of rhetoric, the government stood firm on this issue. But the reality of policy-making in the government, and of policy action resulting from government–MNE dealings, does point to a picture that is much less clear-cut. Through various financial measures that will be discussed in the following chapter on finance, the state-owned MNEs, with the active support and participation of the government, diluted their levels of state ownership with the aim of attracting private injections of capital in order to finance foreign acquisitions. This amounted to partial privatisation, belying the rhetoric of *ni–ni*. In April 1991 the government finally announced that it was willing to see formal partial privatisations in so far as private-sector firms, even foreign ones, could take minority stakes in the state-owned firms. This was seen as a way of encouraging international alliances between the latter and foreign MNEs. Soon thereafter it facilitated the acquisition of a 5 per cent stake in the financially troubled Bull by the Japanese computer company NEC. This policy of permitting the sale of minority stakes in state-owned companies was approved in broader form by President Mitterrand in September 1991.

The above factors do point to some of the dilemmas and inconsistencies that plagued French industrial policy in the 1980s. *Ni–ni* itself was the product of an uneasy compromise between factions of the Socialist Party, whose rationale seems to have been more political than economic in nature. Certainly, there were those on the social democratic wing of the Party, led by the ex-Prime Minister Michel Rocard and the powerful Finance Minister Pierre Bérégovoy, who wanted to see these partial privatisations taken further.[26]

The issue of public ownership was – and still is – linked to that of *French* ownership of the MNEs; for the fear, especially in the electronics sector, was that without the protection of the government a number of French-owned MNEs would fall into foreign hands. In contrast this fear of foreign control was not great among the German MNEs: the strength of their competitive positions and the stability of their (private-sector) ownership structures assured German ownership and control of these firms. Throughout the 1980s, the French government's *concentration, specialisation and internationalisation* orientation was aimed at the promotion of French-owned MNEs abroad, that is, that these MNEs should internationalise while retaining ownership and management control in France. National champions were to become European and world champions. By the end of the 1980s this approach manifested decidedly mixed results.

Elf Aquitaine, CGE and Rhône-Poulenc have all acquired sufficient size internationally in their own right to carry on in the 1990s without having to compromise substantially on present French management control and ownership, providing financial scenarios do not deteriorate sharply. As far as Elf and Rhône-Poulenc are concerned, this scenario was compatible with an ongoing process of diluting the government's stakes in them by increasing injections of private capital in order to finance international expansion; this was taken to its logical conclusion by the majority privatisation of these companies by the Balladur government in 1993–4. The problem cases, however, were and still remain Thomson and Bull, both of whom are heavy loss-makers and a drain on the government's financial resources, while at the same time they face ever more intense international competition, especially from Japanese, South Korean and Taiwanese companies. Bull's losses amounted to FFr6.8 billion in 1990 and the government planned to give it FFr4 billion for 'reconstruction and recovery' expenses as well as FFr2.7 billion for its R&D costs, 30 per cent of the total Bull R&D budget, over four years. Thomson Consumer Electronics made a loss of FFr2.7 billion in 1990 and expected to receive FFr2 billion from the government per annum plus FFr3 billion for R&D to 1995. By 1990 these two companies accounted for the bulk of government support to industry. Table 4.1 gives an indication of the financial positions

Table 4.1 State aid to industry

	Capital subscription by government (FFr bn)			Net profit (FFr bn)		
	1988	1989	1990	1988	1989	1990
Elf	—	—	—	7.2	7.2	10.5
Rhône-Poulenc	—	—	—	3.4	4.1	1.9
Thomson	—	2.0	—	1.2	0.5	−2.7[a]
Bull	1.0	0.5	1.0	0.3	−0.26	−6.8

Source: *Le Monde*, 22 February 1991
Note: [a] For Thomson Consumer Electronics.

and public contributions to the state-owned MNEs in the sample.

There was deep division within the government regarding the extent of support for loss-making state-owned companies such as Thomson and Bull. A more interventionist stance was favoured by the Industry Ministry and a section of the Socialist Party. But the Finance Ministry and the Minister himself, M. Bérégovoy, were reluctant to commit further funds from the public budget, given the continued emphasis on a conservative macroeconomic policy, and were equally opposed to reversing the liberalising, market-orientated trend of industrial policy in the 1980s. Indeed one of the aims of the partial privatisations in 1991 was to raise funds, at a time of slack economic growth, that could be ploughed into other areas of the public budget. The 1991 institutional reforms, which gave the Finance Ministry overall control of industrial policy and tutelage of the relevant ministries, enabled it and M. Bérégovoy to uphold such policy stances against the more interventionist tendencies of the new Prime Minister, Edith Cresson.

Aside from national budgetary constraints, the government's room for manoeuvre in attempting to return to anything like pre-1983 levels of support for industry was hemmed in by tougher EC regulations on state aid to industry and its potential competition-distorting results in the Single Market. Once again, this illustrates the encroachment of a stronger European dimension into national industrial policy. In fact the Commission proceeded with an investigation into the proposed state aid to Thomson and Bull on the grounds that it could have constituted a distortion to competition in the EC market, prompting the French government to put its aid package to Thomson on ice.[27]

For a while, the French government proposed 'European solutions' for Thomson and Bull in order to rescue them from their predicaments: namely wide-ranging strategic alliances or mergers with other European partners, Siemens being particularly envisaged. The latter, however, was by no means favourably disposed to this option, not wishing to dilute and share its control of key activities, quite apart from the integrational problems that would attend such mergers and Siemens's reluctance to becoming burdened with Thomson and Bull's deep-seated competitive weaknesses.[28] French–German differences on such 'European solutions' were highlighted by an interviewee:

These are alliances between weaker companies in weaker countries to pool resources in order to survive in international competition. The large German companies are singular exceptions to this trend – being very unwilling to compromise on ownership and control – because they are only willing to become European as long as they stay German. Unlike the other group, which includes French companies, they start from superior positions and it is therefore perfectly rational to pursue go-alone strategies.

The very fact of countenancing European solutions on the part of the French government and some state-owned MNEs, combined with the ongoing process of partial privatisation with the involvement of private capital and foreign partners, does none the less point to a reinforcement of a trend in industrial policy strongly observable in the 1980s: a continuing dilution of government control and influence in French state-owned MNEs. The evolving nature and status of public ownership of the MNEs has thus become a much more problematic and multidimensioned phenomenon. There are two main advantages to state ownership, from the point of view of management within the MNEs: protection from the threat of takeover; and an indulgent 'shareholder state' aware and supportive of the firms' needs to expand internationally, and therefore willing to take a long-term view which financial markets may not be as willing to countenance. But there are major disadvantages, not least because public ownership restricts access to much-needed funds on capital markets in order to finance expansion abroad. This crucial constraint will be discussed in chapter 5.

Ultimately, the national orientation and logic of industrial policy can proceed to contradict firm-level corporate strategy on the international stage, although public ownership is only one facet of the extremely complex set of relationships between governments and multinationals. The point is that once companies venture abroad they become far less effective as tools of industrial policy conceived in terms of objectives for the home nation-state: they have to function internationally on a commercial basis much like their private-sector competitors. Commercial objectives regarding the activities of foreign subsidiaries – efficiency, market share, profits, and so on – take priority and are similar for all MNEs, whatever their ownership structures.

Pressures to compete with other MNEs tend to reinforce the distinctive corporate identity of the MNEs and correspondingly dilute their state-owned character. As increasingly active MNEs, it is clear that the French firms have increasingly emphasised their individual identities as commercial actors while playing down the role of the French government in them, especially when it comes to doing business abroad. The government, if it is keen to further the internationalisation process of these MNEs rather than hinder it, retreats from active intervention into the role of an increasingly passive shareholder.

Thus, as Anastassopoulos et al. put it in their comprehensive study of state-owned MNEs: 'State-owned enterprises which go multinational will be increasingly privatised, whether formally or in practice.'[29] The above tendency has of course far-reaching ramifications for the structure, content and evolution of government–MNE relations in France, which will be taken up in the second half of this chapter.

Conclusion

Thus the government policy agenda in France with respect to the MNEs has changed quite rapidly, particularly since 1983. Indeed, the pace of change to public-policy orientations is much more evident than in Germany, for the simple reason that previous attitudes within the French government were so 'hexagonial' (insular) and the response to the internationalisation of the firms has had to be that much more urgent. In Germany the government was more outward-looking to begin with, so the injection of a greater international dimension to policy has proceeded at a smoother pace.

Having said that, French–German differences cannot be camouflaged: they arise from the very different position and role of the government in industry in France and Germany. It is abundantly evident from the narrative of the previous section that French government policy towards the MNEs in the 1980s has displayed far more activism than is the case in Germany. Similarly, the policy agendas are differently constituted: in Germany, issue-areas that have been of most concern to the MNEs were identified – environmental regulation, competition policy, telecommunications deregulation; in France, the policy areas of most concern – sectoral restructuring, FDI, public ownership – involve not only a far greater role for the government, but also go far deeper into core areas of corporate policy within the firms. The different industrial structures of France and Germany are also relevant: the German firms are, quite simply, stronger in the international context, and therefore less in need of public help. In France the government has intervened, for good or ill, to attempt to rectify the deficiencies of the firms: capital shortage, bad management organisation, unbalanced product portfolios, inefficient production and sales networks, technological backwardness, and retarded internationalisation.

Even well into the 1990s there remain in France, perhaps due to the very speed of the change that has occurred, policy contradictions and dilemmas that are not so evident in Germany: change in a more market-oriented and internationally aware direction coexists with continuing hallmarks of intervention, industrial promotion/protection of selected companies and other traces of mercantilist thinking – strands of continuity that are products of long-standing attitudes and actions which work through established institutional structures. This is reflected in French–German differences on industrial policy at the EC level, of which the disagreement on 'European solutions' is but one example.

MNE–GOVERNMENT RELATIONS: THE MNEs AS POLITICAL ACTORS

The selected issue-areas which were the subject of negotiation between governments and MNEs in France and Germany during the 1980s have now been exposed. The impact of government policy on the MNEs in these issue-areas has been analysed. It is time to unravel the policy agendas further in order to understand certain variables that translate into eventual policy outcomes: the relative power positions of the MNEs, on the one hand, and the home governments on the other; the structures of government–industry linkage within which these bargaining scenarios took place; and the influence of internationalisation on the evolution of the whole process. Simply looking at government policy will not suffice. To gain a better understanding of the evolution of policy, both public and corporate, the mechanisms of government–MNE relations need to be probed.

First examined for each country are the structure and make-up of relevant policy networks and communities that bring together the MNEs, industry associations and parts of the government apparatus. Then follows an analysis of the MNE–government relationship: on environmental regulation in Germany, concerning Hoechst, Bayer and BASF; on Siemens's role in telecommunications deregulation in Germany; on the roles played by Thomson and CGE in the restructuring of the French electronics industry; on the restructuring of the French chemical industry, especially concerning Elf Aquitaine; and, finally, on the special case of Roussel Uclaf, involving triangular relations between the latter, its German-owned parent Hoechst and the French government.

Germany

Big Business in the FRG has a reputation for being rather conservative and inactive in the political arena, in government relations as well as in general public relations. But such conservatism has recently begun to change as part of a general trend of becoming somewhat more aware of variables outside the firm that, at the very least, have significant indirect, environmental effects on business operations. As Paterson, Grant and Whitston note in their study of the chemical industry: 'Our research shows that the large West German firms are starting to develop their own political capabilities.' Economic sectors, they argue, have a distinctive political identity which is conditioned by the internationalisation of markets. The internationalisation of the political environment together with the development of firm-level political capabilities is manifested by the appointment of European coordinators in Hoechst, Bayer and BASF to handle EC legislation, EC-level activity and to evaluate their impact on the firms concerned.[30]

A handful of corporate captains have led the way in placing more emphasis on *Öffentlichkeitsarbeit* (public relations) as well as on relations with both federal and *Land* governments. Two individuals stand out: the late Dr Alfred Herrhausen of the Deutsche Bank and Dr Edzard Reuter, who, as head of Daimler Benz, has masterminded its transformation from an automobile to a technology concern spanning the cars, electronics and aerospace sectors. Both realised the importance of communicating better and more actively with various stakeholders – financial analysts, the media, interest groups, government – in order to counteract the rising public concern about the power of Big Business in Germany. Catalysts for such concern were the clutch of Daimler Benz acquisitions in the 1980s, particularly those of AEG in 1986 and MBB in 1989, both of which involved the Deutsche Bank and close cooperation between Herrhausen and Reuter. The latter has gone further by engaging senior ex-politicians and civil servants, particularly a number emanating from the Baden-Württemberg *Land* government, to deal with government/public relations. This is quite a departure from long-standing Daimler policy. It should be emphasised here that such a 'government relations' function, particularly in the decentralised German federal system, encompasses closer and wider-ranging two-way contact with the *Land* governments, especially those in *Länder* where the companies are headquartered. This is in addition to relations with the federal government. The intimate relations that have been developed between Daimler Benz and the Baden-Württemberg *Land* government are illustrative in this respect; but it is also true of Siemens's links with the Bavarian government, of Bayer in North-Rhine Westphalia and Hoechst in Hessen.[31]

In five of the six German MNEs a stepped-up political role is discernible, manifested most clearly by expanded *Öffentlichkeitsarbeit* departments. Bayer opened a new 'Communications Centre' in a separate building on its Leverkusen HQ site in 1990. BASF has multiplied its public relations staff in the last few years and has also set up a separate department of mainly scientific experts specifically charged with handling federal and *Land* legislation; although members of the executive board take charge of the most sensitive political matters. Bosch remains the odd one out by sticking to its renowned and long-standing policy of keeping out of the public limelight.[32]

The essence of this enhanced political role was explained in an interview with the director in charge of government relations in one of the MNEs concerned:

A general distance exists between state and industry. In the past as far as we were concerned, the function of dealing with public authorities was not deemed very important. For instance lobbying was considered a dirty word. Now there is greater emphasis by us on dealing with governments, not only here in Germany but worldwide. This is a product of our enhanced international perspective, developing greater sensitivity and antennae to the outer environment ... Governments see the world in national and domestic terms;

we have a global perspective. It is our duty to bridge this gap. Building up our public/government relations capacity in a spirit of cooperation is integral to this process.

Such a standpoint sounds eminently common-sensical and, up to a certain point, can serve a general public interest in addition to the self-interest of the firm. But there are dangers inherent in taking this kind of perspective too far. As was pointed out in the introductory chapter, MNEs can use their influence with governments to close as well as to open markets. Government–MNE relations can be leveraged as a corporate tool to hack away at the regulatory impartiality of public authorities, gain privileged access to subsidies and other forms of industrial policy promotion, and erect barriers against competitors in the market place. Daimler Benz's acquisition of MBB is a clear indication of government relations being used as a market-closing option by the firm. Heavy pressure was put on the federal government by Daimler Benz to reverse the Cartel Office's decision to prevent the acquisition going ahead, due to the dominant market position it would bring to Daimler Benz. A side-package of the deal that was struck was the agreement of the federal government to provide further subsidies for MBB's participation in the pan-European Airbus project in order to cover exchange rate fluctuations.[33]

It is now germane to examine the policy networks and communities through which the German MNEs channel their political action in dealing with public authorities. In chapter 3 it was stressed that the peak industry associations are important as coherently structured representatives of the large member firms to government, having the collective and wholehearted support of the large firms and being privileged insiders in the making as well as the implementation of public policy. Hence the *Verband der Chemischen Industrie* (VCI) and the *Zentralverband der Elektrotechnischen und Elektronischen Industrie* (ZVEI) maintain intimate relations with the relevant divisions within the Federal Ministry of Economics (BMWI) and other sympathetic ministries, having much input on both German and EC policy matters that affect their sectors.

The political representations of the individual firms complement the work of the industry associations. There is, however, more of a tendency for Hoechst, Bayer and BASF to work collectively through the VCI, given their history of tripartite cooperation, roughly equal sizes and power positions, and cumulative domination of the German chemical industry – not only by right of their individual market shares, but also due to having their representatives on the supervisory boards of other chemical companies. Although the ZVEI is powerful and receives backing from its leading member firms, it does have to put up with a somewhat more individualist role (than is the case with the chemical Three) on the part of its dominant member, Siemens. In areas where Siemens is overwhelmingly dominant, for example, in telecommunications equipment and public switching in particular, it tends to deal with government more on a unilateral basis.

Policy networks are decentralised into tighter and narrower communities, uniting ministry divisions, firm business units and product associations, which focus on sub-sectoral issues, for example, agrochemicals, pharmaceuticals, data processing and medical electronics. For instance, the policy community on pharmaceuticals involves: the healthcare divisions of Hoechst and Bayer, two of the leading drug concerns internationally and the two largest in Germany; other smaller companies, including Knoll, the subsidiary of BASF; divisions in the federal ministries of Economics, Research and Technology, and Health; and the industry association, the *Bundesverband der Pharmazeutischen Industrie*, which is allied to the VCI.

The policy communities are integrated upwards into coherently organised pan-sectoral policy networks. These networks are asymmetrically structured, giving the large firm/industry association axis strong power positions: the government is reliant on industry for much self-regulation, partly attributable to the German administrative federal system in which the federal civil service has little responsibility for the implementation of federal legislation on the ground; and it looks to industry as an information-supplier. In the latter respect, the range and depth of expertise available to the large research staffs of the leading firms far outweigh that at hand within the government machine. The German legal system and norms give further leeway for industry in interactions with government: there is full use of administrative law procedure to challenge the decisions of regulatory agencies, for example on the licensing of pharmaceutical products, which is part and parcel of a rule-making culture geared to create flexibility within the legal framework. Far from being regarded as conflictual, this established process is taken by all sides involved as being an additional mechanism for problem-solving and conflict-resolution – through juridical means.[34]

The issue-areas

An increasing political role is more noticeable with the chemical firms due to the greater politicisation of the environment as an issue on the public agenda: they have faced effective criticism from the German environmental movement and the Green Party; they have had to deal with a more environmentally conscious public; and they now face much tighter government regulation on environmental matters. These problems have catalysed Hoechst, Bayer and BASF into becoming more self-conscious political actors on the German scene.

The level of environmental consciousness within Hoechst, Bayer and BASF has increased substantially during the past decade and especially in the latter half of the 1980s. Along with Swiss and Dutch chemical companies, the German Three have the most environmentally advanced corporate policies in the world. Individual executive board members have direct responsibility for matters concerning the environment. Information disclosure and policy explanation is that much more open and fulsome. For instance, BASF was the first company in the world to start publication of a comprehensive annual environmental report alongside its existing annual general and social reports. Dealings with public authorities have become more intensive and professionalised on regulatory matters. Finally, 'environmental thinking' has bitten deep into corporate product planning, with much more emphasis on differentiated higher value-added/ quality products that are both more 'environment-friendly' and suit the customer's changing environmental needs.[35]

One of Hoechst's 'guiding principles' states that 'conditions of safety and environmental protection have equal standing with our objective to perform effectively in international competition'. As of 1988 its environmental protection costs were running at DM853 million. BASF's costs ran to DM1.3 billion in 1989, 11 per cent of investment on plant and equipment. Bayer has a 1988–95 spending programme of DM3 billion on environmental protection and safety, 25 per cent of overall capital investment. Its broadened environmental policy guidelines include a commitment to maintain the same environmental standards abroad as it has at home, regardless of more lax host-country regulations.[36]

According to Paterson, Grant and Whitston, the VCI has a two-tier strategy for dealings with public authorities on environmental regulation. The first is long-standing: it emphasises the economic importance of the chemical industry; the high standards of and spending on environmental protection and safety already applied by the industry; and the importance of maintaining the principle and practice of self-regulation. This approach was used to success-fully defeat Social Democrat-inspired proposals to tighten the regulation of the industry in the Chemicals Act of 1980. VCI input into the formulation of this piece of legislation was highly effect-ive, and the bargaining process was a textbook example of institutionalised government–industry cooperation. Since then, however, regulation has tightened considerably and the issue-area has become heavily politicised. In response, the VCI has added another tier to its strategy: it has broadened its appeal to the public and the media in the realisation that close and intimate relations with the government on environmental regulation, although important, are simply not sufficient. In addition, its own *Leitlinien* (guidelines) for the industry on the production, use and disposal of chemicals and their by-products have been con-siderably tightened, the result of a debate within the industry initiated by the ex-BASF chief executive, Dr Hans Albers.[37]

Overall, the politicisation of the environmental-protection issue-area has catalysed a far more comprehensive political role as an integral component of corporate strategy on the part of Hoechst, Bayer and BASF individually, and collectively through the VCI. The international repercussions are also pertinent, and are mani-fested most clearly in the political action by both the firms and the VCI activated at the EC level on environmental regulation (to be discussed in chapter 6).

In fact it is quite striking to note how underdeveloped in comparison the French chemical MNEs have been in the area of environmental protection, reflecting a more lenient regulatory regime in France and lower levels of public environmental con-sciousness there. Spending levels on environmental protection by Rhône-Poulenc and Atochem, although increasing substantially, are far lower than the sums forked out by the German Three. Admittedly, physical and geographical problems in France are not as acute as they are in Germany: France has a larger and less-populated land mass with more coastal areas; the companies have smaller production sites dotted throughout France in comparison to the greater pollution risks from the concentrated, sprawling sites at Frankfurt-Hoechst, Leverkusen and Ludwigshafen.[38]

These remarks do, however, require some qualification. While undoubted progress has been made by the firms in environmental awareness and public relations, there have been setbacks and instances of corporate failure, Hoechst being the main culprit. A spate of chemical accidents at the latter's Frankfurt sites in early 1993 considerably retarded the chemical industry's efforts to rebuild its corporate image, which had suffered serious damage after spillages of waste material into the Rhine in 1986. There were instances of lax application of regulations and internal safety procedures at Hoechst, as well as a failure to keep the public informed about what was happening. The rest of the chemical industry, including firms such as Bayer, whose environmental protection and public relations policies were more advanced than Hoechst's, were to some extent on the receiving end of public anger caused by Hoechst's incompetence.

Another factor concerning environmental protection in Germany deserves brief mention. As was discussed in chapter 3, complex and detailed environmental regulations in Germany have multiplied since the mid-1980s, imposing a greater burden on chemical firms in terms of costs, with up to 25–33 per cent of annual capital investment spent on environmental protection and legal compliance. These were manageable problems during the 1980s, when firms in the industry enjoyed healthy profits; but they have become more of a competitive disadvantage in the early 1990s, during which period profit margins have been substantially reduced. Hence the more forceful complaints by the VCI of the regulatory situation in Germany, and the more frequent threats by Hoechst, Bayer and BASF to take more of their production to countries with less onerous regulatory environments, at the expense of the German *Standort*.

The second issue-area of MNE–government interaction considered here is the case of the late 1980s' deregulation of the German telecommunications market and the influence of Siemens in the policy process. It has enjoyed a privileged position as the dominant supplier of equipment to the Bundespost (now Deutsche Telekom), which has traditionally relied heavily on it, especially for technological expertise, in a market closed to foreign competition. Given this position, Siemens was for a long time reluctant to see the market deregulated, sticking to this policy position despite debates on market deregulation in the aftermath of US and, later, UK measures from the late 1970s to substantially deregulate their markets. Before its major acquisitions in tele-communications abroad – GPT in the UK and Rolm in the US, both in 1989 – the domestic market accounted for approximately one half of total sales in telecommunications equipment. Its resistance to deregulation and liberalisation of public procurement was but-tressed by a coalition of forces, particularly in the Bundespost and in the company stronghold in Bavaria, with the backing of the *Land* CSU government, subcontractors based around Munich and trade unions.

But Siemens's attitude began to shift around 1987 when it was making concerted attempts, with some success, to penetrate the US market. It became the third public-switching supplier to two Bell operations and, soon after, entered into negotiations with IBM with the intention of acquiring the latter's Rolm public-switching subsidiary. At about the same time, discussions with GEC in the UK were taking place on the subject of making a bid for Plessey, the major object for Siemens being the GPT public-switching operation. It was at this juncture that the company clearly realised that the Rolm and GPT acquisitions would make it a major player in both the US and UK markets and allow it to break out of its German closet. The realisation dawned on the company that its acceptance as a foreign-owned MNE into deregulated markets abroad depended on good 'corporate citizenship' credentials and was hardly compatible with its continued defence of a German market that excluded competition from foreign-owned suppliers. The message was delivered particularly strongly by US federal authorities who were pressurising the German government, on behalf of companies such as AT&T, for market deregulation in Germany. The implicit threat was that a quid pro quo was necessary if Siemens was not to be discriminated against in the US. As a civil servant in the BMWI involved in the telecommuni-cations policy changes of 1989 commented:

> Yes, we were worried about potential US protection. The prevention of this was a major motivation in our delibera-tions on telecommunications reform, in order to prevent our firms, particularly Siemens, from being excluded from the US market. Needless to say, Siemens itself took every oppor-tunity to impress the logic of this argument on us.

From 1987 public company statements by senior management have advocated greater liberalisation of the Bundespost. Such policy stances have also been advanced in dealings with government. Siemens has even lent its voice in favour of liberalisation in submissions to the European Commission on the deregulation of the EC telecommunications market, seeing the opportunities of an enlarged and open West European market. The Siemens policy shift was therefore quite clearly linked to its own internationalisation in telecommunications and played a crucial role in the public policy processes that led up to market deregulation in the *Poststrukturgesetz* of 1989. Since then EC-driven deregulation in the telecommunications sector has accelerated. With the planned opening up of public networks to competition by 1998, Deutsche Telekom will lose its monopoly. By that time it should be partially privatised. Siemens itself has become involved in a number of new ventures at home (for example, in mobile telephony) and abroad. It has thus reconciled itself to a much more deregulated market in telecommunications, with opportunities abroad but more competition in the home market.[39]

In conclusion to this sub-section, the public policy issue-areas of environmental regulation and telecommunications deregulation have been used to show the extent to which the German chemical and electronics MNEs have expanded their roles as political actors in the German political economy: both in terms of dealing with government, where they and their industry associations enjoy privileged insider positions, and in encompassing a broader public relations function.

France

The French MNEs are more advanced in the government relations function at home than their German counterparts. In France the government has a long history of intervention in the corporate affairs of the largest firms that are seen as most connected with the competitiveness of the French economy. For them, therefore, dealing with government at home seems more 'normal' than in the FRG, where the government–firm relationship is more distanced. Public ownership of the firms in France has made this characteristic more marked.

As Charles-Albert Michalet points out, government intervention was dominant up to the early 1960s, but the context of the government–industry relationship began to change with the conscious creation of large indigenous firms, and the opening up of the French economy to the EC and the rest of the world. These firms had to be competitive on international markets, which was dependent not only on their exporting potential from the French market but also on their international networks. This was explicitly recognised in the Sixth Plan. The primary objectives of these emerging national champions had to be efficiency and profitability. It was this implicit acceptance by the government of the primacy of competitiveness factors – that it had to accept the 'rules of the game' in the international market place and conduct itself accordingly 'like any other player' – that defined the terms of the changing relationship between the government and the large firms, serving to loosen the reins of control over the latter.

In his work, *L'État Brancardier*, Elie Cohen makes the point that a number of the large national champions already enjoyed considerable autonomy from government intervention in the 1970s, as well as considerable input to public policy. He emphasises the blocking power of industrialists such as the former head of CGE, Ambroise Roux, who in the late 1960s successfully prevented the government establishing a new national champion in electrical engineering because he judged this measure of government intent as inimical to CGE's interest. Cohen also emphasises the imbalance in government–industry relations which tilts the power relationship to the advantage of the 'private government' of senior management in the firms. Management is more stable, has longer-term presence and in-house expertise. In contrast civil servants are constantly being rotated, thus being in a disadvantaged position to master the details of a particular firm and to exercise influence and control; being on the 'outside' of the firm, they have less knowledge of the firm's products and markets, and very little of the international market place. Given these conditions, management is better able to accommodate itself to government intervention, knowing how to refuse or accept government injunctions, and to get *its* strategies endorsed by the government. In the face of a 'splintered state' with short-term time horizons, rather than a unified, coherently organised one with long-term strategic objectives, firm-level management has more ability to exercise its influence with government over the *longue durée*. Hence Cohen's assertion of 'the pre-eminence of private government in the structure of an industrialised country such as France'.

The above factors were extant in the relationship between the government and the large national champions in the 1970s, well before the period of accelerated internationalisation in the 1980s. But Michalet, writing at a time of existing *dirigisme* in the early 1970s, posed some pertinent questions. Would the larger and internationalising national champions that the government had been so active in creating become more autonomous of the government itself? Would the strategies of the government become subordinate to those of the enterprises? It is these questions, centred on the autonomy of the MNEs from government intervention and their power in influencing public policy, that the following analysis seeks to address in the context of internationalisation in the 1980s.[40]

A look at the contours of the policy networks and communities which envelop the government–MNE linkage is now apposite. As has been indicated previously, the government tends to deal bilaterally with the large firms, for the most part cutting out and bypassing other actors such as the industry associations. This contrasts with plurilateral forms of government–industry cooperation in Germany with the important role of the industry associations within them.

Many analysts put forward the view that the crux of communication between government and industry in France lies in the peculiarly Gallic postwar system of *pantouflage*: the progress of the civil service elite into the top management of both public and private large firms. These *fonctionnaires* share a common education at a handful of select civil service colleges, the *grandes écoles*, of which the *École Nationale d'Administration* (ENA) and the *École Polytechnique* are the most prestigious; they go on to occupy leading positions in the various elite corps of the centralised government administrative machine (*grands corps*), the ministries, of which the *Trésor* in the Ministry of Finance is the most sought after, and in the cabinets of ministers; they are then 'parachuted' into the firms. An increasing number go directly from the *grandes écoles* into the industrial and financial sectors. In a survey in *Les Échos*, it was found that only two of the top 25 French companies had been run consistently by career managers over the previous 20 years. The chairmanship of Elf Aquitaine was reserved for a graduate of the *École des Mines* before the arrival of Loïk Le Floch-Prigent in the mid-1980s, himself a graduate of a minor *grande école* and a senior official at the Ministry of Industry in the early 1980s.

The PDG (*Président Directeur Général* – chairman and chief executive) of CGE (now Alcatel-Alsthom), Pierre Suard, is an *École des Ponts et Chaussées* graduate, like his predecessor at CGE, Ambroise Roux. Two notable *énarques* (ENA graduates) held senior positions at St Gobain before moving on elsewhere: Roger Fauroux, after heading St Gobain, became the Minister of Industry; Alain Gomez has been the charismatic and immensely powerful PDG of Thomson for over a decade.

These government-industry links could not be more different from the German separation of business and bureaucratic elites. The *pantouflage* links, while initially used to transmit government policy to industry and finance, have if anything subsequently served to increase the influence of the top management of the firms in government policy-making. Officials in the ministries face great difficulty in 'controlling' senior management in the firms, who are their superiors in the hierarchy of the elites who have graduated from the *grandes écoles*. Many of these officials are themselves interested in pursuing careers in industry, and members of the *grands corps* within the firms can have a decisive influence on their professional future.[41] Hence the *pantouflage* system of interlocking elites gives management in the firms quite remarkable levels of access and influence, at the very highest levels, to public policy-making that has a bearing on the MNEs. This would be mitigated if the French government was 'strong', 'unified' and 'autonomous', as it has been characterised in much of the Anglo-Saxon literature. Contrary to these interpretations, Helen Milner argues that the government machinery is splintered and divided, as was argued in the section on government policy, presenting multiple points of access for the firms in order to inject their preferences into public policy-making. In addition, the bureaucracy is heavily dependent on the firms for information, policy planning and implementation, as is the case in Germany.[42]

The issue-areas

The changing canvas of French MNE–government relations in policy networks and communities is strongly evident in the restructurings of the chemical and electronics sectors during the 1980s. Accordingly, two major cases that were at the heart of these restructurings are discussed here: the concentration of telecommunications equipment in CGE, and the split of Orkem in 1989 between Elf and Total, which constituted the second major re-structuring of the chemical sector during the decade. The final case examined is that of Roussel Uclaf, the pharmaceutical firm partly owned by Hoechst.

Right through the 1970s the government was very intervention-ist in the telecommunications equipment arena: the powerful and semi-autonomous *Direction Générale des Télécommunications* (DGT), the telecommunications division in the Ministry of Posts and Telecommunications, together with the *Centre National des Études Technologiques* (CNET), which controlled research funding, intervened strongly in shaping the strategies of the two main equipment suppliers, Thomson and Alcatel-CIT, CGE's flagship subsidiary. It was on the DGT's initiative that Thomson was brought into telecommunications manufacturing. Both Thomson and Alcatel were used as equipment suppliers for the DGT's *grand projet* to digitalise the telephone network in the 1970s.

It seems, however, that from 1981 governments consciously strengthened the power of the firms at the expense of a constrained DGT, which was first placed in the Ministry of Industry (1984–5) and then taken out of it again by the Chirac government in 1986. It was the Thomson–CGE swap of operations in 1983 that high-lighted the decline of the DGT's power in relation to the firms. With the restructuring of the electronics sector around firms specialising in poles of competence already in train, a compatability and complementarity of interest was quickly emerging between Thomson and CGE. The Thomson PDG, Alain Gomez, was keen to concentrate his resources in consumer and defence electronics and to make his firm internationally active and competitive in these areas. In order to do that as well as restoring profitability to a loss-making firm, he was set on extracting Thomson from telecommuni-cations. The CGE senior management led by Georges Pébéreau wanted to acquire the Thomson telecommunications operations as the building block of its strategy to jump into the leading division of international telecom manufacturers. With Thomson Telecom-munications acquired, Alcatel would have a monopoly of the French market in public-switching equipment and a near mon-opoly in transmissions equipment. Opposed to this emerging CGE–Thomson consensus was the DGT, which was unwilling to reverse its policy of promoting a Thomson–CGE supplying duopoly as opposed to relying on a sole supplier, CGE.

Two power factors were crucial in the deal that resulted. First, the structural power of the well-established CGE management in government circles, stemming from the firm's continued profitability: unlike the other electronics national champions, it was not a loss-making drain on *Trésor* funds. Second, Gomez and Pébéreau went directly to the Minister of Industry, Laurent Fabius, and President Mitterrand over the heads of the DGT to argue for a Thomson transfer of telecommunications operations to CGE. The policy outcome, with the President's personal blessing, gave the firms what they wanted, with the government underwriting Thomson's losses in telecommunications in order not to burden CGE's balance sheet. According to an interviewee in the Ministry of Industry, the policy outcome at issue here was *'tout à fait la politique des groupes'* (altogether the policy of CGE and Thomson), with the Ministry being practically bypassed by the firms. The direct appeal of the PDGs to the President set a precedent which was repeated on certain occasions when an MNE management wanted its preferences translated into favourable policy outcomes. For example, Jean-René Fourtou of Rhône-Poulenc twice went direct to the Elysée Palace in 1989, once to get approval of the acquisition of the Rorer drugs concern in the US, and the second time to get approval of the transfer of the government minority stake in Roussel Uclaf to Rhône-Poulenc.

The above example of the Thomson–CGE swap was one of the early indications of the changing power relationship between the government and the firms; and it set a standard for government–MNE relations from then on. As a result of the deal, both Thomson and CGE were on the way to acquiring critical mass in their chosen poles of competence; the necessary conditions were being met to pursue international expansion through acquisitions. Those of Thomson Consumer Electronics – Telefunken in the FRG, Ferguson in the UK, RCA in the US – and Alcatel – ITT's telecom operations in Europe – were formulated and implemented within the companies and in interaction with the other firms involved; they entailed minimal input or intervention from the government. Indeed Georges Pébéreau 'informed' the government of the deal with ITT in 1986 after the negotiations had been concluded, despite the fact that at the time CGE was still a nationalised firm. Since CGE's privatisation in 1987, it went on to become the leading telecommunications equipment manufacturer in the world, aided by its many international acquisitions. The relationship with the French public operator, France Télécom (the new name since 1988 for the DGT), and the CNET was turned on its head. Alcatel, from being a relatively small enterprise nurtured and led by the DGT and the CNET, was now internationally active with superior technological and service competences of its own, with the public operator and its research arm increasingly dependent on Alcatel's preferences in the supply of public-network equipment. Indeed it is fair to say that Alcatel has used its finely tuned political skills with the government and the public operator over two decades to further its strategy of transformation from a rather insignificant manufacturer to a world leader in its sector. Other French electronics firms, notably Thomson and Bull, have also exercised great influence on public policy, without any gain in international competitive advantage. In fact quite the reverse (as chapter 6 will discuss).[43]

The next case concerns the second restructuring of the chemical industry in 1989, which involved the *charcutage* (breaking-up) of the state-owned firm Orkem between two other state-owned firms, Elf Aquitaine and Total. The government's aim was to reinforce the concentration of the leading players of the French chemical industry, a process it had set in train with the first restructuring of the sector in 1982–3. The latter entailed much government involvement in the process at the zenith of interventionism, that is, during the 1981–3 period. It was the absence of government intervention in the 1989 restructuring that distinguished it from government involvement in the sector in the early 1980s.

The negotiations on the nature of the split of Orkem between Elf's Atochem subsidiary and Total were overwhelmingly a matter for the firms involved, with the Ministry of Industry on the sidelines and only the very occasional participation of the Minister, M. Fauroux, as a disinterested referee in the intense 'stand-off at La Défense' (where Elf and Total have their HQs) between the Elf and Orkem PDGs, Loïk Le Floch-Prigent and Serge Tschuruk. There is no doubt that these two personalities were the central players around whom the whole process revolved and on whom the final outcome depended.

The monopolisation of the bargaining agenda between the firms on what was a matter of government sectoral policy was, to a great extent, a function of the strong degree of interconnection between senior management elites in chemical industry policy networks. Le Floch-Prigent had been the PDG of Rhône-Poulenc before moving on to Elf, and had also served as a senior civil servant in the Ministry of Industry. During his period at Rhône-Poulenc his deputy was Tschuruk, who then moved on to Orkem. At the time of the negotiations with Elf, Tschuruk was about to leave Orkem to become the PDG of Total, an important factor in the negotiating process. All these elements came into play in achieving the outcome these management elites favoured, and getting that outcome legitimated – dare one say rubber-stamped – by the government. In the process unfavourable outcomes, from the firms' point of view, were staved off, notably a proposal in some Socialist Party circles that envisaged a merger in chemicals between Elf, Total and Orkem.[44]

The last case concerns Roussel Uclaf, France's third-largest pharmaceutical firm at the end of the 1980s, with substantial interests in agro-veterinary and chemical-nutrition products. Hoechst has had an *entente cordiale* with Roussel since 1968, when it acquired a minority shareholding. The Roussel family sold its controlling stake to Hoechst in 1974. The French government at the time, however, was unwilling to sacrifice Roussel's French identity and management autonomy by allowing it to become a fully fledged Hoechst subsidiary. Conditions were therefore attached to Hoechst's acquisition of a majority stake, including a commitment to Roussel's 'distinctive French identity' and its management autonomy. This was enshrined in a legal contract between Hoechst and the French government. Since then Roussel has played a *Sonderrolle* (exceptional role) in the Hoechst international network, united to its parent by a number of R&D and marketing cooperation agreements and joint ventures in France and abroad, without being reduced to a full subsidiary taking its orders from Frankfurt.

In 1981 the new Socialist government intended to nationalise Roussel Uclaf as part of a policy of rationalising the pharmaceutical *filière* around Rhône-Poulenc, Elf Aquitaine and Roussel Uclaf. The government hoped that Hoechst would reduce its stake to a minority and at the same time preserve the range of cooperation agreements it had with Roussel. What it did not reckon with was Hoechst's adamant opposition to giving up its majority stake. Indeed it went so far as to say that it would withdraw from all existing links with Roussel in the event of nationalisation. What followed was an intense round of negotiations which resulted in a compromise agreement in 1982, enforced by another legal contract between Hoechst and the French government. Hoechst reduced its shareholding to a bare majority, with the French government entering Roussel's equity for the first time with a 40 per cent stake. Both sides had equal representation on Roussel's reconstituted *conseil de surveillance* (supervisory board). At the end of the day, the government caved in on its initial demands, judging the cost of Hoechst's exit from the French pharmaceutical industry to be simply too high. By this stage Roussel had gained considerable benefit from Hoechst's financial resources, research expertise and international distribution channels for drug sales. No nationalisation of Roussel, nor the initially planned rationalisation of the pharmaceutical sector, took place. The essence of the Hoechst–Roussel relationship remained intact.[45]

The relations between the French government, Hoechst and Roussel in the aftermath of the 1982 agreement corresponded to a large extent to the overall evolution of industrial policy and government–industry relations in the 1980s. For most of this period, the government had a rather limited role in Roussel's management, being more a passive shareholder than anything else. A new twist to the tale took place in 1989–90, when the government transferred its stake in Roussel to Rhône-Poulenc, mainly as a means of enhancing the latter's liquidity position. Hoechst's condition for accepting this change was that Rhône-Poulenc should be restricted to a portfolio stake, with no involvement in Roussel's management. The government's appointees to Roussel's supervisory board were replaced by Rhône-Poulenc appointees.[46]

Government policy towards Roussel thus came full circle within a decade, initial *dirigiste* intentions giving way in the face of the superior bargaining power of a leading foreign-owned multinational (Hoechst), and finally getting out of the shareholding structure altogether as a direct participant. Even with the changes in 1990, the government could *in theory* have exercised influence in Roussel, given that Rhône-Poulenc was still state-owned. With the privatisation of the latter in 1993–4 this is no longer an option. Rhône-Poulenc's re-entry into the private sector raises questions as to Roussel's future. It could sell its stake to Hoechst and thus permit the latter, for the first time, to dispense with Roussel's management autonomy and incorporate it as a full subsidiary.

The changing context of management autonomy and government intervention

The cases examined here point, it is suggested, to some general conclusions of greater MNE power in the relationship with the government in French policy networks. First, management autonomy from government intervention in corporate strategy and execution has been considerably enhanced, particularly post-1983 after Chevenement's resignation as Minister of Industry. Whereas government intervention used to be the norm, a *modus vivendi* has been established between the government and the companies, both public and private, that makes it now much more difficult for the former to breach the anchored principle of management autonomy, which is staunchly defended by the senior management in the MNEs. And management elites have progessively manoeuvred themselves into a better bargaining position with the government. Previously, government influence in the firms was greater when they were smaller, less-focused on specialised product lines, technologically backward, with defective management organisations and in the throes of financial crisis. By the end of the 1980s these firms had internationalised, thus weakening the ability of the government to control them outside French borders; their balance sheets looked healthier (with the exception of Thomson and Bull); they had a mastery of more-complex technologies and had a better balance and focus of product portfolio; and the structure, competence and commercial orientation of management organisation had been upgraded.

Nevertheless, the government retains important residual powers, particularly with respect to the state-owned firms. First and foremost, there is the power of veto – to say the ultimate *non* to plans presented by the firms to the government – and the right to appoint, renew the contracts of and dismiss the PDGs of the state-owned firms. For example, the renewal of Alain Gomez's contract at Thomson in 1989 was specifically conditional on the government's terms that he sell the Thomson financial market operations subsidiary to Credit Lyonnais and reorganise the management of Thomson Consumer Electronics. Sporadic intervention persists, but only in rare exceptions does the government use the firms as active instruments of public policy, for example in specific generic technology projects such as the Thomson programme in high-definition television (HDTV), which is heavily reliant on public funding. Otherwise, industrial policy has become increasingly passive or has shifted its focus to the EC level.[47] An interviewee summed up a number of these points:

> The extent, limits and mechanics of government intervention are still in a state of flux and uncertainty – a grey area. There is intervention in areas of great political sensitivity that draw in politicians rather than being dealt with by civil servants. The government's only real form of vestigial power is the veto – a blunt weapon. The right of initiative and implementation clearly lies in the corporate domain now . . . It is widely perceived that it is the companies who are competent on industrial matters, not the state. They are looked up to and admired – that gives them enormous clout.

Even these residual powers of intervention in state-owned firms are progressively declining with the Balladur privatisation programme from 1993. This does not mean, however, that the government will lose its influence completely, nor does it signify a dilution of interpersonal links between political, administrative and business elites. The *pantouflage* system remains in force and, moreover, many executives and ex-civil servants with close ties to Prime Minister Balladur have been appointed to take charge of the firms on the current privatisation list (at the time of writing in early 1995).

As far as the selection of firms in this study is concerned, government intervention presented a differentiated picture by the end of the 1980s. There was least intervention in CGE and Elf: their long-standing financial profitability gave them a certain independence from the government. CGE's privatisation in 1987 made a difference in so far as it further reinforced its independence from the government and felt better able to contest government policy when there were conflicts of interest between it and the government. This occurred in 1990 when CGE defied the government by acquiring a majority of the shares in the nuclear power plant construction firm Framatome, which until then had majority ownership by a combination of firms who are state-owned. In the event, CGE had to retreat from majority ownership and outright control by compromising with the government, which was unwilling to see Framatome effectively privatised through the back door. But CGE's very actions in this saga served to prove its credentials of independence from the government as a private-sector company.[48]

Elf, despite having the government as the majority shareholder, by and large acted as a private fiefdom whose independence from the government was well known and well advertised, a state of affairs established by the long-serving PDG Pierre Guillaumat and carried on by his successors. Elf management continued to emphasise that their autonomy was greater than that of other state-owned companies, because the continuity of its government relations had not been disturbed by the trauma of nationalisation in 1981, as had happened to the rest of the French firms studied here (Elf was state-owned throughout the postwar period). If anything, the autonomy of the Elf management from the government was enhanced with the dilution of the government's equity holding in it in the mid-1980s to 54 per cent, with the rest of the shares being publicly listed. This trend was taken to its logical conclusion with Elf's majority privatisation in 1993–4.[49]

Rhône-Poulenc stood in an intermediate position among the French MNEs. Government intervention was active during the early 1980s' restructuring process up to 1982–3. Under the leadership of Le Floch-Prigent and then Fourtou, appointed by the Chirac government in 1987, vigorous internationalisation ran in parallel with increasing assertion of management autonomy from the government.

Government intervention was most active and evident in Thomson and Bull. As loss-makers and recipients of much government subsidy, they were and are more dependent on it and therefore in a weaker bargaining position. Within Thomson, there is more intervention in the defence electronics arm CSF, which is heavily dependent on public contracts, than in the consumer electronics arm TCE, which is not. Furthermore, TCE through acquisition has 90 per cent of sales outside France, with 50 per cent of sales in the US through the RCA acquisition. Given its high levels of internationalisation, it is much less accessible to French government control. Nevertheless, intervention has tended to be more concrete and demanding in Thomson than some other state-owned firms because public funds to it are overwhelmingly targeted at specific technology projects in semiconductors and high-definition television. Subsidy to Bull, for example, is more globally spread and therefore less amenable to targeted government intervention. None the less, the parlous state of Bull's finances with a haemorrhaging balance sheet since 1990 has enabled the government to extract specific commitments from the company, on job shedding and management reorganisation, in return for increased public subsidies.[50]

The second major aspect of greater MNE power in the relationship with the government is the increasing influence of the senior management of the MNEs in public policy-making. The Thomson–CGE swap in 1983 and the Elf–Total split of Orkem in 1989 are crystal-clear examples of the 'semi-privatisation' of government policy exercised by the senior management of the firms involved. Heightened firm-level influence in public policy is manifested in public subsidy extraction in 'strategic' R&D projects; in the more favourable climate and legal regime towards foreign direct investment; and in the restructurings of the chemical and electronics sectors. Interviewees emphasised the greater influence of MNEs in policy networks:

> In the technological arena, it is quite clear that competence and expertise lies with the firms, on which the government is dependent. The initiatives for publicly funded R&D projects come from the firms; only subsequently is it a question of state support and arrangement of cooperation between public laboratories and the firms.

> As a big multinational, we have a qualitatively different relationship with the state than other smaller companies. We have the clout, resources, in-house expertise and specialised knowledge to articulate our positions and preferences; and therefore to be in a position to negotiate from a vantage point of strength with the government on issues of public regulation and control that affect us most.

> We get a better hearing from government these days – it is easier to get leading government members to accept, adopt, expound and promote our positions. It was different ten years ago. Now it is perceived that the priorities of the large MNEs in strategic sectors are also the state's priorities.

CONCLUSION

Not only have public-policy agendas developed more international, and especially European, agendas alongside the internationalisation of indigenous MNEs, but the latter have also become more powerful political actors in their home political economies as a result of their international expansion. Public relations activity has intensified: not only in the German MNEs, to counter the politicisation of issue-areas such as competition policy and environmental regulation; but also in the French MNEs. For instance Rhône-Poulenc recently set up an environmental standards and ethics unit within its international agrochemicals division. It has a heightened media profile and a stated policy aim of developing contacts with 'advocacy groups in political, financial and social circles'. Sanofi has reorganised its communications department, previously very French-centric, on geographical zone lines within its international network: the aim is to present the company as an internationally active, rather than merely a French, concern.[51]

Even before the onset of 1980s' internationalisation, the analysis in this chapter makes it evident that large firms, both in Germany and France, enjoyed privileged positions in policy networks: governments were dependent on them for expertise; and management elites were in positions to both block government intervention and exercise considerable influence in policy formulation and implementation. Within the confines of these intimate insider relationships, it is the MNEs who have gained bargaining power in dealing with governments. The latter have become more dependent on the MNEs' information expertise and human resource pool on crucial policy matters; they are more reliant on the MNEs for the setting of standards and the initiation, definition and implementation of publicly supported projects, particularly in technology. This dynamic of change is especially evident in France. There is less government intervention in French firms, although levels of intervention differ from firm to firm and even differ within the firm.

The MNEs' purview now runs well beyond national boundaries on to the international stage, where the reach of the home governments is weaker than it is in the home market. Imperatives of international competition force the MNEs to give primacy to commercial objectives, so that the French state-owned MNEs increasingly act like private-sector firms, emphasising their individual corporate identities at the expense of the nature of their formal ownership structures. The MNEs are therefore in structurally more powerful positions in policy networks and can thus impress on the home governments the importance of internationalisation not only for them as firms but also in the interests of the home economy's competitiveness: home markets are too small and limited; economic efficiency and the characteristics of certain global industries dictate the imperative of acquiring global scale. This still leaves the danger, however, that MNEs could use their political clout to secure preferential treatment from governments and pursue policies of market closure. This is more evident in France, where economic policy objectives have given preference to large, and now multinational, firms, than in Germany, where a competition-oriented *Ordnungspolitik*, with its ideology of free trade and open markets, and with its instruments of, for example, anti-trust policy, serves to counteract corporatist and cartel-like behaviour.

The preceding analysis also points to enduring French–German differences. To begin with, the structure of policy networks is different. In Germany they involve the powerful sectoral industry associations as well as the MNEs themselves. In France the weak industry associations are largely bypassed and the government deals directly with the MNEs on a bilateral basis. The French MNEs do not pool resources and cooperate on public policy matters and in government relations to the same extent as German MNEs. As far as the government–industry relationship is concerned, the more-distanced German linkage contrasts with the intimate interlocking of elites through the *pantouflage* system in France. German reliance on administrative and legal norms as mechanisms of problem-solving, together with the well-established practice of industry self-regulation, contrast sharply with a more interventionist government culture in France.

Although the pace of change in France is more striking than in Germany, it does not mean that international dimensions to policy agendas and MNE power in government relations have become greater in France than in Germany. Indeed the internationalist credentials of both German government policy and of the German MNEs remain more advanced than in France. But the French started the 1980s from a position of backwardness: insular public-policy orientations and greater government intervention in weakly internationalised national champions. Change in policy agendas and government–MNE relations is linked to the international-isation of the MNEs *à grande vitesse* and has consequently proceeded very rapidly. But the very rapidity of such change brings in its wake contradictions and dilemmas that are not as evident in Germany. Hence the remaining divisions in France, and notably within the administrative machine and the governing Socialist Party, on issues of government intervention in the MNEs – as to whether one should be more liberal, more mercantilist, or simply maintain the status quo on questions such as public ownership, subsidies, protection of the home market against foreign competition, and so on. These French–German comparisons are increasingly evident in emerging EC policy networks, in terms of the MNEs' growing political roles in EC policy-making (the subject of chapter 6), and are manifest in the arena of the financial relationships the MNEs have with banks and the home governments, the subject of the next chapter.

5

THE FINANCIAL FUNCTION AND THE POWER OF THE PURSE

Government–firm, bank–firm relations

What is at issue here is the 'financial function' of the MNEs – their financial needs and the manner in which they go about getting finance – and its linkage to the financial systems in France and Germany. These national systems are differently constituted but work with the same goal in mind: the financial system is basically the intermediary mechanism that transforms short-term savings of individuals, households and firms into long-term investment in goods and services. The main agent of such transformation is the bank which, through operations in various financial markets, channels funds to industry. Financial systems usually involve a role for the government as a regulator; but government intervention can go above and beyond this role, utilising tools of monetary policy, for example, control of interest rates, as well as microeconomic industrial policy, to allocate funds differentially to sectors and firms.[1]

Thus the linkage of the MNEs' financial functions with the national financial systems anchors the MNEs in relationships with external actors in the French and German political economies, notably with the government and with banks. Indeed, it is this political economy aspect of government–firm and bank–firm relations which is of central concern here, and not so much the internal financial systems and operations of the MNEs themselves. One further qualification is required: this chapter concentrates on links with the central governments and the leading commercial-cum-investment banks in France and Germany, and not the financial relationships the firms have with secondary tiers of government, regional banks and other financial institutions. The latter aspects are not unimportant, especially given the significant roles played

132

by the regional and savings banks, and some insurance companies,[2] in the decentralised German financial system. For reasons outlined before, however, these actors cannot be given close scrutiny in this study, which judges the factoring in of central governments and the leading commercial/investment banks as being more important for the political economy of the MNEs' internationalisation.

Finance therefore provides a highly useful focus in analysing the nature of MNE relationships with key external actors in the home political economies: it is one vital characteristic of the embeddedness of the MNEs in the home bases. The argument in chapter 3 emphasised the differences in the constitution of French and German domestic structures, and the differences in national/ home-base embeddedness between French and German MNEs. Chapter 4 proceeded to pinpoint the differences between the two countries in government policy orientation and MNE–government relations. Are similar differences observable in the financial structures of the French and German political economies, and are the links between the MNEs, governments and banks in these countries differently constituted?

Internationalisation factors into these financial relationships. The MNEs have internationalised their production, but there are aspects of related internationalisation: of financial markets, which the MNEs make use of, as well as of the MNEs' own capital structures, for example, equity listings on foreign exchanges. The other task of this chapter is to investigate whether internationalisation provides an element of change in the external financial relationships of the MNEs in their home bases, and whether it alters the bargaining-power variables in these relationships.

MNEs' OWNERSHIP STRUCTURES

There are relatively few German companies that are publicly listed compared with companies in the UK, the US and Japan. Much of the large base of medium-sized *Mittelstand* companies are family-owned and not publicly quoted at all. All the German MNEs examined here, except Bosch, are publicly quoted; the latter is 92 per cent owned by the Robert Bosch Foundation, which devotes a share of the dividends received to various social and cultural projects. The other five have been internationalising their financial

Table 5.1 Major shareholdings in the MNEs, 1988–9

MNE	Major shareholders
German	
AEG	Daimler Benz (56 per cent)[a]
BASF	None >5 per cent
Bayer	Allianz Assurance (10 per cent)
Bosch	Robert Bosch Foundation (92 per cent)
	Bosch family (8 per cent)
Hoechst	Kuwait Petroleum Co. (24.9 per cent)
	Dresdner Bank consortium (10 per cent)
Siemens	Allianz Assurance (10 per cent)
	Siemens family (10 per cent)
French	
Elf-Aquitaine	French government (54 per cent)
	46 per cent of shares publicly listed
(Atochem)	ELF (100 per cent)
(Sanofi)	ELF (57 per cent)
	43 per cent of shares publicly listed
Rhône-Poulenc	French government (100 per cent of voting capital)
	24.2 per cent of equity publicly traded in form of non-voting capital
Thomson	French government (100 per cent)
(Thomson-CSF)	Thomson (60 per cent)
	40 per cent of shares publicly listed
(TCE)	Thomson (100 per cent)
(Thomson-SGS)	Thomson-CSF (50 per cent)
	STET (Italian government holding company)
Bull	French government (100 per cent)
(Bull HN)	Bull (85 per cent)
	NEC (15 per cent)
CGE	100 per cent publicly listed
(Alcatel)	CGE (61 per cent)
	ITT (39 per cent)
(GEC-Alsthom)	CGE (50 per cent)
	GEC (50 per cent)

Sources: *Wer gehört zu wem* (Commerzbank, 16. Auflage, 1988); *Annual Reports*, 1989–90
Note: [a] Daimler Benz: major shareholders Deutsche Bank (28.1 per cent), Mercedes AG (25.3 per cent), Kuwait Government (14 per cent).

bases as a follow-up to the internationalisation of their production networks. Daimler Benz has pursued an active policy of gaining equity listings on major foreign exchanges as a means of providing more liquidity to fund both its diversification into electronics and aerospace as well as its internationalisation in electronics (AEG) and trucks. Hoechst by 1989 had listings on ten foreign exchanges; Bayer was the first German industrial company to get a Tokyo Stock Exchange listing; by 1990 Siemens had listings on all major European exchanges, including the London Stock Exchange. In fact non-German ownership of equity is approaching the 50 per cent mark in a number of leading German companies, including Hoechst and Bayer. In Bayer non-German ownership of the equity base rose from 23 per cent in 1982 to 48 per cent in 1988.

Of the French MNEs CGE, after nationalisation in 1981, was privatised in 1987 and has since been extending its listing on stock exchanges abroad. Public ownership of the others limited their capacity to internationalise their capital bases. By the end of the 1980s the government held 100 per cent of Bull and Thomson, both of whom had some subsidiaries which were either partially quoted (for example, Thomson-CSF) or had stakes held by other parties (for example, Bull HN, Thomson-SGS). The post-1993 Balladur government has both Thomson and Bull on its privatisation list. In a partial privatisation in 1991–2, NEC of Japan acquired a 5 per cent stake in Bull. Although Rhône-Poulenc had 100 per cent of its voting capital in public hands, a quarter of all equity was publicly traded on the Paris Bourse, the US Nasdaq exchange and the New York Stock Exchange. It was the first French company to be quoted on the latter. This was, however, in the form of non-voting capital. The government's stake in Elf was a majority one, with public listing of the rest of the equity. Of Elf's subsidiaries, Atochem was 100 per cent Elf-owned, whereas Sanofi had a minority listing on the Paris Bourse. Rhône-Poulenc and Elf were among the first companies to be privatised by the Balladur government in 1993–4.[3]

GERMANY: BANKENMACHT AND FINANCE–INDUSTRY RELATIONS

Banks have relations with the federal government on the joint committee for export credit and insurance on foreign direct investments. Although there are numerous informal contacts between top bankers and leading politicians and civil servants, the banking system as well as bank–industry relations enjoy considerable freedom from public regulation. As in other areas of public policy, the self-regulation concept is strongly embedded in the German financial system.[4]

The involvement of the main German universal banks in the development of the leading industrial firms goes back to Germany's first bout of late-nineteenth-century industrialisation. Trust banks were formed to provide long-term investment capital and the new universal banks (Deutsche Bank, founded in 1870; Dresdner Bank in 1872; and Commerzbank in 1870) were the joint creation of captains of industry and commerce. These banks were and are 'universal' in the sense that they perform all banking functions under one roof: 'retail' banking for individuals, 'wholesale' banking for firms, 'investment' banking in raising bond and equity capital for firms as well as engaging in the selling and trading of public shares on their own account. The financial concentration around these three banks led, with the necessary financial support, to a wave of industrial concentration in the German economy. The rise of the electrical giants AEG and Siemens, both at home in Germany and abroad, was formulated and implemented in close cooperation with their leading banks.[5]

Such a close intertwining of financial and industrial capital put in place structures of linkage between banks and firms that remain strong today. The banks hold equity stakes in industrial firms, the most famous example being the Deutsche Bank's 28 per cent holding in Daimler Benz. Table 5.1 instances some of the other major shareholdings in the firms in 1988–9, including the 10 per cent stake of a Dresdner-led consortium in Hoechst. The Allianz insurance company has significant stakes in Deutsche, Dresdner and a number of leading manufacturing companies, including Bayer and Siemens. Reciprocally, many of the MNEs have shareholdings in the banks: Hoechst and Bayer-led consortia hold over 20 per cent of Dresdner's capital. Shares deposited with banks by clients allow the banks, unless specific instructions exist to the contrary, to use the proxy voting rights of those shares at shareholders' meetings as they (the banks) wish. Banks lend voting rights to each other, especially in cases where particular banks specialise in particular companies and sectors. Through these mechanisms Deutsche, Dresdner and Commerzbank account for roughly a quarter of all voting shares of publicly listed German companies. In addition, the banks and the Allianz insurance group are represented on the supervisory boards (*Aufsichtsräte*) of the leading firms, just as there are a number of representatives of the latter on the supervisory boards of banks and insurance companies. Traditionally one of the Speakers (executive board chairmen) of the Deutsche Bank heads the supervisory board of Daimler Benz. By 1986 the Deutsche Bank was represented on the *Aufsichtsräte* of 39 of the 100 biggest German companies, the Dresdner Bank on 22, Commerzbank on 15 and the Allianz insurance group on 17 of them.[6]

For these and other reasons it has been vigorously asserted that the banks have considerable power in German industry. This thesis, initially set forth by Rudolf Hilferding,[7] has found widespread expression in modern political economy writings. In his influential *Modern Capitalism*, Andrew Shonfield considers the banks as the grand strategists of the German economy, with a long-term view which is impressed on the industrial firms, that they guide by way of the linkages they have with industry. It is the banks that have an overview of the economy as well as detailed knowledge of the strategies and operations of individual firms. The prefectoral and coordinating role of the banks is the quid pro quo for the risk they take in ploughing long-term and relatively cheap credit into the firms.

John Zysman, writing in the 1980s, accepts the Shonfield thesis without reservation. According to him the universal banks exercise market power over financing sources for industry, controlling access to both equity and bond markets. This version of *Bankenmacht* (the power of the banks) is also accepted by other leading contemporary commentators such as Dyson and Hall.[8] Within Germany such views find expression in Social Democratic and Free Democratic Party circles as well as in successive Monopolies Commission reports. The *Bankenmacht* debate reared its head during the Daimler Benz takeovers of AEG in 1986 and of MBB in 1989: both deals intimately involved the leading Daimler shareholder and 'house bank' to the firm, the Deutsche Bank. Fearing that the power of the banks in German industry is too great and competition-distorting, the FDP, as part of the governing coalition in Bonn, was active in setting up an internal working group within the federal government, with the aim of producing proposals to limit bank power. By the early 1990s, however, no legislation had been introduced to further limit bank shareholdings, proxy voting rights or their representation on the supervisory boards of industrial firms.[9]

It is this thesis of the power of the universal banks in German Big Business, both in terms of providing finance as well as in influencing the strategies and operations of the firms, that is contested here, with reference to this group of six German MNEs. The internationalisation of the MNEs is a crucial variable in the following argument.

Bankenmacht was prevalent in the late nineteenth century and during the post-1945 recovery period. At both times the banks provided much-needed capital, plentifully and cheaply, to industrial firms who were short of it. In these periods the banks clearly wielded a significant 'power of the purse', although their influence in industrial strategies, even during these high points of their power, has been somewhat exaggerated. As Alfred Chandler argues, the management of leading industrial concerns such as AEG, Siemens, Hoechst, Bayer and BASF retained a large degree of independence in pursuing their own strategies, even when dependent on their house banks for the supply of investment funds.[10] Nevertheless, the situation has changed quite dramatically since the mid-1960s.

The key change has been in the increasing self-financing capacity of the large German firms, drawn from withheld profits, exposure on outstanding debts, depreciation and in-house pension funds. Self-financing rates for German *Aktiengesellschaften* (AGs – the equivalent of British public limited corporations or US incorporated companies) were already high in the 1960s, representing 70–80 per cent of total financing. This figure has risen since then and, from the mid-1970s, the leading export-oriented sectors of the German economy have substantially diminished the debt they owe to banks. Figure 5.1 shows the decreasing share of bank credit and loans in the overall capital position of the AGs in the manufacturing economy – from 16.9 per cent in 1974 to 6.6 per cent in 1984; for the chemical and electronics sectors the decrease is even greater.

The financial independence of the MNEs studied here as well as other large German firms goes further than that. By 1984 the own capital of industrial AGs exceeded total credit and loans by 60 per cent, whereas in 1974 it represented only a third of credit-based borrowings. Figure 5.2 shows that some of the firms decreased their debt–equity ratios from the early 1970s onwards, the rate of decrease for BASF and Siemens being particularly striking. Table 5.2 updates the debt–equity ratios to their 1988

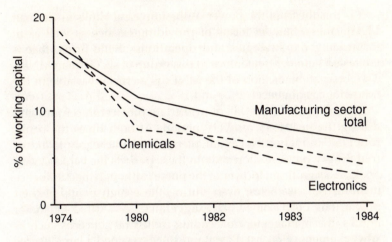

Figure 5.1 Bank credit and loans as percentage of working capital of the
Aktiengesellschaften (AGs), 1974–84
Source: Esser (1990: 23)

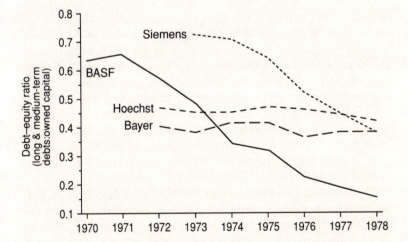

Figure 5.2 Debt–equity ratios of German MNEs in the 1970s
Source: Grou (1985: 123–7)

positions, showing that the downward trend continued apace in the 1980s. Hoechst decreased its net corporate debt from DM10 billion in 1982 to DM6 billion in 1988; in the same period Bayer reduced its total financial obligations from DM13.5 billion to DM4.4 billion. Siemens has had the largest reserves of any German industrial firm: between 1970 and 1985 it increased reserves from DM888 million to DM20.5 billion, from 7.8 per cent to 39.4 per cent of assets. In the same period Daimler Benz raised its money assets from DM326 million to DM7.8 billion, representing an increase from 7.3 per cent to 21.8 per cent of assets. BASF's goal since the 1960s has been to build up its self-financing capacity, in order to finance growth *aus eigene Kraft* (out of own resources) and only to go to external markets 'in cases of real need'. Its last share rights issue in the 1980s was in 1985; whereas in the early 1960s intervals between bouts of external capital-raising were much shorter. As the Siemens chief executive Dr. Karlheinz Kaske has remarked, 'Never have we not made an investment anywhere in the world, which we have judged viable, because of a lack of funds.' Table 5.3 shows the liquidity positions of the German firms as of 1988.[11]

Table 5.2 Debt–equity ratios[a] of German MNEs for 1988

Hoechst	0.54
Bayer	0.20
BASF	0.20
Siemens[b]	0.10
AEG	0.16
Bosch[b]	0.10

Source: Annual Reports, 1988–9
Notes
[a] Long-term and medium-term debts:owned capital.
[b] Figures for 1989.

Table 5.3 Liquid assets of German MNEs in 1988 (DM m)

	Liquid assets
Hoechst	3,369
BASF	6,150
Bayer	4,486
Siemens	21,239[a]
Bosch	4,882

Source: Annual Reports, 1988–9
Note: [a] 1989 figure.

Thus the centrepoint of the *Bankenmacht* thesis – the credit dependence on the banks – did not apply as far as the big industrial firms were concerned, and least of all for the firms examined here. The firms had become less dependent on external financial institutions and had gained more flexibility to follow their own paths. There were also several internationalisation factors at play in the changing power relationship between the firms and the banks.

The postwar internationalisation of the German MNEs can be traced back to the mid to late 1950s. The internationalisation of the German universal banks, Deutsche in particular, is a belated phenomenon of the 1970s onwards. In the intervening period they concentrated very much on a German market which had little competition from foreign-owned banks. In other words, when the industrial firms first expanded abroad, the German banks simply did not have sufficient presence outside Germany to cater for their financial needs. Hence the progressive building-up of ties between the German MNEs and foreign banks, American in particular, whose knowledge of currency management and international financial markets was more developed than that of the German banks. And from the early 1970s foreign banks, with the American ones at the forefront, began to enter the German market.

The cumulative result of these factors was that the firms were by no means preponderantly reliant on the German banks for external financing. They could count on competition at home and abroad among the banks, both domestic and foreign, for their custom. They took advantage of this through increasingly sophisticated internal financial operations. Their *Finanzpolitik* came to be conducted increasingly on the basis of margins, regardless of equity and other structural relationships with the German universal banks, that encouraged ruthless price competition among the banks they dealt with. Indeed competition among the banks intensified with the two-stage establishment of the Single Banking Market as part of the EC's 1992 programme. Financing of overseas investment in particular could thus be undertaken through a mixture of substantial internal financing and raising external capital on home, overseas and increasingly internationalised and deregulated offshore markets, a situation of much greater overall financial flexibility for the firms. The first section in this chapter mentioned that the German MNEs have considerably expanded their international equity bases through public listings abroad. A prime example of diversified financing of international expansion was Hoechst's $3 billion acquisition of Celanese in the US in 1986–7: 40 per cent of the funds required were raised out of the company's own resources, and nearly all the rest was raised on US financial markets.[12]

The other major strand of the *Bankenmacht* argument holds that the banks wield great influence in the corporate affairs of the firms, including in strategies and operations concerning overseas expansion. This argument also seems hardly tenable in modern conditions, given that the necessary condition – the banks' financial hold over the firms – no longer obtains. The following selection from interviews illustrates the above points:

> To do market research in the US regarding entry and expansion, German companies go to one or a few American banks or consultancies, not to German banks. The planning of foreign investments and acquisitions is done in-house by the firms – the banks really do not get involved. Only at the final stage do proposals go to the supervisory board [which has bank representatives on it] for approval, but its power of veto is rarely used – it tends to accept executive board decisions.

> We are not involved in *Geschäftspolitik* (corporate policy of the firms) as in the 1960s. We have been excluded and these are matters for the firms alone ... Our representatives on supervisory boards are not in a position to contest the policy of the executive boards of the companies. Their in-house information and expertise is far superior to what we might have on them.

Indeed the assertion that the banks 'guide' the companies in their strategies, through supervisory board representation and by having detailed financial and other corporate information on the companies, is highly doubtful. First, the supervisory boards are heavily dependent for information on the executive boards of the firms, who are responsible for day-to-day decision-making, and tend to go along with the latter's decisions. Rarely do the supervisory boards steer firm-level corporate decisions. And second, the pool of firm-specific information and expertise lies within the firms themselves to a much greater extent than it does in the banks.[13] It should nevertheless be borne in mind that these trends apply to the large, internationalised manufacturing firms, including the German MNEs examined here; less so to somewhat smaller MNEs who are less internationalised; and not at all to small and medium-sized German firms who are still dependent on the German banks for credit and expertise. In the latter group the universal banks, as well as the cooperative savings banks (*Sparkassen*) and *Landesbanken*, continue to exercise great influence. An interviewee at the Deutsche Bank summed up these differences:

> Conditions have changed in favour of the big firms over time, and at the expense of the banks, including Deutsche. We have more influence in the *Mittelstand* (small and medium-sized firms). It is changing with the 'in-betweens' [for example, Schering, Böhringer-Ingelheim, Benckiser] who are more reliant on the banks [than are the likes of Siemens and Bayer]. But now even they are expanding abroad and building up relations with foreign banks – and they will gradually become less reliant on us [Deutsche].

The same interviewee made the following remarks on Deutsche's relationship with individual firms:

> BASF has the most developed and individualistic of internal financial operations among German companies. They are very aggressive. Bayer's foreign subsidiaries are more financially decentralised and tend to have closer links with locally owned banks abroad [than they do with German banks]. Where financial operations are more centralised, as is the case so far with Siemens, the conditions are better for maintaining a tighter relationship with the *Hausbank*. And engineering the rescue of AEG by Daimler has not given us a concomitant 'financial bonus'. AEG's policy abroad is very clear: build up links abroad with local banks in preference to the *Hausbank* and other German banks.

So where does this situation leave the oft-touted bank–firm links – equity participations, proxy voting rights, supervisory board representation, and so on – that supposedly distinguish the 'German model' from others, especially the Anglo-Saxon varieties of rather loose finance–industry connections? The position held here is that these German finance–industry linkages are important and distinctive, but should on no account be confused with the 'power of the banks in industry'. Such bank power does exist in smaller and medium-sized firms who are more financially reliant on the German banks, but the *Bankenmacht* thesis is difficult to uphold with respect to the large firms. The existing links between the universal banks and the large industrial firms do, however, provide an environment of stability for both financial and industrial institutions, reduce risk and serve common interests in a variety of ways.

First and foremost, the involvement of the banks in the firms provides the latter with substantial protection from takeover. For example it was the banks, particularly Deutsche, which staved off US-owned General Motors's bid for Daimler Benz in the 1960s, and ensured that AEG in the throes of financial collapse was taken over by the German Daimler group as opposed to a foreign-owned concern. Second, there is an extensive two-way flow of information between the firms and their privileged banks. Although the MNEs have historic relations with a lead bank (the so-called *Hausbank*) – for example, Daimler Benz, Bayer and Siemens with Deutsche, Hoechst with Dresdner – they tend to maintain close relations with a select two or three banks. The supervisory boards of the firms represent the highest channelling mechanism of information flow between the firms and the external actors which enjoy close relations with them, not only the banks, but also leading suppliers, customers and unions, who also have representation on the supervisory boards. From the firms' point of view, this phenomenon of drawing in outside actors is a means of better sensitising the firm to its external competitive environment.[14]

The final main advantage of close bank–firm links is that the lead banks are there to aid the firms in situations of crisis – for example what occurred with AEG-Telefunken on three separate occasions in the 1970s and 1980s until its takeover by Daimler Benz. AEG's problems stemmed from a flawed set of corporate strategies: it failed to move into higher value-added electronics products, focusing more on consumer goods and power engineering; it undertook a series of costly acquisitions which did not integrate well into the rest of the group; and it was slow to engage in foreign production. A financial crisis in 1979 led to a rescue package arranged by the long-standing *Hausbank*, Dresdner. Financial aid was given in the form of replenishment of equity capital and new bank loans by a consortium of banks, and old debts were rescheduled, on condition that a restructuring and rationalisation programme was undertaken. This was monitored by the election of the Dresdner chairman Dr Hans Friedrichs to the chairmanship of the AEG supervisory board. The latter brought in a new general manager, Dr Heinz Dürr, who was to stay as chief executive of AEG until 1990.

AEG's problems proved intractable, leading eventually to the company seeking court protection from its creditors in 1982 in order to stave off bankruptcy. It had debts of at least DM5 billion; banks and other creditors faced prospective losses of at least DM2.6 billion. West Germany faced the prospect of its greatest industrial disaster. Once again the banks, led by Dresdner, rallied round and another restructuring effort followed. This involved AEG withdrawing from some major existing joint ventures (for example, with Siemens in nuclear plant construction and light bulbs), ceding the bulk of its telecommunications operations to Bosch and selling the Telefunken consumer electronics operation to the French Thomson group. The company still faced deep financial problems, which came to a head in 1985. After protracted negotiations it was arranged for Daimler Benz to acquire AEG in 1986, once approval from the Federal Cartel Office was forthcoming. Here again the banks were at the heart of the negotiations, particularly the two *Hausbanken*, Deutsche (Daimler's lead bank) and Dresdner (AEG's).[15]

The AEG story does illustrate the point that the banks are there to help the firms in crisis scenarios, as a result of the common ties uniting both sets of actors. Moreover in such situations the banks do exert enormous influence on the firms, both in terms of financing as well as in corporate restructuring strategy and implementation. But once the crisis is over the *status quo ante* of bank–firm relations tends to be restored. Indeed once AEG was subsumed in Daimler Benz, Deutsche and Dresdner did not retain the residual influence arising from the central parts they played in the whole deal. AEG's rather problematic and still incomplete post-1986 corporate restructuring, specialising on its poles of transport systems, microelectronics and factory automation, and proceeding with internationalising its production, became a matter for its own management led by Dürr and the Daimler parent; similarly AEG's financial problems ceased to be those of the banks and became the preserve of Daimler, which has the dubious distinction of being saddled with them to the present day.[16]

The strong linkages between the universal banks and the MNEs remain in force, although they have suffered some weakening as a result of a number of factors: greater inter-bank competition in more deregulated financial markets at home, abroad and offshore; the greater self-financing capacity of the firms; the international-isation of their capital structures; and the increasing sophistication of their internal financial operations.

Whether these linkages can withstand the continuation and acceleration of these trends in the coming decades is an open question. In the early 1990s there has been rising pressure on large industrial firms to pay more attention to shareholders' interests, especially in terms of share price value. Although internal finan-cing remains high by international standards, the recession of the early 1990s has eaten into profits and caused many firms to seek more external capital. The large industrial firms have not, as a consequence, relied on greater bank credit; rather they have tapped cheaper and more flexible sources of funds on inter-national share and bond markets. The price for doing so, how-ever, has been increasing information disclosure and greater focus on shareholder value. There are, therefore, 'Anglo-Saxon' pressures on German firms which might presage a mutation, perhaps even a dilution, of their intimate links with the universal banks and Allianz, without necessarily going to the other extreme of disintermediation à l'anglaise and à l'americaine. Suffice it to say that the record to date does not point to an imminent rupture or even serious weakening of quite distinctive German bank–firm relations.

It is the mutuality of interests and reciprocal dependence between banks and firms, leading to close cooperation between the actors, that sets the 'German model' apart from others, not misconceived notions of bank power in the large firms (as opposed to small and medium-sized firms). As Oberbeck and Baethge point out, the universal banks have increased their economic power in Germany in other ways, especially in the systematic growth of the bulk business with private households, which creates 'a new dimension at the end of the 1980s [of the economic and political influence of banks] that can no longer be analysed using tradi-tional concepts of political influence in industry'. But their de-clining power in relation to large firms 'suggests the banks' limitations in the shaping and organising of capitalism'.[17]

One last point deserves mention. There has undoubtedly been a shift of power from the universal banks to the MNEs in their financial relations, but the continuing closeness of bilateral ties has its costs and benefits. The advantages of protection against takeover and a stable environment for longer-range corporate planning have to be weighed against the anti-competitive and sometimes cartel-like behaviour that can ensue. The conflation of industrial and banking capital in Germany can blunt the market-conforming disciplining mechanisms of otherwise free-wheeling capital markets by erecting barriers to competition from other firms, breeding an aversion to risk-taking and not punishing outright failures of management. The AEG and other cases (such as Metallgesellschaft and Schneider in the early 1990s) show that house banks and supervisory boards have been lax in taking timely action against incompetent managements, only deploying disciplinary measures once crises have arisen and gained public attention.

FRANCE: MNE–BANK AND MNE–GOVERNMENT LINKS, AND GOVERNMENT FINANCIAL POLICY

The French financial system differs markedly in structure from the German, affording a far greater role for the government. As John Zysman states: 'A credit-based, price administered financial system made possible administrative influence and often discretion in the allocation of capital ... finance was crucial in shaping the state bureaucracy's capacity to intervene in industrial affairs.'[18] At the end of the Second World War, it was judged that the financial system was woefully inadequate in allocating capital to industry. Hence the rationale – or the excuse – for the intervention of the government in completely revamping and subsequently playing the leading role in the financial sector. This involved a central role for the *Trésor* (Treasury) in the Ministry of Finance and the Planning Commission, although the latter's influence was to decline gradually, leading to its ultimate marginalisation; a new system of banking regulation with the nationalisation of the Bank of France; and the nationalisation of a considerable part of the commercial banking sector in 1946.

The goal was to selectively allocate capital to targeted sectors of industry by means of government-administered prices set in financial markets for loans, bonds, equity and insurance. Preferential terms were given to recipients through a rediscounting mechanism at the Bank of France and by channelling funds through newly established parastatal financial institutions such as the *Crédit National*, *Caisse des Depôts* and the *Fonds de Développement*

Economique et Social (FDES). The structure and workings of the system were conducive to the mobilisation of investment funds from the commercial and investment banking sectors to be delivered to targeted firms and sectors. One prime function of institutions such as the *Crédit National* was educative: to remove the aversion of the banking community to industrial lending and to inculcate in them an in-house ability to appraise medium and long-term loans.[19] Parastatal funding institutions and inter-ministerial committees (performing much the same function as the former) multiplied. They included: the *Fonds Industriel de Modernisation* (FIM), whose task was to promote the major firms in strategic sectors; the *Compte pour le Développement Industriel* (CODEVI), which attracted finance for industry; and the *Comité Interministériel pour la Restructuration Industrielle* (CIR), which gave aid to firms in difficulty. Indeed it was estimated that there were some 30 public bodies involved in decision-making for the electronics industry, with some 150 different procedures for aiding the industry, funded by different bodies employing different criteria.[20]

It has been argued that this financial system created and nurtured by the government has fostered closer bank–industry relations. Peter Hall presents a widely held view: 'The French banks are in a position to exercise a proportionately greater influence over the affairs of industry ... they generally take an active interest in the production and marketing strategies of the firms they support.' And in a major study of the French banking system, François Morin attributed predominant banking influence in industry to the two leading *banques d'affaires*, Paribas and Suez, who have a history of stockholdings in the large French firms.[21]

This position is misleading. The French banks do not have a tradition of an 'industrial vocation' as in Germany, in the sense that they have shied away from close involvement in firm-level affairs by sharing risks and decisions aimed at long-term growth; rather they have been more concerned with short-term financial profit criteria. As Daniel Lebègue, a former Director of the *Trésor*, has commented: 'One of the traditional reproaches made with respect to the bank in France is that banks are distinct from companies; and it is true that they have without doubt taken fewer risks than their counterparts in other countries in order to favour the creation and development of companies.' This allergy to industrial risk-taking applies not only to the commercial banks, who until recently did not hold major equity positions in industry, but also to the *banques d'affaires*. Paribas and Suez have track records of equity involvement in many leading French firms: Paribas has become involved in oil and venture capital for biotechnology; and Suez has pursued greater investment in agrochemicals, pharmaceuticals and electronics in the 1980s, apart from having had long-standing equity in Thomson, Rhône-Poulenc and CGE. But this has not been translated into bank–firm cooperation along German lines. And in the final analysis, the banks have not rallied round when the firms have been in crisis, quite unlike the illustrative AEG example in Germany. This function has been invariably left to the government. As Elie Cohen comments, banks and financial markets in France have had little sanction on the management of companies; they have not checked or corrected the strategies of firms when the latter have en-countered serious commercial difficulties, leaving only one pos-sibility at the end of the road to save firms from going out of business: government intervention.

There have been many government attempts to foster closer bank–firm links, but results have been at best mixed. Legislative reforms in 1966–7 blurred the division between the commercial banks and the *banques d'affaires*, allowing the latter to engage in commercial banking and the former to take up equity stakes in industry. The nationalisation of 36 private banks, as well as of Paribas and Suez in 1981, was intended to transform the banking sector into a tool of industrial policy by getting the banks more closely involved and in tune with the industrial objectives in-tended for (especially the newly nationalised) national cham-pions. The measures of financial deregulation in the 1980s, starting with the *Loi Delors* in 1983, were intended not only to allow the banks to strengthen their balance sheets but also to use new financial instruments in order to plough extra investment funds into industry. And one aim of the Chirac government's privat-isation programme between 1986 and 1988 was to strengthen bank–industry links: the newly privatised banks – a number of com-mercial banks, as well as Paribas and Suez – were supposed to provide fresh capital and take equity positions in the newly privatised industrial firms such as CGE and St Gobain.

But the intent of the government before, during and after the nationalisations in 1981–2, and after the privatisations of 1986–7, was not translated into practice. Despite the 1966–7 reforms, commercial banks did not take up major equity stakes in industry. Given the lack of tradition and expertise in industrial banking, the banks were unable to act as the government wished, just as the latter had little success in changing the operating behaviour of the banks.[22]

Attempts continued in the late 1980s to forge closer bank–industry relations. A notable example was the government's insistence that Thomson transfer its profitable financial services operation to Crédit Lyonnais, a leading state-owned commercial bank, in return for a 14 per cent Thomson stake in the bank. This was the first such link-up between a major industrial firm and a bank in France. One objective was to inject liquidity into Crédit Lyonnais, but the Thomson PDG Alain Gomez did state another aim: he wanted to establish relations with a close banking partner to help compete against German and Japanese firms in electronics who enjoyed close ties to certain banks and had, in his view, a financial security that Thomson did not enjoy. Furthermore the heads of France's two leading commercial banks, the Banque Nationale de Paris and the Crédit Lyonnais, declared that they wanted to follow a 'Deutsche Bank model' in building up equity participations and other links with selected companies – with the active approval of the government.[23]

With the new privatisation programme of Prime Minister Balladur, there have been renewed attempts to forge closer bank–industry links along German lines. The government is promoting a policy of *noyaux durs* (hard cores), which encourages leading industrial, banking and insurance groups to take long-term stakes as part of 'stable shareholdings' in the newly privatised firms. This has a precedent in the 1986–8 privatisation program. Alcatel-Alsthom and Societé Générale built up a group of core shareholders after their privatisation in 1987. Rhône-Poulenc, Elf, AGF, UAP, Renault and others are in the process of doing the same in the early and mid-1990s, involving mostly French-owned groups but also some foreign-owned concerns such as the German Dresdner Bank (in BNP) and the AMB insurance concern (in AGF). The objectives are, of course, to provide some kind of protection against takeovers and to facilitate long-range planning.[24] It remains to be seen whether these objectives will be fulfilled, but there is another consideration from a competition viewpoint: the construction of the *noyaux durs* involves the further concentration of power among a handful of large French firms in the domestic market, which could well serve to restrict competitive access to non-insiders and blunt disciplinary mechanisms, such as the capital market and other competitors for goods and services, from punishing firm-level inefficiency. These power concentrations and the neglect of competition criteria have, needless to say, a long tradition in French mercantilist policy-making and theorising.

Whatever the state of current policy practice, it would be unwise to predict the flourishing of MNE–bank links along German lines. First, to reiterate, the history of the separate development, rather than the institutionalised cooperation, of banking and industrial cultures in France will continue to be a powerful constraining factor. The large expanse of fertile common ground that exists between the universal banks and the large firms in Germany has no real French equivalent. Despite repeated and continuing government attempts to bridge this gap, there has been no appreciable narrowing of it in the 1980s. Second, the deregulation and internationalisation of financial markets will tend to pressure the further dilution of linkages, as inter-bank competition escalates and banks and firms deal with each other more on arm's-length/price-margin terms – which is the rule rather than the exception in the US and UK financial systems. As Jacques Lesourne comments, 'Bank–firm relations risk deterioration: the strategies of the two sets of actors will be more conflictual than in the 1960–80 period.'[25] The strength of German bank–industry relations may withstand such pressures, but that strength does not exist to begin with in France.

A number of interviewees portrayed the nature of the bank–industry relationship in France:

> Bank–company relations here are more along US lines than German ones, with shareholders, including banks, placing more emphasis on short-term returns on investment rather than long-term growth. French companies are more short-term orientated than in Germany. Indeed we have been more inspired by American corporate practices than German ones. Only a very few leading personalities have been inspired by the German model and preach it in the French context – Raymond Barre [the former Prime Minister] and Jean-Yves Haberer [the PDG of Crédit Lyonnais] at the helm.

On the increasing equity participation of BNP in Rhône-Poulenc:

> This building-up of links with a single bank to reap the

perceived advantages of the German system is not in the nature of French financial and industrial cultures – it is quite a new concept for us.

Government financial policy and government–MNE relations

The involvement of the government in the postwar French financial system and in firm-level financial affairs necessitates consideration of the government–MNE relationship on financial matters – it is far more important in the French context than in Germany. As was argued in the previous chapter, government financial policy *vis-à-vis* the MNEs in the 1980s has been the centrepiece of MNE-oriented industrial policy. It is now time to examine it more closely.

The initial point to make is that public ownership of the MNEs imposes certain financial constraints on the latter in raising the substantial resources required to invest abroad. There are considerable disadvantages in relation to private MNEs. Whereas private MNEs can raise capital on financial markets, public ownership normally precludes this option: capital augmentation can, *ceteris paribus*, only be obtained from specific budgetary grants which, due to prevailing public-spending constraints, are usually difficult to procure. In the French case public ownership has, for these and a number of other related reasons, led to an imbalance in the financial structures of the MNEs: access by the MNEs to international financial markets has been much reduced due to the net foreign debt of France; decision-making processes on financial operations have been made more complex and slower due to government intervention; and ratings on foreign money markets have not been favourable because investors are suspicious of the 'shareholder-state', believing, rightly or wrongly, that the French government actually exercises managerial control of the companies it owns.[26]

Compounding these problems is the history of capital shortage and high debt gearing that has plagued French MNEs, both public and private, in sharp contrast to the high self-financing capability of the German MNEs. This is a factor that has persistently been a source of worry for the French government, concerned as it is with the twin needs of the firms for capital and R&D investment. The capital-shortage problem has been thrown into sharper relief by the escalating investment requirements imposed by the internationalisation strategies of the MNEs, especially in terms of making costly foreign acquisitions.

The MNEs continue to have serious problems with indebtedness, partly as a result of public ownership restricting the access to equity capital. The debt–equity ratio of French companies overall, one of the highest in Europe, was 0.62 in 1984, declining somewhat between 1984 and 1987 due to higher levels of company profitability, and picking up again from then on. In contrast, the German debt–equity ratio peaked at 0.52 in 1981 and declined for the rest of the 1980s. In 1982 24 per cent of the value-added of the nationalised industries in France went to pay interest charges. Rhône-Poulenc, which forked out more for foreign acquisitions than any other French company, had a debt–equity ratio of 0.7 in 1989, representing a net debt of FFr20.6 billion, rising to 0.96 in June 1990 due to its 1989–90 acquisitions which had cost it FFr12.4 billion. Table 5.4 presents the debt–equity ratios of the French MNEs in 1988. These figures are nevertheless an improvement on positions earlier in the decade: for example, Thomson and Bull's peaked at 3.74 and 5.0 respectively in 1984, and Rhône-Poulenc's at 3.9 in 1982. As is evident, the German MNEs have had much lower debt–equity ratios (see Table 5.2) than their French counterparts.[27]

Table 5.4 Long- and medium-term debt:owned capital ratios in 1988

Thomson	0.58
Bull	1.1
CGE	0.71
Rhône-Poulenc	0.5
Elf	0.39

Source: *Annual Reports*, 1988

Indeed the contrast between the powerful self-financing capacity of the German MNEs (see Tables 5.2 and 5.3, Figures 5.1 and 5.2) and the capital shortage/debt-reliance of the French MNEs is striking. In this respect the latter's Achilles Heel is quite different from the competitive advantages of the former: self-financing provides the German MNEs with a large degree of independence from external capital-raising and allows them more flexibility to plan and operate on longer-term business scenarios. The French MNEs' debt reliance and high debt–equity ratios force them continuously to pay off greater amounts of interest and principal, pressuring them to focus on shorter-term profit extraction rather than on longer-term market share objectives. Debt-raising may have been relatively cheap in the mid to late 1980s under lower market interest rates, but the rise in interest rates at the end of the decade ratcheted up the debt-servicing burden of MNEs such as Rhône-Poulenc, in the process undermining investor confidence in them.[28]

The financial strength of the German MNEs also enables them to move faster and further in certain crucial instances, for example in making foreign acquisitions. Thomson was interested in bidding for the British company Plessey but was out-manoeuvred by Siemens, which had the financial resources at hand to join forces quickly with GEC in going ahead with the Plessey bid. Similarly Siemens, with its DM20 billion war chest, had the financial resources to invest heavily in the US public-switching market, and felt able to swallow year-on-year operating losses there in order to build up market share on a longer-term basis. Alcatel, on the other hand, found it difficult to penetrate the US market because the necessary financial investment was too burdensome for its own resources.[29]

Thus the French government throughout the 1980s has been preoccupied with the perceived competitive disadvantages of (especially the state-owned) MNEs and pursued public-policy measures in the attempt to rectify these weaknesses. Given the parlous financial state of the newly nationalised companies in 1981–2 (CGE excepted) and the resources required to undertake the huge restructuring programmes planned for both the chemical and electronics sectors, government subsidy was the policy prescription most commonly applied in the initial years of the first Mitterrand administration. A FFr9 billion package for the newly nationalised industries was announced by the government in 1982; Rhône-Poulenc, Thomson and Bull were among the main beneficiaries. Of that amount, FFr3 billion was in the form of direct public aid; the other FFr6 billion was channelled through the newly nationalised banks in the form of equity capital and subordinated loans. The *Trésor* in the Ministry of Finance played the central role in this process as well as in the financial aspects of the sectoral restructuring programmes. The negotiation of planning contracts in 1983 between the Ministry of Industry and the nationalised firms was followed by a FFr20 billion investment funding programme, of which FFr12.6 billion came from the public budget and the rest from the nationalised banking sector. The main firms received a *panachage* of investment: aid from the public budget, equity/participatory loans and certificates at discounted rates of interest, as well as specific research, employment and development grants. These funds were channelled through the banks and the parapublic lending institutions such as the *Crédit National* and the *Caisse Nationale de l'Industrie*.[30]

A change of policy orientation took place in 1983 for a number of reasons, as was discussed in detail in the previous chapter. Macroeconomic policy became tougher and more conservative along with the general U-turn of retrenchment in 1983 after the failed Keynesian reflationary experiment of 1981–3. Public spending had to be cut back radically, with no real increases in spending levels in 1984 and 1985, partly necessitated by mounting interest charges on a growing public-sector debt and a foreign debt that had reached FFr525 billion by 1985. Given such budgetary stringency, the Ministry of Finance began to cut back sharply on subsidies to the nationalised companies. With the companies getting over the worst of their financial troubles and returning to operating profit, the Finance Ministry called a halt to direct subsidies for the aforementioned firms, and instead focused aid on crisis sectors such as coal, steel and shipbuilding; moreover, it insisted on receiving dividends from firms returning to operating profitability.[31] As an ex-civil servant in the *Trésor* commented:

> The *sauf garde industriel* attitude of the state towards the firms, with industrial criteria to the fore in financial questions, was replaced by the 'state as shareholder' concept. We [in the *Trésor*] then paid more attention to 'balance sheet' questions and put the financial health, rather than the industrial health of the firms, uppermost in our deliberations: wary of subsidies, insisting on dividends from the firms as well as financial rigour on their part.

Post-1983 budgetary constraints and subsidy cutbacks only served to highlight the acute structural financial weaknesses of French MNEs, at a time when investment capital was required in greater quantities due, *inter alia*, to a stronger pace of internationalisation. The need to meet the investment needs of the firms was very much on the government's mind when it embarked on a series of deregulatory measures. Corporate taxation was cut, price controls on industrial products were removed and employers' national insurance charges were reduced. Above all, deregulation was aimed at financial markets. One prime goal was to facilititate the injection of extra sources of private capital into the firms without engaging in outright privatisation and sacrificing the reality of public ownership. Specifically, the government wished to jump-start the underdeveloped Paris Bourse into an internationally performing and sufficiently liquid financial market which would allow funds to flow into the industrial firms.

Major deregulation can be traced to the *Loi Delors* in 1983, extending the *Loi Monory* of 1978 which brought wider access to bond markets through tax credits. The Delors reforms introduced new financial instruments such as the *certificats d'investissements* (non-voting preferential shares), issued up to 25 per cent of a firm's equity and later extended in certain cases to 49 per cent, and the *titres participatifs* (non-voting loan stock). Both these instruments were quickly used by the nationalised companies to the extent of their legal limits.[32]

But as the 1980s progressed, the capital-raising needs of the MNEs became significantly greater: financing requirements for internationalisation through foreign acquisitions were accelerating at a rapid rate, the removal of exchange rate controls in 1986 releasing a pent-up demand by the MNEs to engage in foreign investment. The privatisation of CGE in 1987 gave it greater flexibility in tapping financial markets, but the rest of the firms studied here remained in public ownership. Moreover the incoming Socialist government in 1988 was constrained by the *ni–ni* policy commitment to no further privatisations. Nevertheless, without compromising the principle of public ownership by privatising these MNEs outright, the Rocard administration in President Mitterrand's second *septennat* went out of its way to help state-owned MNEs overcome the *ni–ni* constraints and get access to private capital, thus aiding them in their internationalisation strategies. Hence the continued stages of deregulation and the green light given by the government to state-owned firms to engage in sophisticated financial operations on capital markets; and also allowing them to raise debt capital abroad for foreign acquisitions as well as having the latter listed on foreign financial exchanges with minority quotations. This was the case with Rhône-Poulenc's acquisition of the pharmaceutical firm Rorer in the US: Rhône-Poulenc–Rorer acquired 32 per cent of private equity through listings in New York and Paris.[33]

The Rhône-Poulenc example is illustrative, as it has been especially adept in its financial market operations in order to finance its outstandingly vigorous acquisitions programme, all the while trying to overcome its financial constraints as a state-owned MNE. It was the first firm to use the *certificats d'investissements* (CIs) and *titres participatifs* in 1984, raising FFr1 billion. By 1986 it had reached its legal limit of CIs at 25 per cent of total equity. To finance $1 billion worth of acquisitions in the US, notably of Stauffer Chemicals and Union Carbide's agrochemical division, it pioneered the use of non-equity floating-rate capital notes in the French market in addition to raising $300 million in the US. Its later acquisitions were financed through the imaginative issue of $875 million-worth of participatory notes. A capital augmentation of FFr4.6 billion took place in 1990 with the help of the government's transfer to Rhône-Poulenc of its 35 per cent stake in Roussel Uclaf.[34]

The internationalisation of French MNEs *à grande vitesse* in the late 1980s would not have been possible without the combination of four environmental factors: low market interest rates on borrowings, a strong and buoyant franc, a rapidly developing Paris Bourse as a result of financial deregulation, and a benign government position on overcoming the *ni–ni* financing constraints. The short-term success of the public-sector companies in raising non-government sources of capital is shown by the following figures: between 1988 and 1990 they received FFr183.4 billion in fresh capital, only FFr13.8 billion of which was from the government and FFr21.1 billion in debt write-offs; of the rest, FFr34.3 billion came from financial markets and FFr85.7 billion from reinvested profits.[35]

Such contortions in order to get round *ni–ni* may have filled a short-term gap when external market conditions were propitious, but it is arguable whether they provided any kind of long-term solution to the investment hunger of these internationalising MNEs. Debt-raising can be more expensive and somewhat more risky than equity financing, especially when interest rates rise, as was the case in the late 1980s and early 1990s. Public ownership – and thus restricted access to private equity capital – has in fact served to take debt gearings and exposure to abnormally high and potentially dangerous levels. According to a report by the *Sénat* (the Upper House of Parliament), these methods represent a damaging long-term phenomenon of 'capitalism without capital, cascades of holding companies, and capital without voting rights'.[36] According to one interviewee:

> One cannot do this all the time. Its boost is only temporary. Rising market interest rates make such means less effective and the cumulative effect is to increase the firms' debt burden . . . It is a very unnatural way of going about doing business.

In the final analysis, the long-term investment needs of the state-owned MNEs – given the emphasis of the French government on budgetary rigour and a conservative, disinflationary macroeconomic policy – could only be sated by more access to private equity capital, the corollary of which was wholesale majority or partial privatisation which would serve to dilute the government's voting equity stake in the firms and hence its ability to exercise influence over them as the predominant shareholder. It is in recognition of the exigency of MNE capital requirements that the government made its 1991 announcements that private, including foreign, parties could take stakes in the firms of up to 49 per cent of equity. Plans to transfer government stakes in some of the state-owned MNEs to major banks had the same intent in mind, that is, to facilitate greater investment in the firms, as well as to foster closer bank–firm relations and provide a bulwark against the threat of foreign takeover of the firms in the event of government holdings being reduced below majority control.[37]

Financial market deregulation and a favourable government financial policy stance towards the state-owned MNEs have benefited Rhône-Poulenc and Elf Aquitaine, in terms of the success they have had in overcoming *ni–ni* and raising external finance. As mentioned before, the most pressing problem cases were and are Thomson and Bull, both of which are in competitive and financial difficulties and depend to a much greater extent on government subsidy. Given their weaknesses and the lack of confidence of financial markets in them, it is much more difficult to procure external financing for them.[38]

The above record of government financial policy towards the MNEs should be viewed, it is asserted here, within the context of the overarching interpretation of French industrial policy evolution in the 1980s, as was set out in the previous chapter. The international dimension of financial policy is clearly observable, especially post-1983 with the onset of financial market deregulation. In the previous period, government subsidy was geared to rescuing and restructuring the newly nationalised firms. From then on the government became increasingly aware of the needs of the MNEs to internationalise. This exigency in turn required investment capital, which the MNEs were short of due to the constraints of access to private capital for the state-owned MNEs as well as the newly imposed budgetary constraints on subsidies to them. The requirement of investment to fund internationalisation through costly foreign acquisitions thus was a driving force in the government's largely successful deregulation measures, followed through consistently in the 1980s despite changes of government. Similarly the 1986–8 privatisation programme, although in other ways representing a marked change of policy on the part of the new right-wing government compared to its Socialist predecessor, did have as one of its main goals the injection of private capital to meet the investment needs of France's 'international champions'.

The political compromise within the Socialist Party as embodied in the post-1988 *ni–ni* policy presented further problems for the state-owned MNEs in gaining access to private capital, given that the privatisation option was ruled out. This period coincided with the most ferociously active phase of internationalisation by French MNEs, with the state-owned ones at the forefront in making financially burdensome acquisitions. It is also clear that the government was acutely aware of the MNEs' financing requirements for such measures, and therefore the exigency of attracting further private capital. Thus the Ministries of Finance and Industry, with the backing of the Prime Minister's office and the blessing of the Elysée Palace, went to enormous lengths to get round the constraints of *ni–ni* by acquiescing and indeed promoting the injection of further flows of private capital into the MNEs through increasingly sophisticated financial market operations. This reinforces a key point made in the last chapter: the *ni–ni* rhetoric masked an ongoing process of partial privatisation of MNEs through the back door which gradually diluted the government's financial role in the firms and increased private financial participation in them. Privatisation since 1993 has taken these steps to their logical conclusion.

With increasing levels of private capital in the MNEs, through government-engendered financial-market deregulation in France as well as through the MNEs' tapping of foreign and offshore capital markets, the government's ability to exercise intervention and control of the MNEs has diminished. The firms have become less dependent on government. Thus the power balance in the government–MNE relationship on finance has changed in favour of the MNEs, which reinforces the general argument made in the previous chapter that the MNEs have gained power at the expense of the government. In this respect the argument of Elie Cohen and Michel Bauer is apposite: the government's financial resources and policy orientations have been used to further the *autonomous* strategies of the firms rather than the supposed industrial policies of the government.[39] This point applies applies to Thomson and Bull, whose crisis situations make them more dependent on public subsidy. Despite that fact, government support is directed at promoting the corporate policies that have been devised largely within the firms rather than by the government. The evolution of the government's financial relation to the firms was summed up by an interviewee:

> On financial questions, the state's relation to the firms is more distanced as the firms themselves have become more *celibataire*, for example by the internationalisation of their capital structures, CGE in particular since its privatisation. The state's ability to supervise is not as great as it was. In any case, it is difficult to perform the financial overseeing function in the *Trésor*: there is just one person responsible for the electronics sector and another one for chemicals. With internationalising companies, the task of surveying them in detail becomes impossible.

One final point requires elaboration. In the previous chapter it was indicated that there are differentiated levels of intervention by the government in the MNEs: they were lower in the German MNEs than in the French, but within the latter group differences were observable. CGE and Elf were more autonomous from the government, Rhône-Poulenc was in an intermediate position, and the least autonomous were Thomson and Bull. A major factor of government intervention/management autonomy is the financial relationship between the government and the firm, which represents the central component of the overall government–firm relationship in France. Financial health and independence is a partial guarantor of low levels of government intervention and high levels of management autonomy. Both CGE and Elf were steadily profitable and did not rely on direct public subsidies. CGE's private status further distanced it from government control and involvement in its affairs. Although Elf was state-owned, it regularly paid dividends to the government and its sizeable (46 per cent) minority public listing (until majority privatisation) forced it to pay more attention to the discipline of financial markets, thus further distancing it from government influence.

At the other end of the spectrum were the loss-making Thomson and Bull, who were reliant more on direct government transfers and were 100 per cent government-owned, although some of their subsidiaries had minority private capital participation. They were more susceptible to government intervention, although with them it varied during the course of the 1980s. The greater levels of intervention in the early 1980s and late 1980s to early 1990s, corresponding with worse financial results, contrasted with lower levels of intervention in the mid-1980s, during which time both groups enjoyed a few years of profitability.[40]

Thus financial health and independence as an indicator of government intervention in the French MNEs is akin to the importance of the self-financing capacity of the German MNEs in gaining more independence from the universal banks. In this respect internal business organisation variables – that is, what happens within the MNEs – are replicated at the political economy level in terms of MNE relationships with external actors. For example, Roussel Uclaf maintains a substantial degree of autonomy from its Hoechst parent due, among other reasons, to its regular profitability and cash-cow status within the Hoechst network. Within the Elf holding structure, Sanofi guards its autonomy due to its steady profitability and its separate minority listing on the Paris Bourse; Atochem's less-profitable chemical activities together with its 100 per cent Elf ownership prevent it having the same privileges.[41] These are factors played out within the MNEs' organisational structures, but they are akin to the contingency of financial health and independence of the MNEs in the degree of government and/or bank intervention in them.

CONCLUSION

Both the French and German MNEs have advanced on the road to the internationalisation of their financial functions and capital structures, following in the wake of their internationalisation of production. This was less the case with the state-owned French

MNEs; the very fact of public ownership cramped their financial internationalisation. But these trends were still strongly evident in them, Rhône-Poulenc being the prime example. It was more evident in the privatised CGE as well as with the German MNEs. Bosch's ownership by the Robert Bosch Foundation tightly restricted the ownership of its capital base and therefore made it the exception among the German firms. The privatisation of the other French state-owned MNEs in the mid-1990s should allow them to proceed with the internationalisation of their financial functions at a faster pace.

These dynamics of internationalisation had converging effects on the French and German MNEs. The financial autonomy gained was used to serve their production autonomy in their internationalised networks. This point is strongly made by Charles-Albert Michalet, who argues that the intertwining of production and financial autonomies by MNEs 'at the top of the hierarchy' in the world economy serves to make them more powerful actors and less dependent on governments, banks and other external actors.[42] On financial matters, the German MNEs gained more power in their relationships with the universal banks; the French MNEs wrested more financial autonomy in their relationships with the French government.

These are French–German structural differences – power shifts in relation to banks in Germany and the government in France. First, the make-up of the French financial system differed markedly from the German, although deregulation in both countries and the internationalisation of finance made these differences smaller than they were at the beginning of the 1980s. MNE financial relationships with external actors differed between the two countries: in France, the most important relationship was that between the government and the MNE, most of the French firms studied here having the government as the major shareholder; in Germany the prime financial relationship was that between the MNEs and the universal banks. The structural linkages that bound the two sets of actors in Germany were solid and resilient. In contrast, French bank–firm relations have been and are relatively weak and distant, in spite of continuing government attempts to narrow the gap. These French bank–firm relations, the products of the historical separation of banking and industrial cultures, remained closer to the Anglo-Saxon 'disintermediated' model than the German–Japanese one of tight linkage between industrial and financial capital. The *noyaux durs* policy of the Balladur government is attempting to move in a more German–Japanese direction. It is too early to predict whether outcomes will correspond with initial policy intentions.

Second, the financial structures of the firms themselves manifested French–German differences. The significant competitive advantages of the self-financing capacity of the German MNEs contrasted with the shortage of investment capital and high indebtedness of the French MNEs, something exacerbated by the restriction public ownership imposed on access to private equity capital. On financial questions as in others, therefore, the converging effects of internationalisation had to work through differently constituted French and German domestic structures and government–finance–industry networks.

Finally, the argumentation of this chapter explicitly finds fault with popular models of financial relationships in the French and German political economies. In analysing the external financial relationships of the French and German MNEs, components of certain political economy models were found to be distinctly unhelpful and, indeed, misleading as heuristic devices for empirical investigation. From the evidence gained as a result of the analysis of these MNEs, two major points arise. First, there is little evidence of 'the power of the banks' over the German MNEs. Banks retain substantial economic power in Germany in other ways, for example with small and medium-sized firms and through their growing 'retail' business with individuals and households; but with respect to large industrial firms, their power has declined. Second, it is not tenable to suggest the existence of close bank–firm relations in France on lines suggestive of the German model, let alone to discuss 'the power of the banks' over French MNEs. Links are much looser than suggested or implied, and are being further pressurised by financial deregulation at home as well as by the globalisation of financial markets. And lastly, the French government by its own acts of deregulation and privatisation is in the process of divesting itself of levers of control over both the channelling of funds in the financial system and, ultimately, over the intended recipients of those funds: the firms.

6

EUROPE AND TECHNOLOGY
Cross-border dimensions of political economy

The last three chapters have concentrated on the French and German political economies as the home bases of the MNEs: the embeddedness of the firms in domestic structures; home government policy and MNE–government relations; and MNE relations with external actors on financial matters. This chapter now travels beyond the national confines of France and Germany to take a wider view of the interaction of internationalisation with the role of the MNEs as political economic actors. The focus broadens to encompass a wider geographical dimension, that of the European Community, and a specific functional dimension, that of technology.

As was made evident in chapter 2, the internationalisation of the French and German MNEs in the 1980s took place first and foremost in the European Community, which has become the regional core and springboard for firm-level strategies in global competition. The commercial expansion of the firms in the EC, which has been integrating at an accelerated pace since the mid-1980s, has important political economy implications. First, the policy agendas of the French and German governments have acquired greater European dimensions with the focus of national policy shifting to the EC level, as chapter 4 showed. Second, the 'political' activity of the firms themselves at the EC level has increased significantly, along with their commercial activity of restructuring, rationalisation and concentration through the mechanisms of mergers, acquisitions and alliances. Third, EC policy networks and communities, subsuming the MNEs, supranational and national public authorities, have emerged, gaining more importance relative to existing national policy networks and communities. This chapter expands on each of these three political economy themes, focusing right the way through on one functional part of the value chain for the firms and one arena of public policy: technology.

Internationalisation of research and development (R&D) for the MNEs is an essential component of the overall internationalisation process, especially when it is accepted that the chemical and electronics MNEs studied here are so reliant on technological innovation and diffusion for commercial survival and success. As was discussed in chapter 1, technology is both a primary cause and a motor of internationalisation: necessary R&D costs are escalating enormously, forcing companies to expand their market coverage across the globe to generate enough sales to recoup sunk costs, dependence on national or regional markets no longer being sufficient; and companies expand their own R&D networks across borders, partly in the wake of the internationalisation of manufacturing and sales, and partly to access the most advanced technologies in different 'lead markets', wherever they happen to be located. The late twentieth-century cutting edge, generic technologies of biotechnology and microelectronics have their primary commercial applications in the chemical and electronics sectors respectively. The MNEs examined here are thus among the most active of firms in developing these generic technologies. Therefore, the concentration of this chapter is on the EC dimension of biotechnology and microelectronics for public-policy and MNE activity in policy networks.

ECONOMIC INTEGRATION IN THE EC

With the passage of the Single European Act in 1986, and its subsequent filling out through the agreement on various measures in the White Paper on the Completion of the Internal Market, the EC began a *rélance* of economic integration with the aim of removing barriers to the free movement of goods, services, people and capital within the Community by the end of 1992. The 1992 programme was intended to erode intra-EC barriers to competition in markets such as consumer electronics and telecommunications that had been nationally closed off through different standards and norms, preferential public procurement and government subsidies for privileged national champions, among a host of other protectionist and market-distorting measures. Completing the Internal Market involved efficiency gains for both consumers and producers: consumers gained in terms of the price and quality of goods and services due to greater competition; freer trade allowed producers to relocate and rationalise production in order to reap economies of scale in a larger, more competitive market structure.

The heart of the 1992 programme affecting large manufacturing MNEs such as those examined here thus involved: the harmonisation of different national standards and norms; the abolition of intra-EC frontier controls; the liberalisation of public procurement; the establishment of an EC-wide regime of merger control and competition enforcement; the examination and limitation of state aids to industry that would constitute an unfair advantage over competitor firms; and the abolition of exchange and capital controls. Not only manufacturing sectors, but also those such as financial services and air and road transport were deeply affected. There were also plans to aid the mobility of qualified workers and to harmonise certain aspects of tax and corporate laws and regulations.

Many of these policy-led changes had a deep impact on the MNEs analysed here. Public procurement, representing 15 per cent of EC GDP, was to be opened up, particularly in areas such as the supply of telecommunications equipment and computer hardware. New EC regulations established a framework for the opening and liberalisation of markets in telecommunications equipment and services. In the course of 1990–91, the Siemens acquisition of Nixdorf and the Alcatel acquisition of Fiat's telecommunications operations were among the first cases to be taken up by the Commission in its new role as the Community's prime competition authority. In highly regulated national markets in pharmaceuticals, incremental progress was made towards the approximation of national regimes on new drug approval, price control and patent protection.[1]

These policy-led changes of deregulation and re-regulation at EC level were accompanied by market-led changes by firms as they prepared for competition on a more integrated Internal Market. Chapter 2 detailed the major actions taken by each of the firms in the EC during the 1980s. Corporate restructuring and rationalisation took on new dimensions in the late 1980s. Cross-border merger and takeover activity by EC-headquartered companies both inside and outside the Community, valued at ECU45 billion in 1988–9, took place at record levels. Industry concentration led to the number of major suppliers of telecommunications equipment in the EC declining from ten to four, and the number of major semiconductor manufacturers down from twelve to three; the indigenous European consumer electronics industry became concentrated in two firms, Thomson and Philips.[2]

As Sharp and Holmes point out, the European dimension to public policy has come to take precedence over national policy solutions: 'The degree to which the nation state can seek to carve out for itself an area of industrial space which it can dominate is minimal [as a result of growing interdependence within the EC]. For this reason, within the EC the degree of autonomy available to the individual nation state for the pursuit of industrial objectives is severely constrained.' In France this was evident in the partial disengagement of the government from active intervention in industry: the financial role was increasingly handed over to the domain of private markets, whether by outright or partial 'back door' privatisations; the technological and industrial role became the preserve of the senior management of the firms themselves. Greater scope for action, for national governments, supranational authorities and firms, was perceived to be available at the EC rather than at the national level.[3]

GENERIC TECHNOLOGIES AND R&D INTERNATIONALISATION

In the past, trade, foreign direct investment and financial re-structuring have been the dominant forms of integration in the world economy; now technology is acquiring relatively more importance in relation to existing equity and financial relations, at the heart of a complex structure of networks and alliances that involve both governments and firms. Although the role of government is important in re-regulating, deregulating and setting the 'rules of the game', it is the relentless pace of technological development that is eroding the ability of governments to intervene in industrial affairs. The balance of knowledge and sources of information are shifting away from public authorities and towards internationally competitive firms.[4]

The chemical and electronics MNEs analysed here, being both technology-intensive and internationally active with European home markets, thus provide excellent subjects for the analysis of the power relationships of multinationals with external actors,

especially governments and supranational authorities, on technology matters in the integrating EC. Before tackling such concerns,
it is apposite to provide an overview of the firms' technology
functions and competences, and of their R&D internationalisation
in the 1980s.

Such cross-border expansion of R&D can be characterised as a
mixture of simultaneous moves of centralisation and decentralisation: centralisation of activity in the home market to achieve
economies of scale and scope and to facilitate managerial control;
decentralisation in overseas markets to adapt to local market
conditions, to be close to and integrated with local production, and
to gain a 'window' of access to the latest technological innovations
in foreign 'lead markets'.[5]

The MNEs considered here had R&D budgets that increased
steadily in absolute terms, as a percentage of total sales and in
relation to capital expenditures. Siemens's spending multiplied
ten-fold in 25 years; CGE's eleven-fold between 1980 and 1990.
Siemens in fact had the largest outlay on R&D of any European-
owned firm. Hoechst, Bayer, BASF, Thomson and CGE were also
among the top 15 European-owned R&D spenders. At the lower
end of the scale were the smaller and more product-specialised
AEG, Bosch and Bull, as well as Rhône-Poulenc and Elf Aquitaine.
As Table 6.1 shows, the electronics MNEs typically spent more on
R&D than their chemical counterparts, both in absolute terms and
as a percentage of sales. It is evident that all had quite substantial
R&D outlays, from 11.5 per cent of sales for Bull to 4.1 per cent for
BASF in 1989. Elf's small R&D:sales ratio was due to the fact that
its low research-intensive petroleum activities accounted for half
of group sales: its chemical and pharmaceutical subsidiaries,
Atochem and Sanofi, accounted for the overwhelming bulk of
R&D expenditure.

Spending on R&D tended to be concentrated in 'high-tech' areas
such as microelectronics, pharmaceuticals, agrochemicals and
advanced materials. Forty-three per cent of Hoechst's and 32 per
cent of Bayer's R&D budgets went on health research in 1989; for
Thomson 25 per cent of sales in components had to be spent on
R&D. These are also companies which were heavily dependent on
continuing streams of innovations: for instance 50 per cent of
Bayer's sales in 1989 accrued from products and processes that did
not exist in the mid-1970s. Four of the German MNEs – Siemens,

Hoechst, Bayer and BASF – were among the leading ten companies worldwide in registering patents in 1988.

Internationalisation of R&D was very intensive in the 1980s. As with the internationalisation of production, it took place through a mixture of internal growth and acquisitions for the German MNEs; whereas the French MNEs took foreign R&D activities under their control, preponderantly through the acquisition of large manufacturing companies abroad. Thus as a result of the acquisition of ITT's European telecommunications operations, CGE doubled its R&D outlay in 1986–7. And Thomson Consumer Electronics increased its company-funded R&D by 140 per cent in 1988 due to the RCA acquisition in the US. Its two major basic research centres came to be located outside France: one in Villingen, West Germany, and the other at Princeton in the US. Over 50 per cent of Rhône-Poulenc's R&D was conducted outside France by the end of the 1980s. The German MNEs remained relatively more centralised at home in their R&D. For BASF and Bosch, 90 per cent of R&D took place in tightly centralised laboratories in Germany. And some of them only really began to venture abroad for substantial R&D in the mid-1980s, especially BASF, Bosch and AEG. But the trend in the direction of internationalisation was clear: 40 per cent of Hoechst's R&D was conducted abroad by the end of the 1980s, compared to 5 per cent

Table 6.1: R&D expenditures in 1988–9 for MNEs

German MNEs	R&D spending (DMm)	R&D spending as % of sales
Siemens	6,875	11.2
Bosch	1,640	5.9
AEG	1,090	8.1
Bayer	2,460	6.0
Hoechst	2,416	5.9
BASF	1,789	4.1
French MNEs (FFrm)		
CGE	10,735	8.4
Bull	3,641	11.5
Thomson	7,600	10.2
Rhône-Poulenc	3,823	5.9
Elf Aquitaine	2,944[a]	2.3

Source: Annual Reports, 1988–9
Note: [a] Of which Sanofi accounted for 44.4% and Atochem 26.5%.

in 1970; for Siemens the figures were 20 per cent in 1990 compared to 0.5 per cent in 1970; and the US accounted for 20 per cent of Bayer's R&D, up from 1.5 per cent in 1973. As in production, research was becoming concentrated on a North American/West European/Far Eastern axis.[6]

Following this outline of the R&D internationalisation of the MNEs in the 1980s, it is now possible to go on to examine the European and technology dimensions of their activities in the generic technologies of biotechnology and microelectronics.

Biotechnology

Attention in this section is devoted primarily to the biotechnology activities of the German chemical MNEs in the 1980s: their expansion of research in this area in the US and its repercussions in the German political economy for public policy and government–industry relations.

The long-run potential for realising commercial gain from bio- and genetically engineered innovations, especially in pharmaceuticals and agrochemicals, became clear only late in the 1970s. By the early 1980s Hoechst, Bayer and to a lesser extent BASF (less involved in biotechnology, as its pharmaceutical division was much smaller than those of the other two) became acutely concerned about the weak state of biotechnology research in Germany in comparison to the 'lead market' of the US, which was and remains home to the 'state of the art' in biotechnology. The root cause of the problem was the continual postwar weakness of molecular biology research in Germany, together with insufficient cooperation between pure research in universities and public research institutes on the one hand, and applied research in the companies on the other. The failure of federal government-supported biotechnology initiatives in the 1970s was testament to a weak German *Standort* in this generic technology. In contrast, the climate for research in the US was favourable to innovation, with established and well-functioning links between university and corporate research.

These factors informed Hoechst's landmark decision in 1981 to begin biotechnology research outside Germany by establishing a research partnership with the Massachusetts General Hospital and the Harvard Medical School. Bayer followed closely by concluding a cooperation agreement with Yale University and beefing up the biotechnology operations of one of its main US subsidiaries, Miles Laboratories. The Hoechst decision was followed by the company's very public complaints on the state of the German *Standort* in biotechnology, together with virulent criticisms of federal government policy. It raised the spectre of a mass migration of biotechnology research abroad by German companies at the expense of the German *Standort* if measures were not taken to rectify structural weaknesses, the implication being that a 'hollowing out' of critical R&D in Germany would have negative knock-on effects in production and commercialisation. It was not a question of either concentrating biotechnology research at home or locating it abroad lock, stock and barrel; rather it was whether ineluctable and ongoing internationalisation of R&D in a core technology would proceed in tandem with upgraded biotechnology activity at home in Germany or, conversely, at the expense of the home base. For internationalisation of the companies' research in biotechnology was inevitable, especially focusing on gaining a 'window on foreign science' in the lead markets for this technology in the US and Japan.

Given these actions by the two leading biotechnology firms in Germany, the German research establishment was rapidly provoked, indeed shocked, into action. In particular, federal government policy conducted by the Ministry of Research and Technology (BMFT) changed its orientation. It started to stimulate cooperation programmes between the main companies, universities and other public research centres much more actively, informed by a *Verbundforschung* concept of public–private research cooperation between institutions. Links were built up between Hoechst and the University of Frankfurt, Bayer and the Max Planck Institute in Cologne, and BASF and the University of Heidelberg. At the same time the BMFT's emphasis veered away from direct intervention in research programmes, more indicative of its approach in the 1970s, to one of leaving the initiative to the firms, universities and research institutes engaged in federally sponsored programmes.[7]

Although the environment for biotechnology research in Germany subsequently improved somewhat, the structural problems of the *Standort* persisted in the production of bio-engineered innovations, and particularly in the field of genetic engineering. First, there was tremendous sensitivity to genetic engineering in Germany, stemming from the experience of the Nazi period and the fear of some of the possible applications of successful research in this area. Second, companies found some aspects of the legal regime either unclear or inimical to the production of genetically engineered drugs and other substances. From the firms' viewpoint a secure and clear-cut legal framework was essential, given the long lead times from innovation to production and commercialisation in this area of activity, with significant costs and risks involved in the process.

Indeed it was the lack of a legally explicit framework permitting production of genetically engineered substances, together with more cumbersome and long-drawn-out procedures in getting government approval for production as a result of new federal legislation (the *Bundesemissionsschutzgesetz* of 1988), that precipitated BASF's establishment of genetic engineering facilities in Boston, in the process halting work on its genetic engineering project at its Ludwigshafen headquarters. This represented a turning point for BASF in its highly centralised R&D operations: for the first time, the company had ventured abroad to do substantial basic research. Due to the unfavourable legal climate in Germany, Bayer also decided to concentrate its genetic engineering operations, especially the production of its Factor VIII drug, with its Miles subsidiary in the US. Hoechst, which alone of the three gambled on concentrating its genetic engineering in Germany without resort to activities in the US, found its plans to produce human insulin blocked by an administrative court in its home *Land* of Hessen in 1989, on the grounds that existing federal legislation did not explicitly provide for the production of genetically engineered substances.

Once again the actions of Hoechst, Bayer and BASF, in transferring core technology operations to the US and voicing criticism of the weaknesses of the German *Standort* in this area, put the spotlight on public authorities and federal government policy towards biotechnology. There was much pressure exerted on the federal government to change the law and explicitly permit genetic engineering production by the companies, their industry association and the scientific community. Relevant legislation passed through the Bundestag in 1990. Nevertheless, the high political sensitivity of genetic engineering and regulatory obstacles to production persist in Germany. The MNEs studied here continue to concentrate their core biotechnology activities in the US. This is also the case with the Swiss pharmaceutical MNEs headquartered in Basle, who face similar political and regulatory problems in Switzerland.[8]

This section has sought to bring to light specific cases of interaction between internationalisation and domestic structures in a core technology. In both biotechnology research and genetic engineering production, Hoechst, Bayer and BASF international-ised their value-adding activities to the US, partly because the US happened to be the lead market in these areas, and partly to overcome the weaknesses of the German *Standort*. Such firm-level actions worked their way back to pressure changes in public policy in Germany, although politico-regulatory problems are still a great source of worry for the MNEs.

Biotechnology: France and the EC

The French chemical and pharmaceutical MNEs were all active in different areas of biotechnology. Elf's biotechnology activities were concentrated in Sanofi and geared to product development in pharmaceuticals, cosmetics and petrochemicals. Rhône-Poulenc's subsidiary Institut Merieux geared its biotechnology research to the development of vaccines, in which it was the world leader. Through North American acquisitions such as those of Rorer in pharmaceuticals and Connaught BioSciences by Merieux, Rhône-Poulenc internationalised its biotechnology research. Finally, Roussel Uclaf was also very active in biotechnology, geared towards its drug and agrochemical product portfolio and in cooperation with its majority owner Hoechst.

The research infrastructure in biotechnology in France was arguably better than in Germany: the legal climate was far more favourable; and there was a long tradition of molecular biology research in a number of firms as well as in established government-funded institutes such as the *Centre nationale de la recherche scientifique* (CNRS), the *Institut nationale pour la santé et les recherches medicales* (INSERM) and the *Institut nationale pour les recherches agronomiques* (INRA). Throughout the 1980s biotechnology re-search was prioritised through the government's civil research budget. A number of government reports accorded great emphasis to the *filière biologique* with the aims of capturing 10 per cent of world biotechnology markets by 1990 and making France the third force in this area after the US and Japan. The *Program Mobilisateur* in 1982 proposed to achieve these objectives through a policy mix of increased public funding, which rose from FFr670 million in 1982 to FFr1501 million in 1987, channelled through inter-ministerial committees and parapublic financial institutions such as the *Agence nationale de valorisation de la recherche* (ANVAR), the *Délégation générale à l'aménagement du térritoire* (DATAR) and the *Comité interministériel pour le développement des investissements et le soutien de l'emploi* (CODIS); enhanced cooperation between the public research institutes and the firms; and the designation of Elf, Rhône-Poulenc and Roussel Uclaf as the main corporate 'poles of development' in this field.

Government biotechnology policy was not particularly success-ful in the 1980s, primarily due to the lack of enthusiasm and participation by industry in policy formation and implementation, especially by the major firms, Rhône-Poulenc, Roussel Uclaf and Sanofi. They largely went ahead with their own in-house research programmes, giving little attention to government policy objec-tives. They did not involve themselves to any great extent in the government's prioritised area of research geared to the agro-food sector; and the government's stated aim of improving R&D collaboration inter-firm, and between the firms and the research institutes, had very marginal impact: the major firms jealously guarded their intellectual property rights and kept their key research competences to themselves, shying away from major collaborative ventures.

The biotechnology experience in France in the 1980s is a telling example of the limitations of government technology/industrial policy measures that inspired neither enthusiasm nor active participation on the part of the major corporate actors. Public policy was ineffective precisely because the major firms, in which the core technological competences were housed, lacked interest in public initiatives and proceeded with their own corporate policies. For these reasons, government biotechnology policy after 1985 de-emphasised the *filière* concept and placed more import-ance on improved scientific training programmes and greater European cooperation.[9]

At a more aggregated regional level, the European biotech-nology industry was and is much weaker than its US and Japanese counterparts. Some of the weaknesses of the German *Standort* already instanced were replicated at the European level: bad university–firm links on research, aversion to risk-taking, and relatively few companies engaged in commercialising innovations. Governments and firms had difficulty in agreeing on a major common EC programme in biotechnology to complement existing national programmes. Above all, the major European companies active in this field were disinclined to engage in major collaborative efforts, being reticent to share their key in-house R&D capabilities. Biotechnology applications were also widespread, ranging from petrochemicals through food and nutrients to pharmaceuticals and agrochemicals. Companies engaged in biotechnology research thus had diverse backgrounds and found it difficult to agree on common priorities for cooperation at the European level. As will be evident in the next section, EC policy and programmes on inter-firm R&D cooperation in microelectronics progressed at a much faster pace than any equivalent in biotechnology. The Commission's *Research and Development in Advanced Communications Technology in Europe* (RACE) programme housed EC-funded biotechnology R&D projects, but they were of marginal interest to the major European firms.

By the end of the 1980s the EC regime on biotechnology and EC policy towards the industry remained weak, with continuing discord between the major firms and the Commission. In a paper submitted to the Commission by leading European biotechnology firms through the EC/EFTA chemical industry federation, the *Conseil européen des fédérations de l'industrie chimique* (CEFIC), it was claimed that public policy was partly to blame for the structural competitive weakness of the European biotechnology industry: national regulatory systems were incoherent and adversarial, especially in genetic engineering, with excessive costs and risks involved in engaging in research and production; and the Commission itself was divided on its approach to the industry.[10]

Microelectronics

The state of the French and German infrastructures in microelectronics was indicative of the overall conditions of their technological bases. In contrast to the situation in biotechnology, the German research base in microelectronics was more advanced than in France: *Verbundforschung* was practised in terms of close and generally well-functioning links between universities, public research institutes and firms, for example between Siemens and the University of Erlangen, and between AEG and Ulm University. In France there was a divide – between the pure research ethos of public research institutes and the more commercially geared applied research culture in the major firms – that prevented an effective flow of personnel and information between the two sets of institutions and limited the viability of research co-operation. Furthermore, there were French–German differences in public policy on technology. Invariably the large technology-intensive firms had public policy and government subsidies geared primarily towards their research priorities, but the industrial and social tissue was somewhat more balanced in Germany: the BMFT formulated and implemented policy with more attention to upgrading the technological base, particularly in microelectronics and advanced materials, as a public good in order to diffuse innovations throughout the economy. Hence it was more sensitive to the needs of small and medium-sized enterprises and to research carried out in universities, rather than being completely 'captured' by the preferences of the large firms. In France research policy was overwhelmingly geared towards the large national champions, especially their high-profile research projects that were considered to be strategically important for national competitiveness. Therefore, Thomson and Bull had nearly half of their R&D budgets financed through subvention by the French government by the end of the 1980s; whereas German government subsidy represented only 3 per cent of Siemens's R&D expenses; and combined BMFT and EC funding accounted for 5 per cent of AEG's R&D budget.[11]

In the 1980s the leading European-owned electronics MNEs felt the necessity to improve massively their in-house capacity in generic microelectronics technologies in order not to slip behind American and Japanese competitors. Consequently this entailed escalating expenditure by the firms on R&D. Siemens took a strategic decision to prioritise a semiconductor chip research and manufacturing capability in 1983–4, soon followed by Thomson and Philips; AEG specialised in the niche area of applications-specific semiconductors; Bosch in mobile communications; Thomson devoted much attention to developing a capability in high-definition television; Alcatel in optoelectronics; and the digitalisation revolution dominated the research programmes of Siemens and Alcatel in telecommunications.

Due to the costs and risks associated with these necessarily heavy technology investments, and the competitive need to turn innovations more quickly into the viable production and commercialisation of products, a number of electronics MNEs increasingly resorted to strategies of R&D collaboration with other firms from Europe, the US and Japan. Given the specificity of microelectronics applications in the electronics sector, companies found more common interest and were better able to define concrete objectives and work together on common projects than was the case in biotechnology. These factors informed the decision of Siemens and Philips to cooperate on research for the Megachip (4 megabit semiconductor) project, subsidised by the German and Dutch governments; and of Siemens, ICL and Bull to establish a joint computer research centre in Munich. As Lynn Mytelka points out, such 'strategic partnering', in a production process that is becoming ever more knowledge-intensive, is changing the parameters of international competition in electronics; not least by shifting a technological paradigm to the core of government industrial policies.[12]

Thus R&D collaboration in Europe between large electronics firms was on the increase in the 1980s, providing the basis for such collaboration to be institutionalised by policy initiatives and programmes at the EC level from the mid-1980s onwards. But it was also the awareness by national governments, the Commission and the large firms that the European electronics industry was suffering from increasing competitive weakness in relation to the US and Japan that spurred public policy initiatives on the basis of a common EC policy on information technology. The redundancy of national policy solutions in the face of the internationalisation of production, technologies and competition, focused attention at the EC level as a means of attempting to rectify competitive weaknesses in the European electronics industry and to upgrade the European technological base. As will be discussed in the following sections, it was on information technology policy issues that the political activity of the MNEs was most active; and it was on these policy foci that the strongest policy communities at the EC level emerged in the mid to late 1980s.

Table 6.2 shows that in two key branches of the electronics sector, semiconductors and computers, European-owned firms were very weakly represented on the world market by 1988–9: in semiconductors Philips was at the bottom of the top ten companies; in computers Olivetti and Bull were among the smallest of the top ten. European-owned semiconductor manufacturers' share of European and world markets fell to 36.5 per cent and

Table 6.2 World rankings of European electronics companies

| Computers (1989) | | | Telecommunications (1988) | | | Semiconductors (1989) | | |
Company	Country	Sales ($ bn)	Company	Country	Sales ($ bn)	Company	Country	Sales ($ bn)
IBM	US	62.71	AT&T	US	10.24	NEC	Japan	5.01
DEC	US	12.74	Alcatel	France	9.41	Toshiba	Japan	4.93
Fujitsu	Japan	11.88	Siemens	Germany	6.81	Hitachi	Japan	3.97
Unysis	US	10.10	NEC	Japan	5.82	Motorola	US	3.32
NEC	Japan	10.02	Northern Telecom	Canada	5.40	Fujitsu	Japan	2.96
Hitachi	Japan	9.84	Ericsson	Sweden	5.04	Texas Instruments	US	2.79
Hewlett-Packard	US	8.10	Motorola	US	3.02	Mitsubishi	Japan	2.58
Olivetti	Italy	7.26	Philips	Netherlands	2.80	Intel	US	2.43
Bull	France	6.47	Fujitsu	Japan	2.49	Matsushita	Japan	1.88
NCR	US	5.96	Bosch	Germany	2.16	Philips	Netherlands	1.72

Source: The Financial Times, 25 July 1990

9.5 per cent respectively by 1989; only SGS-Thomson, Philips and Siemens of European-owned companies had over 5 per cent of the European home market and none of them had over 5 per cent of the world market. In data processing there were only two European-owned companies, Siemens-Nixdorf and Bull, with 5–10 per cent of the European market; neither of them had more than 5 per cent of world market share. Only in telecommunications equipment of the major electronics industry branches was the representation of European-owned companies creditable (see Table 6.2). Overall, as Figure 6.1 shows, Europe had a declining percentage of world production in electronics, standing in 1989 behind the US and Japan, and an increasing trade deficit of over $33 billion in 1988, mostly accounted for in bilateral deficits with the US and Japan (see Figure 6.2). As Table 6.3 shows, only three European-owned companies, Siemens, Thomson and Philips, had 1–5 per cent of world market share in the world electronics industry; in the European home market, only Siemens had over 5 per cent of market share.[13]

Many of the competitive disadvantages of European-owned electronics companies stemmed from their historic national champion dependence on their home markets, with insufficient coverage and presence in the wider European market and glaring weakness in markets outside the EC, particularly in the other key regional markets of North America and East Asia. In industries that required pan-regional strength and were also globalising rapidly, the competitive gap between European-owned companies and a number of US and Japanese competitors became very large. As Table 6.3 shows, companies such as IBM, Matsushita and Hitachi had strong market shares not only in their home markets in the US and Japan, but also in the other regional cores, including Europe, and on the world market overall. In broad swathes of the electronics sector such critical world market shares were becoming the necessary condition for commercial success, posing monumental challenges for the leading European-owned MNEs.

The first and still the most important of the major European R&D inter-firm collaboration programmes was ESPRIT (European Strategic Programme for Research and Development in Information Technology), established in 1985 and aimed at 'pre-competitive' research cooperation in which the participating firms and the European Commission each paid 50 per cent of the project costs.

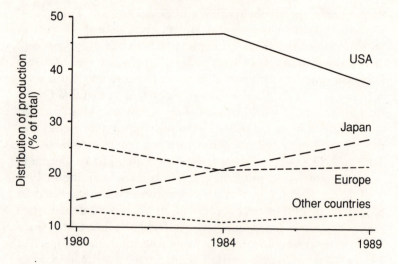

Figure 6.1 Distribution of electronics production: US, Japan and Europe
Source: Electronics International Corporation (1989: 16)

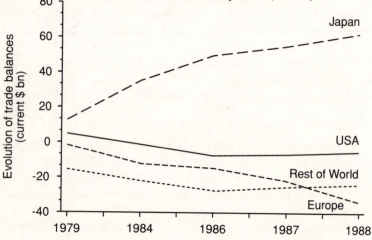

Figure 6.2 Evolution of trade balances: US, Japan and Europe
Source: Electronics International Corporation (1989: 32)

Table 6.3 Principal companies in the electronics industry, 1988

Market share	Europe	US	Japan	World
> 5%	IBM Siemens	IBM	Fujitsu Hitachi IBM Matsushita Toshiba NEC	IBM
2–5%	CGE Philips Thomson	AT&T DEC GM	Mitsubishi Sony	Hitachi Matsushita NEC Philips
1–2%	Bosch Bull DEC Ericsson GEC HP Matsushita Nixdorf Olivetti Plessey STC Unysis	GE HP Honeywell Matsushita Motorola Philips Raytheon Rockwell Texas Thomson Toshiba Unysis Xerox	Oki Sanyo Sharp	AT&T DEC Fujitsu GE GM HP Siemens Sony Thomson Toshiba Unysis Xerox
Top 5 hold:	24%	19%	39%	16%
Top 10 hold:	33%	26%	50%	25%

Source: Electronics International Corporation (1989), p. 35

An Information Technology Task Force within the Commission, attached to DG XII, steered the programme. The Commission also directed other R&D programmes on a smaller scale, notably Basic Research in Industrial Technologies in Europe (BRITE), aimed at smaller companies and concentrating on research in new materials and automation; and RACE, aimed at research in broadband telecommunications and biotechnology, *inter alia*. The electronics MNEs in this study, except Bosch, were all extensively involved as major participants in ESPRIT which they, along with a handful of other leading European-owned electronics firms, played a key part in establishing. The roles and influence of the MNEs in the policy

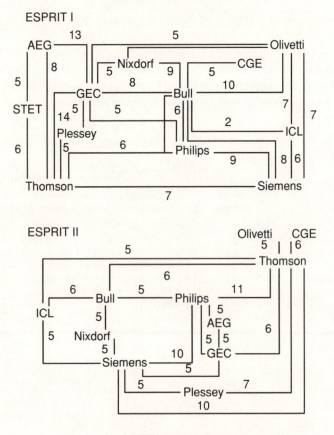

Figure 6.3 Inter-firm linkages in ESPRIT
Source: Mytelka (1990 b: 202–3)

communities dealing with ESPRIT and other European collaborative research projects will be addressed more specifically later in
this chapter.

Although EC R&D subsidy was quite small compared to the
R&D budgets of the large firms – total funding for ESPRIT, RACE
and BRITE was less than the annual research budget of Siemens –
there was a financial incentive to participate: 5 per cent of Bull's
1986 R&D budget came from ESPRIT funding, for example.
Indeed Bull was involved in 32 ESPRIT I projects which in total
accounted for one-fifth of total programme spending of ECU1.5
billion. Bull, Thomson, Siemens, GEC and Philips were the most

active participants with myriad linkages to each other and to other companies on a whole range of projects. These core members, except GEC, reinforced their positions in the renewed ESPRIT II that ran from 1989 to 1993.[14] Figure 6.3 illustrates the linkages between the companies in ESPRIT, and Table 6.4 shows the extent of their participation in the projects of the programme.

Table 6.4 Participation of the 12 information technology majors in ESPRIT I and II

	ESPRIT I		ESPRIT II		TOTAL	
	No. of projects	*% of total*	*No. of projects*	*% of total*	*No. of projects*	*% of total*
GEC	41	18.2	16	10.5	57	15.1
Thomson-SGS	38	16.9	43	28.1	81	21.4
Bull	32	14.2	22	14.4	54	14.3
Philips	26	11.6	27	17.6	53	14.0
Siemens	25	11.1	27	17.6	52	13.6
Olivetti	24	10.7	10	6.5	34	9.0
ICL	24	10.7	8	5.2	32	8.5
AEG	22	9.8	17	11.1	39	10.3
Alcatel	17	7.6	20	13.1	37	9.9
STET	16	7.1	8	5.2	24	6.3
Plessey[a]	15	6.6	8	5.2	23	6.1
Nixdorf[b]	12	5.3	7	4.6	19	5.0
Total	225		153		378	

Source: Mytelka (1990), p. 201
Notes
[a] Jointly acquired by Siemens and GEC in 1989.
[b] Acquired by Siemens in 1990.

Based on a detailed survey of ESPRIT's track record, Lynn Mytelka concludes that firms derived the following benefits from the programme: the range of application of technologies was extended; firms had a better idea of the future shape of the market in long-term R&D projects; and critical mass in R&D was promoted through inter-firm collaboration. ESPRIT was particularly useful to French firms, encouraging them to improve hitherto insufficiently developed ties to small and medium-sized enterprises, universities and research institutes within France and the rest of Western Europe. Above all, many of the French participants advanced the importance held by R&D within the firm's overall planning process: longer-term R&D projects became more common, as were repeated alliances with other firms in ESPRIT on new projects both inside and outside the programme. Mytelka thus argues that ESPRIT achieved notable successes in both enhancing the R&D capacities of the European multinationals who participate in it and in upgrading the European technological base.

It has also been argued that the programme may well have acted as a competitive weapon in addressing some of the weaknesses of European-owned firms compared to US and Japanese ones. Nowhere was such weakness so evident as in alliances between European-owned firms with American and Japanese counterparts. Electronics firms reared as national champions on protected national markets within the Community found difficulty in co-operating with each other, given different organisational cultures between the firms, an inability to think and act in a 'pan-European' sense as a result of home-market dependence, and similar product portfolios in competition with each other. The failure of the UNIDATA project in computers between Siemens, Philips and Bull in the 1970s was testament to this sad record of intra-European cooperation. All too often these companies concluded alliances with American and Japanese partners in preference to other European firms, frequently being junior partners in such alliances due to their relatively inferior R&D capacities and competitive disadvantages in other areas of the value chain. Technological dependence on US and Japanese firms in many cases followed: the reliance of Bull on NEC and of Siemens on Fujitsu and Hitachi, through joint ventures in which they marketed the mainframes of the Japanese firms, were prime examples.

The ESPRIT programme thus, it was argued, acted as a midwife in promoting intra-European collaboration between firms, both inside and outside the programme, that was so lacking up to the mid-1980s. The intention was to help them acquire a better 'entrance ticket' in cooperation agreements on a more equal and less dependent basis with non-European partners. The latter were still important: more than half the research alliances of the French firms in ESPRIT were with non-EC partners; 43 per cent of non-ESPRIT collaborations by the programme's German members were also with non-European partners.[15]

These arguments in defence of a policy of selective intervention, going beyond the *de minimis* rules regulating competition and privileging certain firms with public subsidies, cannot proceed unchallenged. First, it is problematic to justify the distinction between pre-competitive and competitive research in economic terms. In fact most of the resources were devoted to applied, rather than basic, research and there again to research carried out in close contact to the market. EC-promoted 'pre-competitive' R&D collaborations were used as an instrument to get round EC competition laws, particularly the general prohibition of cartels in Article 85 of the Treaty of Rome. Second, it is difficult to show that large firms increased their research staffs and budgets on a longer-term basis due to the financial incentive of ESPRIT and similar programmes. Third, cooperation did not tend to outlast the period of subsidisation. And finally, small and medium-sized firms proved to be handicapped in getting into the game, lacking the political lobbying power of the larger firms. Indeed the common feature of all these programmes was the domination of them, in terms of project definition and implementation as well as the disbursement of subsidies, by a handful of European-owned MNEs.[16]

Aside from ESPRIT there were other important European collaborative programmes in technology, involving some of the electronics MNEs studied here, which displayed even more noticeable 'vertical' features of industrial policy favouring a core of privileged large firms. Some high-profile and high-cost projects were housed within the intergovernmental European Research Coordination Agency (EUREKA) programme, which was established on the initiative of the French government and came to be dominated by French companies, which received large-scale funding from the French government. The Commission in Brussels had no authority for EUREKA, which encompassed projects that involved inter-firm collaboration going beyond basic research into product development and in some cases even further into production and marketing. EUREKA's two most notable projects were JESSI (the Joint European Submicron Silicon Initiative) for semiconductors and the one for high-definition television (HDTV). Both entailed substantial funding from member governments, particularly the French government, with the stated objective of building up an independent European capability in generic technologies to counter what was seen as a Japanese threat. Domination by Japanese firms of the manufacture and supply of semiconductors, the building block of manufacturing across the electronics industry and a crucial input to production across a range of industrial sectors, was seen in some quarters as threatening the competitive advantages of European-owned electronics firms, as well as the fundamental competitiveness and independence of the European electronics and wider manufacturing base. The same argument applied to HDTV, in which Japanese firms were advanced in developing a standard for something that had potentially widespread application (computer peripherals, broadcasting equipment as well as consumer electronics) in a market that was predicted to be worth $18 billion by 2010, and which provided a huge market for semiconductors: HDTV required ten times more microchips than basic TVs as inputs to manufacturing. These arguments were propounded forcefully by the French government and firms such as Thomson, Philips and to some extent Siemens, who were engaged in these projects as indigenous semiconductor and consumer electronics producers. The next section on firm preferences will explore the company positions in greater detail.

The JESSI programme thus involved Thomson-SGS, Siemens and Philips, the three remaining large-scale indigenous European semiconductor manufacturers, as the core participants, with 50 per cent funding of each firm's costs coming from the home governments. Each firm's investments in semiconductors, inside and outside JESSI, amounted to over $1 billion. The HDTV project was similarly constructed, with Thomson Consumer Electronics, Philips and Bosch as the core members sharing the aim of developing a common European and world standard for HDTV. The French government's subsidy from 1990 for Thomson's HDTV ventures, inside and outside the EUREKA programme, totalled FFr2bn.

These programmes were the clearest indication of French-style technology policies being applied on a larger European canvas. As events in the early 1990s have made clear, the JESSI and HDTV projects, after the expenditure of much public subsidy, have turned out to be major disasters of EC industrial policy. In HDTV the Commission was unable to impose the analogue standard being developed by Thomson and Philips on reluctant broadcasting and multimedia industries; and in any case the development of digital technology in the US and Japan was making European efforts out of date. The JESSI programme was unable to prevent the accelerating decline of semiconductor market share held by its major member firms in the face of Far Eastern competition – to the extent that both Philips and Siemens severely cut back their production of mass market DRAMs (dynamic random access memories) and SGS-Thomson transferred some of its production from France to South-East Asia.

The electronics firms also had important inter-firm technology ventures outside the scope of these publicly funded European programmes. As a rule the higher-risk, more upstream projects tended to come within the compass of programmes such as ESPRIT and EUREKA. More concrete ventures closer to production and marketing possibilities, especially when it was a case of intimate cooperation between only two firms, tended to be set up and carried through bilaterally by the firms involved outside public R&D programmes: the intention was to retain management control of these projects exclusively by the firms involved away from the gaze and scrutiny of governments and supranational authorities. Hence Siemens had key agreements with Philips in the Megabit project, Toshiba for 1 megabit chips and IBM for 64 megabit chips, all outside the JESSI semiconductor project. Thomson-SGS and Philips had set up a joint HDTV venture outside the EUREKA–HDTV project, with considerable subsidy from the French and Dutch governments respectively.[17]

POLICY PREFERENCES OF FIRMS

Having looked at the R&D capacities of the firms and at the public programmes in technology in which they were involved at national and EC levels, it is now apposite to consider the public-policy preferences of the MNEs on EC policy. The following sub-sections will deal with the input of corporate preferences in EC technology policies, but first an analysis of the firms' general positions on 'external' EC policy, that is, with respect to third country markets, is relevant. As we shall argue later, corporate preferences in EC foreign economic policy are intimately related to their preferences on 'internal' EC policy.

In *Resisting Protectionism* the American political economist Helen Milner argues that increased international economic interdependence has wrought changes in the policy preferences of industries and firms:

Strengthened international economic ties in the form of

exports, multinationality and global intra-firm trade have raised the costs of protection for internationally-oriented firms. These firms have thus resisted seeking protection even in times of serious import competition.[18]

The French and German MNEs analysed here internationalised their production networks in the 1980s on a West European–North American axis, with the core of expansion increasingly concentrating on the integrating regional home market of the EC. Their roots and linkages in these two regional cores of the world economy through exports, intra-firm trade, value-adding R&D, production and sales therefore deepened, in the process making their own public-policy preferences more open-market-oriented with respect to West Europe and North America. Protectionist preferences adopted by company headquarters to protect the French and German home markets from competition emanating from other EC member countries and the US more clearly endangered the interests of the same firms' operations in those very markets. Home market protection made little sense in the context of an integrating EC to which the firms and the member governments were committed in their own interests. Protection either at national or EC level aimed against the US would have threatened retaliatory action against the firms' US subsidiaries by US authorities, and impeded the integration and commercial progress of the firms in the US market. Furthermore, EC protection against the US could have disrupted intra-firm flows between integrated European and American operations of the same firms as well as the exports of their US subsidiaries to the EC.

For these reasons Siemens changed its policy preferences in favour of telecommunications equipment deregulation both in its German home market and in the EC, given that it had internationalised through strategic acquisitions in both the US and the EC, as was discussed in chapter 4. The most manifest transformation in policy preferences during the 1980s was shown by the competitively weakest of the firms, Thomson and Bull. Both were national champions reared on a previously highly protected home market in France: Bull had a guaranteed third share of all government purchasing contracts for computers; and Thomson dominated the insulated consumer electronics market behind the barriers created by a peculiar French TV standard, quotas and restrictions on inward investment that kept out foreign competition. Since then both companies have expanded through acquisitions in the EC and the US; and barriers closing the French market from the outside world were eroded through the EC Single Market programme, with its liberalisation of foreign investment and public procurement, and harmonisation of standards and norms; there was also penetration of inward investment from Japan and the US. Consequently, Thomson and Bull came round to the view that policies of purely national protection were inefficient and unworkable.[19]

Milner is therefore correct up to a point: the internationalisation of firms has induced more open-market-orientated policy preferences on their part. But such a dynamic is differentiated: anti-protectionist preferences are geared towards regional/national markets in which the firms have established integrated production which is frequently linked in cross-border networks with production in the home market. But that does not mean that liberal firm preferences are applied to all international markets. As will be evident in the following discussion, there was a high incidence of protectionist preferences at the EC level on the part of the electronics MNEs, particularly Thomson, directed against competition from Japan and the Far East. Such bilaterally focused protection was a result of two forces: these MNEs faced the brunt of competition from East Asia, particularly Japan; and the MNEs themselves did not significantly expand their markets and production networks into this region of the world economy. Their commercial weakness in this regional area, in contrast to their increasing strength in the US, meant that they could better afford EC protection directed against these markets without having their own existing production and sales networks greatly damaged. Thus, as Figure 6.4 illustrates, firm preferences on public policy were differentiated and could be placed on a liberalism–protectionism continuum: more open-market-orientated towards markets in which internationalisation was concentrated (West Europe, North America); more protectionist where firm-level presence was weak and whence the international competitive threat was greatest (Japan, Far East).

This context thus provides the background to a discussion of the promotional/protectionist elements of the European programmes in microelectronics in which the electronics MNEs were leading participants; and the variations of overall firm preferences between and within the MNEs.

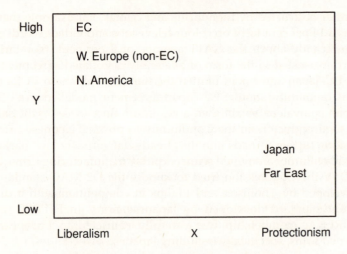

Figure 6.4 Differentiated firm preferences
Note: X axis = firm preferences; Y axis = levels of internationalisation.

Protection and promotion: European programmes in microelectronics

It is argued in this sub-section that the policy orientations for publicly supported European inter-firm collaborative research projects in microelectronics were far from clear-cut and showed deep contradictions; at any event they were couched in elements of EC-level protection and promotion for the multinationals who dominated these projects against competition from the Far East, especially from Japanese firms.

First, these technology programmes involved large-scale EC and national government funding which amounted to ECU1.75 billion in 1990 alone. Second, the focus of the projects and the funding involved were geared to the preferences and participation of the handful of large electronics firms who dominated the programmes: the twelve main firms in ESPRIT; Thomson and Philips in HDTV; Siemens, Thomson-SGS and Philips in JESSI. Such public promotion of an unofficial producers' cartel was complemented by EC-level protection directed primarily against Japanese firms. Anti-dumping duties, rules of origin and local-content requirements were imposed on goods produced by Japanese, Taiwanese and South Korean firms. Imports were further obstructed by high tariffs and quotas. For example there was a 14 per cent tariff on colour televisions and video recorders, significantly above the GATT average of 8 per cent. Non-tariff barriers existed in the form of bilaterally negotiated agreements: an EC–Japan agreement limited the import of Japanese VCRs to the Community; another EC–Japan agreement, modelled on a US–Japan equivalent, established a minimum floor price on the sale of semiconductors in the Community to prevent Japanese firms making further inroads into the already dangerously low market share of European-owned semiconductor manufacturing firms. In HDTV the Commission tried to impose the D2 MAC standard, developed by Thomson and Philips in competition with a different standard developed by Japanese firms. In ESPRIT and EUREKA, membership was carefully restricted to European-owned firms, specifically excluding Japanese-owned ones.

Such policy orientations enjoyed whole-hearted support from the French government at the EC level in defence of an 'independent' European capability against the prospect of dependence on Japanese firms in a strategic sector such as electronics; and more to the point, in defence of competitively weak French national champions who were most threatened by Japanese competition. Thus the French government shifted its protectionist stance from the national to the EC level. Protection and promotion of indigenous 'European champions' in electronics was also supported by elements within the Commission.

But other parts of the Commission, as well as the German government, sympathised with a set of views that took a critical attitude towards EC technology policy. This liberal position started from the premise that the integration of the EC should correspond to a regional market open to the rest of the international economy as part of a strengthened multilateral order. Go-it-alone strategies for the EC were considered negative and incompatible with the internationalisation of markets and production, as well as the global mobility of technology and capital. Such an anti-'Fortress Europe' position held that the logic of the 1992 programme, emphasising deregulation and greater competition in the Internal Market, required trade and other foreign economic policies that were open-market-orientated, and EC competition policies that were vigorously enforced. The combination of EC protection and promotion on which a number of European-owned firms were dependent, it was argued, contradicted the market-orientated direction of the 1992 programme, and provided the cushion that prevented these firms from tackling the root cause of their competitive problems: production, sales and distribution networks that were inferior in comparison with more efficient non-EC firms and which required drastic restructuring and rationalisation.

Indeed a Commission report on industrial policies in 1990 argued very much along these lines: greater liberalism – freer trade, reduction of trade-distorting subsidies, open public procurement, abolition of remaining national quotas – should accompany a reorientation of approach towards programmes such as ESPRIT. There should be more emphasis on upgrading the public good of the European technological base, concentrating more on basic research in universities and small and medium-sized enterprises, and on improving the diffusion and application of technology through stronger links between the latter actors and the large firms. There should also be a better focus on skills, standards and environmental rules. The corollary to this approach should be a de-emphasis on using these projects primarily to promote individual European/national champions. Some went further in arguing that membership of publicly funded European R&D collaborative projects should be opened to non-European-owned firms, including Japanese and American ones, who through inward investment increasingly contributed to EC value-added, rather than having these projects confined by 'nationality' criteria to indigenous firms. Despite these criticisms and the patent failure of projects such as JESSI and HDTV, the main features of programmes like ESPRIT – project and subsidy domination by a small number of European-owned MNEs – continued well into the 1990s.[20]

At all events, this discussion highlighted the point that technology policy not only came to dominate industrial policy questions, but also that its focus was taken up to the EC level at the expense of the national level. This European dimension became all-pervasive, whether the arguments employed were protectionist/promotional or liberal, and complemented the European dimension of policy on Single Market matters. Unlike the consensus on the Single Market, however, EC technology-cum-foreign economic policies brought out differences between actors. The differences between the French and German governments on 'Fortress Europe' have been noted; now it is time to concentrate on the preferences of the firms themselves and how they varied within and between the firms.

Variations between the firms' policy preferences

It would, in the first instance, be misleading to infer that the liberal/ protectionist divide between the French and German governments on EC foreign economic policy was reflected in a similar divide between the French and German MNEs. It is accurate to say that there was a partial divide along these lines: in certain subsectors of the electronics industry, the French firms were notably more protectionist than their German counterparts. But firm preferences were somewhat more complex and could on no account simply be extrapolated from the policy positions adopted by their home governments. For there are cross-cutting differences that emerge on examination of each of the firms and that are contingent on the competitive positioning of the firm in international competition, sectoral and intra-sectoral characteristics, and the coherence of the firm's internal organisation. These lines of analysis bring out comparisons between and within the firms studied. Only some of the differences are between the French MNEs on the one hand and the German ones on the other; more often than not, there are characteristics that span this notional 'national' divide and are more clearly predicated on business and industrial organisation variables than on the mere 'nationality' of the firm. Hence the importance of studying the business organisation of the firm in order to comprehend the nature of its preferences on key issues of public policy.

The first point to make is that the French and German chemical MNEs took positions that were broadly more open-market-orientated than their electronics counterparts. These differences were inter-sectoral, not inter-national. Chapter 2 analysed some of these sectoral differences. The chemical MNEs had historically less government intervention and regulation than their electronics counterparts; their home markets were less protected and they subsequently internationalised earlier and more extensively. Their competitive positioning was stronger: European chemical MNEs, with the German Hoechst, Bayer and BASF at the forefront, followed by multinationals from the UK, Switzerland and France (notably Rhône-Poulenc among the French companies), were among the world leaders with strong market shares in the

European home market, significant and expanding presence in the US and long-established operations in other parts of the world. Furthermore, there was little competition from Japanese chemical/pharmaceutical firms on the world stage as the latter did not substantially internationalise out of Japanese and East Asian markets.

Given such relative competitive strength and more advanced internationalisation, the chemical MNEs, regardless of national origin, adopted more open-market policy preferences in the EC and in the international economy. This was clearly shown by the representations made by the chemical industry to the Uruguay Round of the GATT, favouring the trade-liberalising aims of the Round with concrete proposals.[21]

The electronics industry, however, was far more differentiated than the chemical industry in terms of the competitive positioning of the firms and their policy preferences. First, there were differences between the German firms, Siemens, AEG and Bosch, and two of the French firms, Thomson and Bull. The German three were competitively stronger on the international stage, most notably Siemens which was represented across the range of activities in electronics; AEG came to have the formidable backing of its owner Daimler Benz, although it remained competitively weak in a number of its product areas; and Bosch was the world leader in automotive electronics and was expanding in telecommunications. Siemens, Daimler and Bosch had in addition very substantial in-house financial resources.

Thomson and Bull in the first instance suffered from the French 'path to internationalisation' as documented in chapter 2: home market dependent national champions who had attempted to jump directly to world class level through a spate of foreign acquisitions in the 1980s, without having gone through an intermediate internationally orientated 'learning' stage. This the German MNEs had through an export orientation in many, but not all, of their activities. Given this situation, Thomson and Bull found themselves attempting to integrate foreign acquisitions without first building a national power base to compete globally. They were disadvantaged 'followers' in a competitive game whose rules they did not control, without mastery of core products and technologies. In alliances with US and Japanese firms they were in situations of technological dependence, as was the case with Bull–NEC in computer mainframes and Thomson–JVC in

VCRs.[22] They suffered from a host of other weaknesses. Both were concentrated in sub-sectors in which the European electronics industry was structurally weak and being eroded by Japanese competition: Bull in computers, Thomson in consumer electronics and semiconductors. They were not diversified enough to offset losses and long-term investments in these areas through profits from other areas of activity, whereas Siemens was able to pursue such strategies given its profits in areas such as medical electronics, automation and, above all, telecommunications. And lastly, both Thomson and Bull were short of capital resources, dependent on French government and EC subsidy for costly technology investments.

Given such competitive weakness, Thomson and Bull had lobbied strongly for 'European solutions' of promotion at EC level through privileged positions and subsidy in European R&D collaboration programmes. Such defensive strategies to hold existing market shares from weak positions also led to preferences for merging with other European companies with public support: Bull with Siemens-Nixdorf in computers, Thomson-SGS with Siemens in semiconductors. Thomson went one stage further with open and strongly worded calls for across-the-board EC protection against East Asian competition. Indeed, among the twelve firms studied here Thomson was quite clearly the most extreme in calls for protection/promotion at EC level, given its preferences in consumer electronics, semiconductors and HDTV. As Alan Cawson puts it: '[Philips] and Thomson seem to be more interested in lobbying for protectionist measures than in addressing their own fundamental lack of competitiveness [in product innovation, technologies, length of product cycles and global strategies].' Siemens, Bosch and AEG, being less reliant on such shields of promotion and protection, had different policy preferences: they were especially less protectionist-oriented *vis-à-vis* Japanese firms, given their developing alliances with some of them; they also eschewed exclusive and defensive 'European solutions' of inter-firm mergers given the extra cards they had to play, for example alliances with US and Japanese firms (Siemens with IBM, Toshiba and Fujitsu, AEG with Mitsubishi, Bosch with Nippondenso and Matsushita). The wide-ranging alliance between Siemens and IBM on research, development and (planned) production of the 64 megabit chip was rapidly acquiring more importance relative to Siemens's links with Philips and Thomson-SGS on semiconductors.[23]

The notable exception among the French electronics MNEs was CGE. It was competitively stronger than Thomson and Bull: Alcatel had extended its home market domination in tele-communications equipment to become a world leader through acquisitions, in a sector which faced little Japanese competition; and Alsthom, through the merger with GEC, was one of the leaders in the European mechanical engineering/transport systems market. Thus CGE was less dependent on EC promotion/protection and accordingly had somewhat different policy prefer-ences.

The EC–Japan agreement setting floor prices for semiconductors also highlighted intra-sectoral and inter-firm differences: the chip producers, Thomson-SGS, Siemens and Philips, were in favour, as the agreement was designed to keep prices buoyant; but other European companies who were chip users, including Bull, Alcatel and Olivetti, were against because it threatened to raise their input costs artificially. Furthermore, the agreement brought out dif-ferences within firms: the chip-using divisions within Thomson Consumer Electronics and Siemens were noticeably less keen on the accord than the chip-producing divisions, Thomson-SGS and Siemens's semiconductor division.[24]

Finally, consideration of the coherence of the firms' internal organisation is merited. The Thomson group was a highly illus-trative example of an organisation that had historically lacked internal coherence, given that it was the product of a series of mergers and takeovers that had, to a great extent, remained separate empires rather than being fully integrated with each other. As an interviewee in SGS-Thomson commented:

> The problem is that Thomson is a very unintegrated group. CSF and TCE have little to do with each other. TCE, itself the product of a number of domestic and foreign acquisi-tions, is internally unintegrated. This makes it a problem for SGS-Thomson to supply it with components. Our R&D culture is very different from TCE's, and frankly we have stronger supplier relations with external clients such as IBM and Philips than with TCE. We lack a DRAM [dynamic random access memory chips, the most widely used as inputs for mass market consumer electronics] manufac-turing capacity, in contrast to Siemens; and it is DRAMS that are most needed by TCE.

The very lack of internal integration posed serious competitive problems for Thomson. But it also affected the cohesion, or rather the lack of cohesion, of the firm's stated public-policy preferences. There were well-advertised positions taken in favour of EC protection and promotion at group and TCE headquarters at La Défense in Paris. But there was remarkable discord within Thomson on these very positions, flowing from the group's malintegration. Many quarters of TCE were not fully behind Thomson-SGS's calls for EC protection/promotion in semiconductors, given the weak links between the two. And the more strident and virulent anti-Japanese statements made at group HQ were not necessarily shared by executives in some of the recent foreign acquisitions. For instance, a former chief executive of Ferguson (acquired by TCE in the UK) and adviser to TCE was reported in *The Financial Times* as welcoming Japanese investment in the EC: 'All major Japanese firms have European content in colour television manufacture – that puts them beyond criticism.' Another Ferguson general manager commented that the Japanese firms in the UK had done 'a fantastic job' with superior production and technical quality.[25] Both statements clearly contradicted HQ policy in Paris.

With Siemens there were differences between divisions on the group's policies, for example on the EC–Japan semiconductor agreement; but the degree of discord was severely constrained by the internal cohesion and integration of the group. This was indicative of another French–German firm-level difference: vertical integration was much more evident in the German firms, who relied more on internal growth; it was much less the case among the French firms, who expanded both at home and abroad through a reliance on acquisitions.

Hence firm preferences on public policy were contingent on the following business/industrial organisation factors which pointed to differences inter- and intra-firm: competitive positioning, inter- and intra-sectoral differences, and internal firm organisation. Firm-level differences did not invariably divide on French–German lines, and did not necessarily correspond to positions taken by the home governments.

POLITICAL ACTIVITY BY THE FIRMS IN EC POLICY NETWORKS

MNEs based in the EC had significantly stepped-up their 'political' activities at the EC level from the mid-1980s as a result of a number of forces: the accelerated pace of integration in the Community, with the accompanying increase of supranational legislative activity after the passage of the Single European Act; and the shift from national to European dimensions of industrial and technology policies, encapsulated by the establishment and working of programmes in inter-firm R&D collaboration. Such political activity by the firms and their industry associations encompassed lobbying and maintaining ongoing relations with Directorates General of the Commission, the cabinets of Commissioners, the national permanent delegations to the EC, and other supranational institutions such as the European Parliament and the Economic and Social Committee. Nearly all the firms examined here had established their own offices in Brussels to handle EC-related matters. Hoechst, Bayer and BASF appointed European coordinators in 1986 to improve the management of their European strategies, including the political function of dealing with EC authorities, programmes and legislation. The German industry associations for chemicals and electronics, the VCI and the ZVEI, set up offices in Brussels and Strasbourg – in the latter city to liase with the European Parliament and its committees. Rhône-Poulenc had established an in-house management centre in Brussels for the discussion and formulation of strategies specifically geared to preparation for the Single Market in the EC.[26]

Interviewees summed up the reasons for the take-off of such political activity at the EC level by the firms and the industry associations:

> The 1992 programme was a catalyst to a greater European role for the VCI. There is more EC legislation to deal with, both absolutely and relative to national legislation. In the not too distant future 80 per cent of legislation of relevance to the chemical industry will probably emanate from the Community. There is therefore a functional necessity for us to be in Brussels on the ground.

> Before we [in Bull] made our representations to the French government, which in turn would take matters up with the Commission. This approach is no longer feasible given the increasing activity at Community level. We have to deal directly with the Commission.

> The heightened importance of a European dimension to public

policy of relevance to the MNEs, combined with their greater roles as political actors at the EC level, led to the creation and emergence of EC policy networks and communities that steadily gained in importance relative to national policy networks/communities. EC policy networks enveloped the firms, industry associations, national governments and supranational authorities, all relating to one another on specific policy foci. The influence of the firms in two policy initiatives, the 1992 programme and ESPRIT, provided the basis for both an enhanced political role for the firms at the EC level and the emergence of EC policy networks in which these firms were to become prominent members.

In 1983 the *Round Table of European Industrialists* was formed, presided over by the Volvo chairman Pehr Gyllenhammer and having as members the chairmen/chief executives of 17 leading European companies from a number of different industrial branches. The group included Alain Gomez of Thomson, Dr Karl-Heinz Kaske of Siemens, Dr Hans Merkle of Bosch and Professor Werner Breitschwerdt of Daimler Benz. The *Round Table* served a double interest: it was a forum for European companies to discuss their ideas on political action at a European level; and it was a sounding board for the Commission, with its members acting as a strong lobby in favour of European initiatives within their own national contexts. The *Round Table*'s work was and is ongoing, but its influence was most crucial in helping to initiate and guide the debate on a *rélance* of European economic integration that led to the Cockfield proposals, the Single European Act and the White Paper on the Internal Market. A landmark in the debate was the *Round Table*'s second report *Changing Scales*, published in June 1985, which surveyed the economies of scale that would issue from a genuine unification of the Common Market.

The Gyllenhammer Group was crucial in influencing the 1992 programme; but another 'Round Table' was to become even more influential in the creation and progress of common EC policies in information technology. This group was formed in the late 1970s by Étienne Davignon, then EC Commissioner for Industry, with the exclusive membership of the twelve largest European-owned electronics firms. All the electronics MNEs studied here except Bosch – that is, Thomson-Brandt, now TCE, AEG, Siemens, CIT-Alcatel and Bull – were founder members. In 1983 the twelve sent a letter to the Commission presenting a dramatic view of the state of the European information technology industry and emphasising the inadequacy of existing national programmes within the EC. Combined pressure from the twelve and the Commission led to the Council of Ministers accepting the establishment of the European Strategic Programme for Research and Development in Information Technology (ESPRIT). The twelve contributed in a decisive fashion to the shaping of ESPRIT: the new Information Technology Task Force in the Commission relied preponderantly on expertise from the companies to make the ESPRIT proposals and formulate the final programme. To monitor the execution of the programme an ESPRIT Advisory Board was set up, of which half the members were representatives of the twelve 'IT Round Table' companies. Since 1985 managers and technicians from the twelve became heavily involved in ESPRIT, dominating the channels of influence from industry within it. It is therefore not surprising to observe that the projects of the programme were often tailor-made for this handful of firms: in 1985 one or more of the 'founding fathers' participated in 70 per cent of all ESPRIT projects.[27]

The influence of individual electronics firms in the inter-governmental EUREKA programme was even greater than in ESPRIT, especially in the high-profile projects on semiconductors and HDTV. In these there were smaller numbers of lead firms – Thomson and Philips in HDTV, Thomson-SGS, Siemens and Philips in JESSI – for which these projects were specifically designed and which they overwhelmingly dominated. The influence of a handful of French electronics firms was especially evident in EUREKA.

Very broadly speaking, a division of labour between the firms and the industry associations in EC-level political activity evolved. The bulk of the industry associations' work in the late 1980s entailed dealing with the various measures of the White Paper on the Completion of the Internal Market, and primarily through the pan-European umbrella associations. For example the VCI became increasingly involved in the work of CEFIC, the federation of West European chemical industry associations. Its primary objective was to handle environmental protection, genetic engineering and biotechnology legislation where possible at the EC level rather than in Germany, so that harmonised Community-wide regulations would bring German regulations into line. This was seen by the German chemical industry as a means of circumventing increasingly stringent German legislation that impacted negatively on the industry (see chapter 4 on environmental protection legislation and this chapter on biotechnology and genetic engin-eering), that is, using the EC level to achieve domestic objectives. CEFIC's internal structure had been changed to permit the direct participation of leading multinational firms as corporate associate members, in addition to its legal members who were the national chemical industry associations. There was intense involvement in CEFIC of Hoechst, Bayer and BASF individually and in co-operation with the VCI, most evident in CEFIC's Special Advisory Group on the Environment (SAGE).[28]

Thus policy areas with industry-wide implications tended to be dealt with through the national and pan-European industry associations, with varying degrees of involvement by individual firms. Firms tended to deal bilaterally with the Commission and other authorities, bypassing the industry associations, on more discrete policy foci which impacted largely on them individually or on a reasonably small group of firms of which they were members. Hence R&D collaboration programmes such as ESPRIT and EUREKA, which hinged on cooperation between the large member firms, were conducive to direct firm-level participation without the involvement of larger collectivities such as industry associations. The powerful positions that were wielded by this handful of electronics firms in these tightly cohesive and intimate policy communities gave them a vested interest in keeping membership and involvement as restricted as possible, so that individual firm preferences gained maximum input into the policy process on agendas that were effectively amenable to their control. Most noticeable was the extraordinary hold over EC consumer electronics policy by the two dominant indigenous firms in the industry, Thomson and Philips. Their preferences – on protection from Japanese competition and promotion in ESPRIT, JESSI and HDTV – effectively blocked a more liberal EC policy orientation.[29]

There were French–German differences in firm/industry asso-ciation political activity at EC level that reflected and replicated the workings of differently constituted French and German domestic structures. The German industry associations, the VCI and the ZVEI, were far more active in Brussels and Strasbourg than their French counterparts, the UIC and the FIEE. The German associations were more prominent in the workings of the pan-European associations, with the full backing and involve-ment of their leading firms. This was especially the case with the complementary participation of Hoechst, Bayer, BASF and the VCI in CEFIC. Such relations corresponded to cooperation between large firms and industry associations in Germany. As an interviewee in the FIEE commented:

> As our member firms have Europeanised commercially, there has been a natural extension of political activity to the European level, for the firms individually and for the FIEE. But our [the FIEE's] weaknesses at the EC level are correspondingly extensions of our weaknesses in France. We are not as active in the pan-European federations as the ZVEI. Unlike them we do not have an office in Brussels. Whereas they get full backing from Siemens in Brussels, we have real problems in getting support from our large member firms, especially in providing expertise on areas such as standard harmonisation and other 1992 measures. It is the Germans who make the running here. Our firms have different priorities: their disinterest in industry-wide matters stands in contrast to their intense activity in R&D programmes, in which they deal directly with the Commission.

French–German differences in firm–industry association relations, as outlined in chapter 3, were mirrored by the activity of the same French and German actors at the EC level. The French firms preferred bilateral dealings with EC authorities just as they preferred to deal with the government bilaterally in France, bypassing plurilateral forms of cooperation with other firms and industry associations. And the French firms were more prominent political actors at the EC level than their German counterparts, when it was a case of firms acting individually rather than through industry associations. French electronics firms formed the largest and most influential group within ESPRIT and were even more powerful within EUREKA. Thomson and Bull were among the most active and effective of corporate political actors at Community level. They were most effective in enlisting the whole-hearted support of the French government for their preferences in dealings with the Commission. Thus the highly developed 'government relations' function on the part of French firms with intimate ties to the French government spilled over into EC activity; whereas the political function of the German firms was less developed as a result of the more distanced government–industry linkage in Germany.

CONCLUSION

This chapter has shown convergence on both European and technology dimensions. The background of accelerated integration in the EC in the mid to late 1980s forged a consensus uniting the MNEs, the French and German governments and EC authorities on measures to integrate the Internal Market. In addition the MNEs internationalised their R&D networks to varying degrees, as with production on a West European/North American/Far Eastern axis, with the core of their R&D located in their national bases and in the EC. This was especially the case in microelectronics, but less evident in biotechnology: the structural weakness of the German and West European biotechnology/genetic engineering bases led the chemical/pharmaceutical MNEs to concentrate and expand many of their key activities in this area in the US. Internationalisation of microelectronics was manifested by the proliferation of inter-firm alliances between European, US and Japanese firms in this generic technology. Convergence on a European dimension in microelectronics was most marked in the mid to late 1980s with the establishment and development of common EC technology policies, the core of which were inter-firm R&D collaboration projects, especially the EC's ESPRIT and the intergovernmental EUREKA.

Convergence is further identifiable in the policy preferences of these internationalising MNEs. The French and German firms all came to have progressively liberal, open-market orientations with respect to West European and North American regional markets, these preferences being most marked in the home market of the integrating EC. One major factor informing these preferences was the concentration of the MNEs' international expansion in these regions of the world economy.

Finally, there was increasing political activity of these French and German MNEs at the EC level in emerging and stronger EC policy networks and communities. Firm-level political action in the *European Round Table* was important in the lead-up to the Single European Act and the 1992 programme. The firms' participation and influence was strongest in EC technology policy communities dealing with collaborative R&D projects. Technology was thus highly illustrative of both a rising European dimension to public policy, at the expense of nationally conceived measures, and of increasing MNE power in policy networks, especially in relations with national governments and supranational authorities who were dependent on the MNEs for the formulation and execution of technology policy. Witness the ineffectiveness of government biotechnology policy in France when the leading corporate actors did not support and participate fully in government-designed programmes. Now another layer of MNE power at the EC level was added to that already explicated in the context of French and German domestic structures.

Such European and technology convergence was limited by French–German differences. First, the German *Standort* in biotechnology exhibited peculiar weaknesses that impacted on the German chemical MNEs, quite different to the more clement situation in France. There were also differences between the French and German electronics MNEs on EC protection and promotion. The competitively weaker French firms campaigned more strongly for 'European solutions' of protection and promotion. The competitively stronger German firms, less reliant on public-policy cushions and with other bargaining cards to play, exhibited somewhat more open market preferences. But there were other differences in firms' preferences, between and within firms, that had less to do with nationality (that is, French–German differences) and more to do with sectoral, sub-sectoral and internal firm organisation characteristics. This makes it all the more important to treat firms as unique and differentiated administrative structures rather than as unitary actors in political economy analysis.

French–German differences also emerged in political action by firms and industry associations at the EC level, reflecting the manner in which the firms interacted with external actors in differently constituted French and German domestic structures.

The change induced by convergence, limited by the continuity of enduring French-German differences, has been threaded through the chapters of this book: we started with firm-level internationalisation, then went on to analyses of French and German domestic structures and the relations of the MNEs with home governments and banks within them, and finally arrived at the cross-border dimensions of Europe and technology. Internationalisation and technological development have induced a process of change in the political action of multinationals and in government-industry relations. It is the MNEs that are the primary carriers of such change with increasing power relative to external actors. This makes it all the more vital to place the political role of multinationals at the centre of the study of European and international political economy. But, as Webber, Cawson *et al.* add: 'National differences remain as major influences on this uneven development.'

7

CONCLUSION
Micropolitical economy, the 1980s, the 1990s and the way ahead

This study has centred on the political economy of a number of French- and German-owned multinational enterprises in chemicals and electronics. The selected MNEs are not only leading corporate actors in France and Germany; they have become significantly more important actors on the European and international stages, active in sectors characterised by technology-intensiveness and globalising markets. Given this focus, the study has sought to contribute to interdisciplinary scholarship at the crossroads of political economy and business organisation. Individual firms, especially MNEs with production networks spread across the world to cater for globalising markets, are in their own right increasingly influencing the structure and dynamics of a more integrated world economy; they are indeed the main mechanisms of such integration. The corporate activities of these firms have become crucial determinants of outcomes in the world economy. Important aspects of such corporate affairs concern the embeddedness of the firm in its external environment in relations with other important actors such as governments, trade unions, banks, industrial associations, as well as with its sub-contractors, suppliers and clients. It is precisely this area of interaction between multinationals and other actors, which affect both the competitive advantages of the firms, the competitiveness of the economies in which they do business, and variables of relative power and policy choice, that has been neglected in social science research. Economics and political economy underemphasise the role of the individual firm, and business studies does not sufficiently address the role of the firm in its external environment. This book has attempted to disaggregate the black box of the firm and examine its power relationships with external actors, thus continually

206

treating the firm as a political economic actor. Hence the approach utilised here is intended primarily as a contribution to the field of what can be called the 'micropolitical economy' of the firm.

The MNEs studied here internationalised their production during the period studied, the 1980s; at the same time they remained most strongly implanted in the domestic structures of their home bases in France and Germany, where they had a series of historically conditioned relationships with external actors. These relationships were affected by firm-level internationalisation, just as the latter process was coloured by the embeddedness of the MNEs in domestic structures. The interaction of internationalisation with domestic structures is thus threaded through this study, and is used to make a comparative argument.

The first section presents a review of the argument of this study. The following section contains some propositions on the cross-cutting pressures of cosmopolitanism and national origin to which the firms analysed have been and are subject. The third section is somewhat more theoretically inclined: it seeks to identify and draw out the lessons of this study for future theoretical and empirical research in the micropolitical economy of the MNE.

REVIEW OF THE ARGUMENT

Chapter 2 looked at the internationalisation of the MNEs in the 1980s, with some general interpretations on different paths to internationalisation. First, there were inter- and intra-sectoral differences played out within and between MNEs. Sub-sectors within electronics and chemicals internationalised in different ways and at different speeds; most importantly, the chemical MNEs were at more advanced stages of internationalisation than their electronics counterparts, due to the effects of government promotion and protection of national champions that retarded internationalisation in the electronics industry. Second, there were French–German differences. The German MNEs had internationalised their production on the strength of previously serving world markets through exporting from Germany. For these firms *Export-modell Deutschland* and international production strategies proceeded hand in hand, mutually reinforcing each other. The French MNEs, in contrast, were in general smaller and competitively weaker than their German counterparts. One aspect of such competitive disadvantage was home market dependence with insufficient international presence. From this starting point the French MNEs internationalised very rapidly in the 1980s in an attempt to catch up with their main competitors, relying preponderantly on the mechanism of acquisitions to acquire critical mass abroad as quickly as possible.

Despite these differences the MNEs internationalised along converging paths, after markedly different points of departure. Most characteristic of such convergence was the common concentration of international expansion on Western Europe, North America and, increasingly, South East Asia. The mid to late 1980s showed that the core of geographical expansion took place in the European Community, increasingly regarded as the MNEs' 'home market' in global competition.

Chapter 3 went on to examine the embeddedness of the MNEs in the domestic structures of France and Germany, homing in on the linkages between the MNEs and other actors in the domains of government, finance, industry and labour. At an economic level of analysis, it was found that the postwar convergence of the French and German economies was reinforced in the 1980s, particularly in terms of macroeconomic policy, although the reunification of the two Germanies at the end of the decade led German macroeconomic policy down a different path.

At the political economy level of analysis, clear differences emerged in the institutional make-up of the French and German political economies. The German MNEs were rooted strongly in a market economy with well-established and highly organised links to external actors such as federal and *Land* public authorities, banks, industry associations, medium-sized firms, universities, research institutes, trade unions and chambers of commerce. These linkages anchored the German MNEs in long-term commitments to the German *Standort*, which provided a launching-pad for internationalisation strategies and was at the vortex of the firms' cross-border production networks.

MNE links with external actors in France were much weaker and more conflict-oriented than in Germany. There were therefore deep and enduring differences in the microeconomic embeddedness of the MNEs in French and German domestic structures, standing in contrast to, limiting and qualifying the convergence phenomena and effects induced by internationalisation.

The subsequent chapters concentrated on the interaction of internationalisation with domestic structures. Chapter 4 elaborated on the notion of the MNEs as political actors, especially seen in terms of relations with the home central governments; also examined were home government policy approaches towards the MNEs. It was initially argued that government policy approaches in Germany were qualitatively different to the greater incidence of sectoral and firm-level government intervention in France. These differences led to contrasting government policy agendas in the 1980s of most relevance to the MNEs. Despite these differences, there was a common infusion of an international dimension to these agendas, the core of it being the increasing absolute and relative importance of the EC as a focus of industrial and technology policy of concern to the MNEs.

The second part of chapter 4 focused on MNE–government relations. The structure and composition of policy networks and communities differed between France and Germany. The senior management of the French MNEs enjoyed intimate relations with key parts of the government apparatus, whereas there was a more distanced relationship between government and industry in Germany. German policy networks also accorded more importance than in France to the powerful sectoral industry associations, who enjoyed the backing and resources of their leading member firms.

Internationalisation enhanced the bargaining power of the MNEs in dealings with governments. Relationships with home governments were increasingly characterised by asymmetrical dependence: MNEs wrested greater autonomy from governments, given the diminishing ability of nationally bounded public authorities to control and influence footloose companies with global reach; and governments became more dependent on MNEs in the formulation and implementation of public policy. Moreover, this shift towards greater MNE power in policy networks was especially observable in the French case: not only had MNE autonomy increased in the 1980s in tandem with lower levels of government intervention; but the influence of the senior management of the firms in a number of public-policy areas and issues also increased. The privatisation of many leading French firms in the early and mid-1990s, including some of the sample of firms studied here, only served to reinforce this trend.

Chapter 5 concentrated on the MNEs' financial function, particularly in so far as it affected their relations with banks and the home governments in Germany and France. The structure of the

French and German financial systems differed, allowing more leeway for government intervention in France than in Germany. The bank–firm relationship was stronger in Germany, given the myriad linkages uniting the universal banks with the large manufacturing firms; whereas the ties between the French MNEs and French banks were more disintermediated. Differences also existed in the financial structures within the firms. The high liquidity and substantial self-financing capacities of the German MNEs contrasted with the debt-reliance of the French MNEs, exacerbated by the limitations of access to private capital as a result of public ownership.

The MNEs gained power in their relations with external actors on financial matters. In the German case, the internationalisation of finance together with the self-financing capability of the German MNEs gave them increased power in relations with the universal banks. French government policy manifested acute sensitivity to the capital needs of the French MNEs, first to restructure in the early 1980s, then to internationalise. Governments relied on financial market deregulation to inject private capital into the state-owned MNEs, setting in train an ongoing and accelerating process of partial and 'backdoor' privatisation. The interlude of the Gaullist-led government saw the full-scale privatisation of CGE in 1987. Creeping privatisation, whether *de facto* or *de jure*, meant that capital markets increasingly displaced the government as ultimate disciplinary and control mechanisms of the firms, and enabled the management of the MNEs to reinforce their autonomy from the government. The 1990s privatisation programme has seemingly brought this process closer to its logical conclusion.

These findings contest theories that postulate the power of the German banks over the large industrial firms; and others that emphasise the power of the government and/or banks over the large industrial firms in the French financial system.

Chapter 6 concentrated on two related cross-border dimensions of political economy: Europe and technology. The accelerated integration of the EC in the mid to late 1980s factored into a number of developments: the geographical expansion of the MNEs in the EC as the core of their internationalisation strategies; the greater European dimension to public policy agendas; and the increase of MNE political activity at the EC level in emerging policy networks and communities. These technology-intensive MNEs also internationalised their research and development functions. Inter-firm research collaboration also increased at the EC level, especially in microelectronics.

Associated with these trends were firm preferences that became more liberal and open-market-orientated with respect to West Europe and North America, given that the MNEs' international-isation was concentrated in these regional cores. Lastly, the political activity of the MNEs at the EC level increased enor-mously during the 1980s. Such activity was particularly evident in the strong policy communities that dealt with R&D pro-grammes such as ESPRIT and EUREKA, in which these and a handful of other European-owned MNEs had privileged and dominant positions in policy formation and execution. These communities provided further evidence of the dependence of public authorities on MNEs in technology matters.

These common trends were limited by French–German dif-ferences. Some of the French electronics MNEs, particularly Thomson and Bull, were competitively weaker than their German counterparts and adopted policy preferences of public promotion and protection at the EC level, especially against competition emanating from Japan and the Far East. There was a similar liberal/protectionist divide on these issue-areas between the French and German governments. Not all differences within and between MNEs on policy preferences and political action were nationally grounded: many resulted from variations between and within the chemical and electronics sectors, the competitive positioning of the individual firms, and the degree of integration and coherence within the firms' organisations – that is, variables of business organisation with political economy implications. Finally, there were French–German differences in firm-level political action at the EC level which replicated differences in MNE action in French and German domestic structures.

This study has therefore sought to uncover and lay bare a complex bundle of continuity and change in the 1980s: inter-nationalisation induced a converging dynamic that influenced the evolution of MNE activity in French and German domestic struc-tures; on the other hand, these differently constituted domestic structures retained some of their enduring, historically conditioned characteristics. The balance between continuity and change differed between Germany and France during the decade. The inter-nationalisation of the German MNEs proceeded at a smoother pace; they remained more competitive; and German domestic structures showed themselves to be more stable and resilient. In short, more continuity was evident in Germany, manifested in government policy, MNE–bank and MNE–government relations, alongside the changes that were detailed. Greater incidence of change was evident in France: in the manner of MNE internationalisation; the shifts of government policy; and the altering power balance in the MNE–government relationship. Such rapid change did not however completely overturn many established policy approaches and reactions. Hence the existence of greater inconsistency and division in France than in Germany: in choosing between market orientation and EC promotion/protection, as a matter of both government policy and corporate strategy; and in the degree of government intervention in the firms, most evident in the issue of privatisation vs. public ownership. It can conceivably be argued, however, that the strands of German continuity were called into question by the fall of the Berlin Wall in 1989, the reunification of the two Germanies and the painful process of transforming the old East German economy and integrating it with West Germany. The bottlenecks and rigidities of a more weakly competitive German *Standort* also became more visible and acute in the early 1990s.

THE NATIONALITY AND/OR COSMOPOLITANISM OF THE MNE

Implicit in this study is what can be termed the Janus-face of the MNE: it is a global actor with representation in many countries and with cross-border production networks, and at the same time is deeply embedded in its home base. This study has shown that the internationalisation of all the MNEs has endowed them with global interests as increasingly cosmopolitan actors, and at the same time made them more important national/regional actors in the areas where international expansion has been focused, especially in the EC but also in North America. Nevertheless these MNEs remain French and German given their strong implantation in their home bases, where value-added is still asymmetrically concentrated and where management control of their international networks resides. What, therefore, is the trade-off between these two aspects concerning the MNEs' cosmopolitanism and national origin?

What it does *not* entail is the following: either a loss of their

Frenchness and Germanness, given the extent and pace of their internationalisation; or the essential retention of such Frenchness and Germanness in its old form before 1980s' internationalisation, only now projected on to the world stage. That trade-off is too simple, too crude and does not accord with the complex reality. The hedged answer to the question posed, it is argued here, is that the firms, both within their organisations and in relation to their external environments, are evolving as multinational actors as a result of a reciprocal interaction between their internationalisation on the one hand, and their embeddedness in French and German domestic structures on the other. To be sure, their Frenchness and Germanness suffer an element of dilution, particularly as their global interests come to the fore, as do their interests as national corporate citizens in their leading overseas markets; and internationalisation, as has been continually emphasised, has worked its way back to change the nature of their behaviour in France and Germany, especially in relating to external actors such as governments and banks. Equally, it has also been underlined that the MNEs' essential Frenchness and Germanness – their peculiar embeddedness in the structures of the French and German political economies – has externalised itself in their increasingly important overseas and cross-border activities: the French MNEs relying on acquisitions abroad just as they have done at home; the German MNEs placing more emphasis on vertical integration, training, quality standards, build-up of long-term market share, and reliance on steadier internal growth abroad, in keeping with well-established domestic procedures. Even in terms of their political functions, such externalisation has occurred at the EC level: the German firms working with their industry associations; the French ones preferring to deal on their own and bilaterally with EC authorities.

Thus there is no straight and simple trade-off, and by extension an inverse correlation, between cosmopolitanism and national origin. MNEs are neither 'national' firms with foreign appendages, nor are they, as Robert Reich seems to argue, relatively undifferentiated global actors who, regardless of national origin, take their mobile resources to the best possible locations.[1] Nationality and cosmopolitanism coexist and interact with each other in myriad forms. More cosmopolitanism and greater identification as European and American actors proceed alongside the maintenance of Frenchness and Germanness, especially in the home

213

bases but also abroad. In contrast to other studies of MNEs, this research effort has continually stressed the importance of the home base as a major determinant of MNE behaviour. MNEs are distinctive in terms of their national origin. And it is this aspect of differentiation among MNEs, arising from their implantation in different national/regional political economies and the manner in which they relate to other actors in their external environments, that gives a cutting-edge to political economy analyses of the multinational firm. For all too often studies in international business organisation and strategy tend to assume, indeed over-estimate, a certain homogeneity among MNEs, regardless of national origin and overlooking differences in the make-up of the domestic structures in which they are embedded.

THEORETICAL IMPLICATIONS FOR THE STUDY OF MICROPOLITICAL ECONOMY

This final section seeks to locate the implications of this study for research in political economy. As was pointed out in chapter 1, political economy scholarship tends to focus on 'what govern-ments do'. This study focuses on 'what firms do' in interaction with other actors, including governments, in the international political economy. The firm is thus the unit of analysis here. Bringing the multinational firm into the heart of political economic analysis is more exigent now than it ever has been. As the report from the United Nations Centre on Transnational Corporations, *The Triad in Foreign Direct Investment*, makes abundantly clear, the global strategies of firms are playing a crucial role in economic development and in shaping the world economy, and are set to play a heightened role in the future. Whereas trade powered international economic growth in the 1950s and 1960s, the inter-national investments, intra- and inter-firm trade, technologies and alliances of American, European, Japanese-owned and other MNEs are acquiring relatively more importance at the end of the twentieth century. The global and regional strategies of firms not only pose challenges for corporate management, but also for governments in managing their economies.[2] The integration of the EC and the increasing European dimensions to public policy are poignant examples of this phenomenon.

The series of relationships between multinationals and govern-ments is perhaps the single most important political economy dimension of the role of MNEs in national and regional economies as well as in the international economy. As Alan Rugman comments: 'The very nature of the MNE makes conflict with government inevitable.' The MNE's objective is to maximise its return – profits, market share – on its firm-specific advantages through international operations in trade, foreign investment and licensing. Sovereign governments, on the other hand, regard the MNE in the context of the broader economic, political, social and cultural goals of the nation-state.[3] The interests of the two sets of actors can be complementary, when MNEs and governments agree on measures which contribute to national competitiveness; or they can conflict, when the global interests of firms diverge from the national priorities of governments. Inevitably, governments and MNEs have to deal with each other: MNEs are important contributors to national wealth and offer the advantages of being global in terms of worldwide market access and leverage of cutting-edge technologies; just as governments modify the strategic options available to MNEs, both in their external environments and with respect to their internal coordination.

Both sides have and activate relative bargaining power in their dealings with each other. Governments are sovereign regulators of the economies in which MNEs operate, they contribute to long-term factor creation and upgrading, are important customers through public procurement, and set product standards; and there are constellations of policy bundles, such as subsidies, tax concessions, credit terms and public ownership, that affect MNEs. But the internationalising firm dilutes the ability of governments to exercise control of it, especially outside the national territorial boundaries where governmental jurisdiction holds sway. When value-adding networks are integrated cross-border within the MNE, there are repercussions in national economies which governments may be able to do little about without endangering the competitive viability of the firm. Thus for governments there is a policy trade-off between the efficiency gains arising from internationalisation and the diminution of control, of the MNE and its environment, that accompanies this process. As far as the MNE is concerned, its bargaining power lies in the firm-specific advantages it commands in product and process technology, manufacturing, marketing, capital, management skills, firm size and worldwide commercial intelligence. Of these it wants to retain in-house control, but governments have to be accommodated on their national economic and non-economic goals if the MNE is to be able to function effectively wherever it operates.[4]

As Susan Strange and John Stopford assert:

> The growth of global competition can be seen as moving the world towards a position where events are conditioned more by an emerging managerial technocracy than by traditional notions of state power. In this new technocracy, firms feature prominently but are only one component of a wider network ... Competition is increasingly among different production and institutional systems and contrasting social organisations.

The differences of MNE embeddedness in domestic structures brought out in this book illustrate the great impact of institutional organisation in international competition. Inter-state competition is part and parcel of this process: British, French and German models of capitalism compete in the ongoing saga of European integration; the *face-à-face* between American, German and Japanese models of capitalism is more sharply observable in the post-Cold War environment.[5] Anchored in emerging structures of such competition are 'triads of relationships' between companies and governments, as Figure 7.1 shows. In the pursuit of global market shares there are growing interactions and forms of collaboration

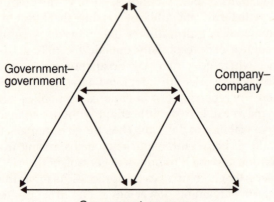

Figure 7.1 Triads of relationships
Source: Stopford and Strange (1990: 22)

between governments and firms, as the magnitude of 'what multi-national firms do' has grown to the point of directly affecting the outcomes of governments' economic policy choices.

For both governments and MNEs, the agenda of their inter-action has shifted with changes in the international political economy. Governments are losing the power to pursue indepen-dent policies; they, like firms, must master the 'new diplomacy' of bargaining, testing the intellectual skills and administrative ca-pacities of both sets of actors, within government bureaucracies as well as within MNE organisations. As Yves Doz argues, this represents a shift from an agenda of regulation (of MNEs by governments) to one of negotiation, in which a recognition of relative bargaining power is more sharply impressed on multiple agendas of interaction.[6]

Future directions for research

The role of the MNE in national, regional and international political economies is more important than ever before. What occurs within firms, and in relations and competition between firms, is a greater determinant of political economy processes and outcomes. Bringing the firm into interdisciplinary research at the crossroads of political economy and business studies calls for fresh conceptualisation, given the inadequacy of existing theoris-ing in economics, political economy and business organisation, and new pastures of empirical investigation. This study has adopted one theoretical framework of the interaction of inter-nationalisation with the embeddedness of MNEs in domestic structures, and applied it to analyse the political economy of a deliberately selected group of French and German MNEs in the 1980s. It should be emphasised that this is just one approach in micropolitical economy as applied to a rather microscopic focus. Interdisciplinary political economy/business studies research should be catholic in encouraging a variety of theoretical ap-proaches on many different empirical foci. But this study is, in the mind of the author, suggestive of further areas of research in the micropolitical economy of the firm, particularly issue-areas of increasing relevance to the 1990s.

First, the broad approach used here can conceivably be applied to MNEs active in different sectors and headquartered in different countries. This study has shown the importance of characteristics that vary between and within the chemical and electronics sectors, leading to differences between MNEs and within MNE organisations. Sectoral variables do matter and affect the business organisation of MNEs. Thus MNEs active in other sectors touched in varying degrees by the globalisation of competition, such as food and drinks, aerospace, cars, any number of service industries (for example, banking, insurance), can be considered.

Equally, the study has emphasised the importance of the MNE's implantation in the domestic structures of the home country. The literature on MNEs, in contrast, almost exclusively focuses on MNEs in host countries and the relations of MNEs with host governments. France and Germany have been the home nation-states at issue here, but other home bases for MNEs can be analysed: within the North American/West European/East Asian Triad, where foreign direct investment is concentrated and whose countries are both source and host to the overwhelming number of the world's leading MNEs; outside the Triad, for example home countries such as India and Brazil which are the launching pads for smaller but newly emergent multinationals; and countries of different size. The latter aspect needs elaboration. US and Japanese MNEs, coming from home markets which are the largest integrated national markets in the world, have been conditioned in different home environments and undergone different paths to internationalisation compared to MNEs from medium-sized countries, especially the UK, France and Germany, which in turn are different from MNEs with small home markets, such as Holland, Sweden and Switzerland. In any case, each country has unique, historically conditioned domestic structures inserted in different ways into the international economy, which in turn leads to inter-country differences in MNE embeddedness in the home bases.

Thus a combination of sectoral and national variables can be used to study the interaction of internationalisation with domestic structures.

Second, it is also valid to analyse the implantation of MNEs in their core overseas markets. This study has shown that the internationalisation of French and German MNEs has been concentrated in other West European markets and in North America. How have these MNEs become 'embedded' in the US and in other member nations of the EC; for example German MNEs in France, French MNEs in Germany? How are they developing as political actors in these markets, especially in terms of their relations with the host governments? How do the domestic structures of these host markets condition the MNEs? What are host government policy approaches towards these foreign-owned MNEs? These vital questions do indeed touch on the issue of the national origin of MNEs. Should public policy deliberately support nationally owned firms to the exclusion of foreign-owned ones operating in the domestic market? Or, as Robert Reich has forcefully argued, should criteria of nationality – where owner-ship lies – be relegated in favour of other criteria which emphasise the value-added contribution of firms, both indigenous and foreign-owned, to the domestic economy?[7] These questions of MNE activity in host-country markets are more important in the 1990s, given the increasing implantation of European, American and Japanese-owned MNEs in each others' markets: for example, the issue of nationality versus value-added contribution criteria lies at the heart of disagreements on promotion and protection of European-owned firms in EC information technology policy, as chapter 6 showed.

Third, MNEs should be studied as specifically political actors in the sense that there should be extensive analysis of their rela-tionships with external actors in policy networks/communities, addressing issues which have some relation to public policy. Relations between multinational firms and industry associations, banks, smaller and medium-sized firms, trade unions and, last but by no means least, governments, should be studied separately (for example, MNE–bank relations, MNE–government relations) and/or collectively (MNE relations with a whole range of external actors). These areas have received far too little attention in any systematic fashion in the existing literature, and the same can be said of the specific 'government relations' function within MNEs. How do different MNEs deal with governments? How is the government relations function organised within the MNE? Are relations with different governments coordinated centrally at headquarters level, or dealt with in a decentralised manner by national subsidiaries on a country-by-country, local-for-local basis? Or is there a detectable trend of mixtures of centralisation and decentralisation, as there is in other functions and parts of the value chain for 'transnationalising' MNEs? And what are the main variables that inform and shape this government relations function (for example, sectoral, sub-sectoral, national origin, path to internationalisation, intra-firm organisational characteristics)?

Such political action on the part of MNEs certainly needs much more study at the level of the European Community, for since the mid-1980s especially European-owned MNEs, but also US, Japanese, South Korean and Taiwanese firms, have rapidly built up a presence in emergent EC policy networks and communities, as chapter 6 portrayed. MNE positions in these networks and their interactions with other actors such as national governments, industry associations, trade unions and supranational authorities deserve special attention.

These then are a number of broad yet reasonably discrete areas in the political economy of the multinational firm that have been identified as fertile plots for future interdisciplinary research by political economists and business organisation specialists in the 1990s. In essence they all boil down to the fundamental interaction between internationalisation and domestic structures, and touch on the question of the MNE's evolving mixture of national origin and cosmopolitan influences. Certainly, conceptualisation and abstraction on the political economy of the firm need to be significantly advanced to keep track of the changing role of the firm in the coming decade. But it is firmly argued here that such theorising can only be of any real utility, for both scholars and practitioners, if it is predicated on solid and wide-ranging empirical research. It is in this spirit that this research effort has been conducted.

NOTES

1 INTRODUCTION

1 For definitions of the MNE and international production, see Rugman *et al.* (1986), p. 7; Dunning (1988), p. 1.
2 Gilpin (1986), p. 11; Strange (1988); Lindblom (1977).
3 Grosse and Behrman (1992), pp. 93–96, 118.
4 Cawson *et al.* (1990), p. 8.
5 On the sociological concept of embeddedness and its application to the MNE, see Sally (1994 a), pp. 167–170.
6 UNCTNC (1991).
7 Julius (1990); Robock and Simmonds (1989); United Nations Centre on the Transnational Corporation (1991); Stopford and Strange (1991), pp. 15–16; Ostry (1992), p. 9.
8 CGE's name was changed to Alcatel-Alsthom in 1990. Given the fact that the name change took place at the very end of the period covered in this study, the company is referred to throughout as CGE.
9 UNCTNC (1991); *The Financial Times*, 29 July 1991.
10 Hymer (1976); Bain (1956); Dunning (1988); Caves (1982).
11 Coase (1937), pp. 386–405; Williamson (1975).
12 See Michalet and Delapierre (1971, 1981); Michalet (1973); Rugman and McIlveen (1985); Group of Thirty (1984).
13 Porter (1986), p. 19; also see Porter's 'Introduction and Summary' in the same volume.
14 Pelkmans and Winters (1988); Hodges, Woolcock and Schreiber (1991), pp. 3–5.
15 Junne and van Tulder (1988), pp. 16–17; Stopford and Turner (1988), pp. 28, 32; on further technological explanations of internationalisation, see Mytelka (ed.) (1990); Williams (1984).
16 On chemicals and biotechnology, see: Junne and van Tulder (1988), pp. 12, 56; Paterson, Grant and Whitston (1988), pp. 4–7, 42; *The Financial Times*, 14 February 1990 (feature on speciality chemicals); 31 August 1990 (survey on the chemical industry); Sally (1993 b).
17 Electronics International Corporation (1989).
18 Junne and van Tulder (1988), pp. 8–12, 36–7; Hodges, Woolcock and Schreiber (1991), pp. 60–61; *The Financial Times*, 20 March 1990; 25

221

August 1990; and 30 August 1990 (features and surveys on the electronics industry); Sally (1993 a).

19 On such 'structuralism' and 'institutionalism', see: Katzenstein (1977), 'Introduction' and 'Conclusion'; Hall (1986), 'Economic Policy and Paradigms of Politics' (chapter 1).

20 The above discussion on interactions between actors in national political economies draws heavily on Wilks and Wright (1987), 'Introduction', pp. 3–6.

21 Ibid., 'Conclusion', pp. 297–299.

22 Paterson, Grant and Whitston (1988), p. 10.

23 Dunning (1992), pp. 162–163; Stopford and Strange (1991), pp. 22, 29, 204–205; Doz (1986), pp. 226, 231, 258.

24 Boddewyn (1988), p. 348; Boddewyn and Brewer (1994).

25 Porter (1990); Albert (1991).

26 The 'Germany' referred to in this book is, of course, the 'West Germany' that existed right throughout the period covered here and up to political reunification in 1990. Then as now, it is the 'Federal Republic of Germany', with five newly constituted federal states as well as Berlin (that is, the old East Germany) joining the eleven states of the former West Germany. 'Germany' instead of 'West Germany' is used in this thesis because it is the term commonly used for the FRG post-reunification.

27 *The Financial Times*, 23 April 1990.

28 On the continuity of cooperational mechanisms in the polity and the economy of the unified Germany carried over from the old West Germany, see Sally and Webber (1994 b).

2 THE INTERNATIONALISATION OF FRENCH AND GERMAN MNEs

1 'Direct investment refers to investment that is made to acquire a lasting interest in an enterprise operating in an economy other than that of the investor, the investor's purpose being to have an effective voice in the management of the enterprise.' This is the broadly accepted IMF definition of foreign direct investment, distinguishing it from portfolio investment, whose intention is to invest without the intention to control or influence production and management. See Julius and Thomsen (1988), pp. 3–4.

2 *The Financial Times*, 27 July 1990; *Le Monde*, 12 September 1990; OECD (1990), pp. 6–7.

3 Juhl (1985).

4 Michalet and Chevallier (1985).

5 Stopford, Dunning and Haberich (1980), company profiles.

6 *Annual Reports* to 1989; Olle and Oesterheld (1985); Oesterheld and Wortmann (1987).

On *Bayer*: *Bayer Berichte* – 'Hermann J. Strenger zur unternehmenspolitischen Themen' (on company strategy), 'Bayer in den USA', Heft 61/1989. On US expansion: *Wall Street Journal*, 14 October 1988; *Börsen*

Zeitung, 14 October 1988; *Frankfurter Allgemeine Zeitung*, 30 December 1988; *The Financial Times*, 29 September 1989; *Handelsblatt*, 1 March 1990. On long-term strategy: *Frankfurter Allgemeine Zeitung*, 11 October 1988 (article by the Bayer chief executive, Hermann J. Strenger).

On *Hoechst*: On US expansion: *Frankfurter Allgemeine Zeitung*, 14 April 1987, 'Forbes Magazine figures list Hoechst as the leading foreign investor in the US, Bayer (4), BASF (18), Siemens (36), Bosch (99)'; 19 June 1989; *The Financial Times*, 4 November 1986 and 1 September 1989. On international expansion and strategy: *Handelsblatt*, 1 March 1990; *Die Neue Ärztliche*, 29 January 1988; *FAZ Blick in die Wirtschaft*, 12 April 1989; *Industrie Magazin*, 1 June 1988.

On *BASF*: On US expansion: *Frankfurter Allgemeine Zeitung*, 5 January and 14 March 1989; *Börsen Zeitung*, 6 April 1990. On international expansion and strategy: *Die Neue Ärztliche*, 9 April 1990; *Süddeutsche Zeitung*, 4 May 1990; *Frankfurter Allgemeine Zeitung*, 5 September 1989, 29 March 1990; *Industrie Magazin*, 1 April 1990.

On *all three firms*: *The Economist*, 19 December 1987, p. 19; *International Herald Tribune*, April 1980 (survey on West German technology) and 17 April 1985 (special report on West Germany); *New York Times*, 28 October 1981; *The Financial Times*, 17 August 1979.

7 Stopford, Dunning and Haberich (1980), company profiles.

8 *Annual Reports* to 1989; on Siemens-Nixdorf: *The Financial Times*, 11 January 1990; *Frankfurter Allgemeine Zeitung*, 23 March 1990.

9 *Annual Reports* to 1989; *Manager Magazin*, 1 November 1989; *The Financial Times*, 16 May 1990.

10 *Annual Reports* to 1989; *Frankfurter Allgemeine Zeitung*, 16 May 1986 (editorial by Dr Jürgen Jeske) and 9 October 1990.

11 *Annual Reports* to 1989.

On *AEG*: *Frankfurter Allgemeine Zeitung*, 21 September 1989.

On *Bosch*: *The Financial Times*, 13 September 1989.

On *Siemens*: *The Financial Times*, 3 March 1989 and 21 June 1990; *Frankfurter Allgemeine Zeitung*, 29 January 1990 (Dr Lorenz Göslich in an editorial).

12 Olle and Oesterheld (1985); Oesterheld and Wortmann (1987).

13 *Annual Reports* to 1989.

On *AEG*: *Frankfurter Allgemeine Zeitung*, 13 December 1989; *Süddeutsche Zeitung*, 8 December 1989; *Handelsblatt*, 19 December 1989.

On *Bosch*: *Börsen Zeitung*, 19 July 1990; *Manager Magazin*, 1 November 1989.

On *Siemens*: *Frankfurter Allgemeine Zeitung*, 12 March 1990; *Manager Magazin*, 1 September 1989; *The Financial Times*, 23 March 1990; *Handelsblatt*, 5 March 1990; *Die Zeit*, 25 August 1989; *Börsen Zeitung*, 10 March 1990. (On GEC-Plessey): *FAZ Blick in die Wirtschaft*, 9 July 1990; *The Financial Times*, 12 January 1990; 15 March 1990; 22 March 1990; 4 April 1990; 3 July 1990.

14 On *Elf* and *Rhône-Poulenc*: *Annual Reports* to 1989; Stopford, Dunning and Haberich (1980), company profiles; *The Financial Times*, 4 January 1990; 5 July 1990 and 12 November 1990.

15 *Annual Reports* to 1989. On *Rhône-Poulenc*: *Informations Chimie*, no. 316, April 1990 (interview with the company chief executive Jean-René Fourtou); *L'Expansion*, 17/30 May 1990; *Chemical Week International*, 14 March 1990; *The Financial Times*, 22 February 1990 and 11 July 1990; *Frankfurter Allgemeine Zeitung*, 22 February 1990.

16 *Annual Reports* to 1989.

On *Rhône-Poulenc*: *C&EN*, 29 January 1990; *The Financial Times*, 20 December 1988; 25 February 1989; 12 September 1989; 21 September 1989; 27 September 1989; 15 December 1989; 20 January 1990; 13 March 1990; 16 March 1990; 7 September 1990; 19 September 1990; *Le Monde*, 25 August 1990; 12 October 1990; *The Economist*, 19 December 1987; *Les Échos*, 14 June 1990.

On *Elf*: *The Financial Times*, 6 August 1981; 24 June 1988; 31 January 1990; 7 September 1990; 10 January 1991; *Le Monde*, 23 July 1981; *International Herald Tribune*, 29 July 1981.

17 Roussel Uclaf: *Annual Report*, 1989.

18 *Annual Reports* to 1989; Stopford, Dunning and Haberich (1980), company profiles.

19 *Annual Reports* to 1989.

On *Thomson*: *The Financial Times*, 7 October 1989; 15 December 1989; 4 January 1990; 9 February 1990; 11 May 1990; 16 May 1990; 16 July 1990; 24 July 1990.

On *Bull*: *Neue Zürcher Zeitung*, 18 January 1990; *The Financial Times*, 18 April 1990; 30 July 1990; 3 October 1990; 8 November 1990; *La Tribune* 19 June 1990; *Le Monde*, 31 July 1990 (interview with Bull chief executive Francis Lorenz); 14 September 1990.

On *CGE*: *Süddeutsche Zeitung*, 24 November 1989; *The Financial Times*, 19 March 1990; 3 April 1990; 5 October 1990; 10 January 1991.

20 On the evolution of company organisational structures and the 'transnational' recentralisation/decentralisation debate, see Chandler and Daems (1980); Dyas and Thanheiser (1976); Bartlett and Ghoshal (1989); Prahalad and Doz (1987).

21 For the organisational developments in the MNEs, see:

On *BASF*: *FAZ Beruf und Chance*, 17 February 1990; *Frankfurter Rundschau*, 12 February 1990.

On *Bayer*: *Wirtschaftswoche*, 15 August 1986.

On *Hoechst*: *Die Welt*, 27 June 1989; *Frankfurter Allgemeine Zeitung*, 19 June 1989; *Manager Magazin*, 1 November 1988; *The Financial Times*, 2 June 1988.

On *Siemens*: *Börsen Zeitung*, 10 March 1990; *Manager Magazin*, 1 September 1989; *Stuttgarter Zeitung*, 2 October 1990; *The Financial Times*, 3 March 1989.

On *Rhône-Poulenc*: *Les Échos*, 14 June 1990.

On *Bull*: *Neue Zürcher Zeitung*, 18 January 1990; *Le Monde*, 14 September 1990; *The Financial Times*, 30 July 1990 and 8 November 1990.

On *CGE*: *Le Monde*, 6 April 1990.

22 See *The Financial Times*, 'Survey on the European Top 500', 11 January 1991.

23 *The Financial Times*, 5 October 1990 (on Siemens-Nixdorf); *Die Zeit*, 5 October 1990 (feature article by Konrad Seitz); Seitz (1990).
24 Anastassopoulos, Blanc and Dussuage (1983), p. 65; Junne and van Tulder (1988), pp. 135–136.
25 Ibid., p. 207.
26 Bain & Company (1989); see also *The Financial Times*, 9 November 1989 and 9 May 1990.
27 DREE/Ministère de l'Industrie (1989).

3 MNEs IN DOMESTIC STRUCTURES

1 Porter (1990), pp. xii, 1, 6, 11, 15, 69, 590, 736.
2 Porter unfortunately conflates nations and firms with the all-embracing term competitive advantage. For a criticism of this, see Samuel Brittan's review in *The Financial Times*, 28 June 1990.
3 Zysman (1983), pp. 146–151, 251.
4 OECD (1990).
5 Jean-Marie Rausch in *Le Monde*, 14 December 1990.
6 Verband der Chemischen Industrie e.V. (1990); Union des Industries Chimiques (1990).
7 'Quels remèdes au deficit industriel?', Lettre d'Information Trimestrielle de la Fédération des Industries Électroniques et Électrotechniques, April 1990 (Paris: FIEE).
8 Dicken (1987), pp. 380–381.
9 Michalet and Chevallier (1985), p. 95; Juhl (1985), p. 133.
10 On the German *Standort* debate, see: Bundesverband der Deutschen Industrie (1988); Biedenkopf und Miegel (1989); Fels (1987); Dyson (1989).
11 See especially the OECD *Economic Outlook* issues of 1988; also OECD (1983).
12 Ibid.; also *Die Zeit*, 27 October 1989.
13 Interview.
14 Interviews; also see *Frankfurter Allgemeine Zeitung*, 13 June 1989; Professor Dr Ulrich Steger in *Die Zeit*, 21 September 1990.
15 Interview; *Handelsblatt*, 27 February 1990; *Frankfurter Allgemeine Zeitung*, 31 August 1989; 5 September 1989; *Die Zeit*, 8 June 1990.
16 *Die Zeit*, 27 October 1989; OECD (1990 and 1991).
17 Porter (1990), pp. 317, 640; Ergas (1984), pp. 22–24, 30.
18 Junne and van Tulder (1988), p. 151; Ergas (1984), p. 28; Maurice, Sallier and Sylvestre (1982).
19 *Annual Reports*.
20 Dyson (1989), p. 154; *Die Zeit*, 27 October 1989.
21 Lesourne (1985), p. 88; Ergas (1984), p. 20; Phau-Khac and Pigelet (1979).
22 Adams (1989), pp. 98–105.
23 Milner (1988), pp. 195–196.
24 See *Economic Outlook*, June 1990 (Paris: OECD).
25 Ergas (1984), pp. 22–24.

26 *Annual Reports; Elf Social Report*, 1989; Junne and van Tulder (1988), p. 113.
27 OECD (1990).
28 For an overview of the historical developments of French and German domestic structures, see Katzenstein (ed.) (1977), 'Conclusion', pp. 323–332.
29 Smith (1986).
30 On the social market economy and the role of the state, see Sally (1994 b).
31 Porter (1990), p. 622.
32 On the structure of German financial markets and bank-industry relations, see Zysman (1983).
33 Markovits and Allen (1989), pp. 292, 298–299, 303; Hall (1986), p. 236.
34 Porter (1990), pp. 103, 105; Katzenstein (1990), 'Conclusion', p. 318.
35 Andrew Shonfield makes the point that the present-day peak associations have a structure modelled by the industrialist Alfred Krupp during the Nazi era: he fashioned them on the lines of an industrial army. Shonfield (1965), pp. 242–243. On industry associations in Germany: Braunthal (1965); Varain (1977); Ehrmann (1980).
36 Katzenstein (1990), 'Introduction', pp. 10–11.
37 Allen (1990), p. 162.
38 Porter (1990), p. 592.
39 Allen (1990), p. 158; Katzenstein (1990), p. 346.
40 Junne and van Tulder (1988), pp. 114, 155, 146–147; Katzenstein (1990), 'Conclusion', pp. 329–330, 333–334.
41 Siemens, notably, has been willing to pay out *Lehrgeld* (learning money) to its US operations for a long period, in the meantime taking substantial losses there. *Frankfurter Allgemeine Zeitung* (editorial), 29 January 1990.
42 Andrew Shonfield drew attention to the extension of time-horizons in the business planning of German firms in the 1960s: his paragon was Siemens. Shonfield (1965), p. 259.
43 Chandler (1990).
44 On these recent trends in German corporatism, see Sally and Webber (1994 b).
45 Machin and Wright (1985). On the structure of the French political economy and the role of the government, see Wright (1983); Katzenstein (1977), 'Introduction' and 'Conclusion'; Zysman (1977); Machin and Hall (1990); Hayward (1973).
46 Suleiman (1974 and 1978).
47 The Bank of France was made formally independent of the Ministry of Finance in 1993 as part of the preparations to move to Economic and Monetary Union under the terms of the Treaty on European Union ratified by the member-states of the EC.
48 Chozel and Payet (1963).
49 Adams (1989), p. 115; Hayward (1986), p. 21; Green (1983), p. 161.
50 See the chapter 'Provincial Pressures in the Jacobin State' in Wright (1983); also Lesourne (1985), p. 87.
51 See *Le Monde*, 20 September, 1990 for an analysis of the Constant

Report; also see Lesourne (1985), p. 57; Lecerf, Drancourt *et al.* (1985), p. 38.
52 Lecerf, Drancourt *et al.* (1985), p. 38; Elf Aquitaine, *Social Report*, 1989.
53 Machin and Wright (1985), 'Introduction', p. 28; Hall (1986), pp. 244, 247–248; Wright (1983), pp. 238–239, 247. On French trade unions in general, refer to Réynaud (1975).
54 See Zysman (1983).
55 Hall (1986), p. 169; Wright (1983), pp. 240, 249; see also Ehrmann (1957).
56 *The Economist*, 'France Peers into the German Soul and its Own', 24 October, 1987.

4 GOVERNMENT POLICY AND MNE–GOVERNMENT RELATIONS

1 On anti-trust and telecom deregulation developments, see Junne and van Tulder (1988), pp. 198, 201.
2 OECD (1989).
3 On *Modell Deutschland*, see Küster (1974), pp. 65–77; Schiller (1968). On promotion of the electronics industry in Germany, see Junne and van Tulder (1988), pp. 159–160.
4 Esser and Fach (1983), pp. 103–111, 120, 125–126.
5 On the structure of the BMWI and its relation to both industry and other ministries, see Paterson, Grant and Whitston (1988), pp. 84–96.
6 Paterson, Grant and Whitston (1988), pp. 264–268.
7 On Daimler-MBB, see *The Financial Times*, 13 September 1989; on Siemens-Nixdorf, *Frankfurter Allgemeine Zeitung*, 13 January 1990 (editorial by Dr Fernando Wassner).
8 Junne and van Tulder (1988), p. 200.
9 Hodges (1989), p. 8.
10 Aujac (1986).
11 *The Financial Times*, 19 February 1990.
12 Cawson, Holmes and Stevens (1987), pp. 12–14, 28; *The Financial Times*, 24 May 1991.
13 *The Financial Times*, 12 December 1989.
14 *International Herald Tribune*, 1 June 1987 (survey on France); for changes in French outward investment policy, see Katzenstein (1977), 'Conclusion', p. 301; Hall (1986), pp. 212–213.
15 Cohen and Bauer (1985), pp. 95–96; Stoffaës (1984), p. 290; *Business Week*, 16 January 1980; *Fortune*, 13 March 1978.
16 *Program Commun de Gouvernement du Parti Communiste et du Parti Socialiste* (Paris: Editions Sociales, 1972).
17 Savary (1984), pp. 159, 163; Webber, Moon and Richardson (1984), p. 39.
18 Cohen and Bauer (1985), p. 88; François Morin, 'Nationaliser', in *Le Monde*, 13 June 1981; Stoffaës (1980 and 1983).
19 Webber, Moon and Richardson (1984), p. 23; Savary (1984), p. 188;

Hall (1986), pp. 205–206; Anastassopoulos, Blanc and Dussauge (1987), p. 40.

20 Savary (1984), p. 165; Cohen and Bauer (1985), pp. 98–99, 101–108.

21 Savary (1984), p. 166; *The Financial Times*, 4 January 1990.

22 Farnoux (1982), especially Annexe VII, 'Les Axes d'une Stratégie Globale'; Savary (1984), pp. 158, 161, 169; Anastassopoulos, Blanc and Dussuage (1987), pp. 8, 122.

23 Interview; also see Hall (1986), pp. 204–205; *The Financial Times*, 21 and 22 July 1982.

24 Wilkinson (1984), p. 53; *The Financial Times*, 13 January 1986.

25 Cohen (1989), pp. 321–323.

26 On the *ni–ni* debate, see *The Financial Times*, 15 December 1989; 19 March 1990 (editorial); 5 April 1991 and 13 September 1991; on Bull-NEC, *The Financial Times*, 15 June 1991.

27 On state aid to Thomson and Bull, see *The Financial Times*, 17 May 1990; 24 July 1990; 12 February 1991; 28 March 1991; 5 April 1991; *Le Monde*, 25 July 1990. On EC constraints on state aid to Thomson, *The Financial Times*, 20 June 1991.

28 SGS-Thomson finally dropped attempts to merge with Siemens, given the latter's opposition and its (Siemens's) developing links with IBM on semiconductors; *The Financial Times*, 15 October 1991.

29 Anastassopoulos, Blanc and Dussuage (1987), p. 181; see also pp. 65, 95, 148–149.

30 Paterson, Grant and Whitston (1988), pp. 1, 10, 309.

31 See *Die Zeit* ('Die Chefs'), 23 March 1990; *FAZ Blick in die Wirtschaft*, 14 March 1989.

32 Bayer *Annual Report*, 1988; Interview; *Die Zeit* (on Bosch), 1 December 1989.

33 See references in notes 7 and 8.

34 Paterson, Grant and Whitston (1988), pp. 44, 59, 62, 66, 71, 84, 286; Hancher and Ruete (1987), pp. 167, 174.

35 See *The Financial Times*, 5 March 1990 and 12 March 1990; *Die Neue Ärztliche*, 14 June 1989.

36 *Annual Reports*, 1988–9.

37 Schneider (1985), p. 182; Paterson, Grant and Whitston (1988), pp. 256–259.

38 *The Financial Times*, 5 and 12 March 1990.

39 On the Siemens policy shift, see Junne (1990), pp. 271–273; Junne and van Tulder (1988), p. 189; Webber (1986); Morgan and Webber (1986), pp. 56–79.

40 Cohen (1989), pp. 36, 245–247; Michalet (1974), pp. 115–125.

41 On *pantouflage*, see Suleiman (1974) and (1978); Thoenig (1973); Barsoux and Lawrence (1990); also see *The Financial Times*, 25 October 1990; Junne and van Tulder (1988), p. 197.

42 Milner (1987), pp. 656–657, 664. On versions of the 'strong' state in France, see Shonfield (1965) and Zysman (1983).

43 On the CGE–Thomson swap in 1983 and the evolution of Alcatel as a commercial and political actor in its home base, see Sally (1993 a).

44 Interviews; see also *The Financial Times*, 1 December 1989; 12 December 1989; 14 December 1989 (review on France); 15 December 1989.
45 Interviews; Hack and Hack (1985), pp. 314–318; *Le Monde*, 10 July 1981, 6 November 1981, 24 February 1989; *Frankfurter Allgemeine Zeitung*, 25 February 1982; *The Financial Times*, 9 July 1981, 25 November 1981.
46 Interviews; *Frankfurter Allgemeine Zeitung*, 12 October 1989, 8 November 1989; *Le Monde*, 26 June 1990; *The Financial Times*, 20 February 1990.
47 Interviews; also see *The Financial Times*, survey on France, 26 June 1990.
48 On the CGE–Framatome affair, see *Le Monde*, 27 June 1990, 18 September 1990; *The Financial Times*, 24 April 1990, 31 October 1990.
49 Interview.
50 Interviews.
51 *Annual Reports*, 1989.

5 THE FINANCIAL FUNCTION AND THE POWER OF THE PURSE

1 See Hu (1984), p. 28.
2 An exception is made for the Allianz insurance company, given its widespread links with large German industrial firms.
3 *Annual Reports*, 1989 and 1990; on Daimler's financial policy, see *The Financial Times*, 6 December 1990; *Handelsblatt*, 5 March 1990.
4 Dyson (1986), pp. 120, 126.
5 Esser (1990), pp. 19–20.
6 Ibid., pp. 25–26; *Die Zeit*, 16 July 1991.
7 Hilferding (1968): 'The mobilisation of capital and the constantly strong expansion of credit gradually but completely changes the hierarchy of capitalist actors. The power of the banks grows; they become the founders and finally the overlords of industry, whose profits they extract for themselves, just as the usurer of old once charged his interest by expropriating a portion of the produce of the farmer and the income of the landlord' (p. 310).
8 Shonfield (1965), pp. 246–255, 261; Hall (1986), pp. 235, 240; Zysman (1983), pp. 260–265; Dyson (1986).
9 Esser (1990), pp. 18, 24–7; Monopolkommission (1977, 1987 and 1988); Bundesminister für Wirtschaft (1979); see also *Frankfurter Allgemeine Zeitung*, 17 May 1990.
10 Chandler (1990).
11 Esser (1990), p. 23; *Frankfurter Allgemeine Zeitung*, 10 April 1990; *Börsen Zeitung*, 6 April 1990; *Manager Magazin*, 1 November 1989; *Annual Reports*, 1988–9.
12 Esser (1990), pp. 23–24; Paterson, Grant and Whitston (1988), p. 120; Interview; also see *The Financial Times*, 5 November 1986 and 17 May 1990.
13 Esser (1990), p. 27; Paterson, Grant and Whitston (1988), p. 120.

14 Esser (1990), p. 27; Grant, Paterson and Whitston (1988), p. 118; Hu (1984), p. 2.
15 On the involvement of the banks in the AEG crises, see Esser and Fach (1983), pp. 118–121.
16 Interviews.
17 Oberbeck and Baethge (1990), p. 280.
18 Zysman (1983), pp. 168–169.
19 Ibid., pp. 104–133; Hu (1984), p. 32.
20 Machin and Wright (1985), p. 10; Hall (1986), p. 217.
21 Hall (1986), pp. 242–243; Zysman (1983), p. 266; Morin (1974).
22 To support this argument on bank–industry relations, see Cohen (1989), pp. 60–63, 106, 109; Cox (1986), pp. 30, 51; Green (1986), pp. 92, 96, 99–100, 102; Lesourne (1985), p. 105.
23 On Thomson–Crédit Lyonnais, see *The Financial Times*, 24 October 1989; interview.
24 See Albert (1991); Sally and Webber (1994 a).
25 Lesourne (1985), p. 56.
26 Anastassopoulos, Blanc and Dussauge (1987), pp. 69, 71, 97–98.
27 *The Financial Times*, 9 November 1989, 10 September 1990; Hall (1986), p. 222; *Annual Reports*, 1988–89.
28 Interview.
29 Anastassopoulos, Blanc and Dussuage (1987), p. 70; *The Financial Times*, 24 October 1989.
30 Hall (1986), pp. 205–206; *The Financial Times*, 7 April 1982; 12 May 1982; 29 May 1982; 23 July 1982; 10 August 1982; 12 November 1982; 10 February 1983; *Le Monde*, 11 April 1982; 12 May 1982; 13 May 1982; 15 May 1982; 9 June 1982; 10 February 1983; 11 February 1983; 19 February 1983; 24 February 1983.
31 Hall (1986), p. 212; *The Financial Times*, 9 May 1985; 24 July 1985; *Le Monde*, 24 July 1985.
32 Hall (1986), p. 212; Green (1986), pp. 94–95, 113; *Le Monde*, 1 March 1985.
33 *Le Monde*, 21 September 1990.
34 *The Financial Times*, 16 September 1985, 25 September 1989; *International Herald Tribune*, 1 June 1987 (survey on France); *Le Monde*, 14 July 1990.
35 *The Financial Times*, 26 June 1990 (survey on France).
36 Ibid.
37 *Le Monde*, 29 September 1990; *The Financial Times*, 18 February 1991 and 13 September 1991; interview.
38 *Le Monde*, 22 February 1991.
39 Cohen and Bauer (1981); Hayward (1986), pp. 34–35. This point of less government control and less MNE financial dependence on the government is made by Lesourne (1985), p. 82 and Michalet (1985 a), p. 176.
40 Interview.
41 Interview.
42 Michalet (1985 a), p. 177.

6 EUROPE AND TECHNOLOGY

1 On the 1992 programme, see Cecchini *et al.* (1988); Pelkmans and Winters (1988); Hodges, Woolcock and Schreiber (1991), pp. 18–20, 25, 66; Economist Advisory Group (1988). On the competition implications of Siemens–Nixdorf and CGE–Fiat, see *The Financial Times*, 12 January 1990 and 25 April 1991.

2 *The Financial Times*, 15 March 1990; 20 March 1990 (survey on European high technology); 24 September 1990.

3 Sharp and Holmes (1989 a), pp. 220–221.

4 Michalet (1990), pp. 47–48; Sharp and Holmes (1989 a), pp. 221, 223.

5 Hack and Hack (1985); Hack (1990); National Academy of Engineering (1987); Doz (1987).

6 *Annual Reports*, 1988–9; Hack and Hack (1985), chapters on Siemens and Hoechst, Bayer, BASF; *Frankfurter Allgemeine Zeitung*, 28 May 1990; *Börsen Zeitung*, 19 June 1990; *Handelsblatt*, 17 March 1990.

7 On the initial moves by Hoechst and Bayer into the US for biotechnology research, and the changes in BMFT policy induced by them, see Junne and van Tulder (1988), pp. 173–174; *The Financial Times*, 4 May 1983 and 12 November 1984; *International Herald Tribune*, April 1982 (survey on West German technology) and 3 April 1984.

8 On the genetic engineering debate, see *Die Neue Ärztliche*, 22 September 1988 and 14 November 1988; *Frankfurter Allgemeine Zeitung*, 23 November 1988 and 13 October 1990; *Handelsblatt*, 18 January 1990 and 31 January 1990; *Die Zeit*, 18 November 1988; *Stuttgarter Zeitung*, 16 November 1989; *Industrie Magazin*, 1 April 1990. On the biotechnology activities of the Swiss MNEs, see Sally (1993 b).

9 On biotechnology in France, see Sharp (1989), pp. 137–155.

10 On biotechnology at the EC level, see Junne and van Tulder (1988), pp. 142, 176–177; *The Financial Times*, 31 January 1990; 4 July 1990 and 29 November 1990.

11 Junne and van Tulder (1988), pp. 164, 208; *Annual Reports* of AEG, Siemens, Thomson and Bull, 1988–9; *Industrie Magazin*, 1 October 1990.

12 Junne and van Tulder (1988), pp. 38, 85; Mytelka (1990 a), pp. 15, 24.

13 *The Financial Times*, 25 July 1990; Electronics International Corporation (1989), pp. 16, 31, 35, 64, 153.

14 Mytelka (1990 b), pp. 190, 192, 204; Junne and van Tulder (1988), pp. 222–224.

15 On the supposed advantages of ESPRIT and EC–US–Japan inter-firm cooperation, see Junne and van Tulder (1988), pp. 41–42, 244–252; Mytelka (1990 b), p. 187.

16 On criticisms of EC R & D collaborative programmes, see Streit (1993), pp. 400–402, 406; Curzon Price (1992).

17 On the EUREKA programme and such inter-firm cooperation in semiconductors and HDTV, see Junne and van Tulder (1988), pp. 223–224, 231; *Börsen Zeitung*, 12 June 1990; *Libération*, 2 July 1990; *Le Monde*, 17 May 1990; *The Financial Times*, 7 November 1989; 26 January 1990; 7 March 1990; 16 May 1990; 17 July 1990; 5 July 1991.

18 Milner (1987), p. 564; and (1988).
19 Cawson *et al*. (1990), pp. 273–275.
20 *The Financial Times*, 29 May 1990 and 27 July 1990 (editorials). On the EC promotion/protection debate in electronics, see *The Financial Times*, 28 February 1990 (Patrick Messerlin on trade and competition policies); 22 October 1990; 31 October 1990 (on the EC Industrial Policies Report); 29 April 1991 (HDTV); *Le Monde*, 21 July 1990; 24 July 1990; French Electronics Industry Report (1988), Introduction by Jean Caillot, p. 6 (French views on the debate). For further criticisms of protection/promotion, see Sharp and Holmes (1989 a), pp. 229–233.
21 *The Financial Times*, 25 September 1990 and 28 September 1990.
22 Delapierre and Zimmerman (1990), p. 105.
23 Cawson (1989), p. 77; *The Financial Times*, 29 May 1990 (editorial) and 29 April 1991.
24 Interviews.
25 *The Financial Times*, 26 September 1990.
26 Paterson, Grant and Whitston (1988), pp. 195–196; interviews; Rhône-Poulenc, *Annual Report*, 1989.
27 On such firm-level political action in the Gyllenhammer *Round Table* and ESPRIT, see Junne and van Tulder (1988), pp. 213–215, 225; Zysman and Sandholtz (1989).
28 Paterson, Grant and Whitston (1988), pp. 182, 195; interviews.
29 Cawson (1989), p. 72.

7 CONCLUSION

1 Reich (1990).
2 United Nations Centre on the Transnational Corporation (1991).
3 Rugman, Lecraw and Booth (1986), p. 253.
4 On the above aspects of the MNE–government relationship, see ibid., chs 11–14; Doz (1986).
5 Albert (1991).
6 Stopford and Strange (1991), pp. 22, 29, 204–205; Doz (1986), pp. 226, 231, 258.
7 Reich (1990 and 1991).

BIBLIOGRAPHY

Adams, William James (1989), *Restructuring the French Economy: Government and the Rise of Market Competition since World War* II, Washington, D.C.: Brookings.

Adams, William James, and Stoffaës, Christian (eds) (1986), *French Industrial Policy*, Washington, D.C.: Brookings.

Albert, Michel (1991), *Capitalisme Contre Capitalisme*, Paris: Seuil.

Allen, Christopher S. (1990), *The Political Consequences of Change: The Chemicals Industry*, in Katzenstein (1990).

Altvater, Elmar (1980), *Deutschland – eine Modellskizze*, in Hannover and Gremliza (1980).

Anastassopoulos, J.-P., Blanc, Georges, and Dussuage, Pierre (1987), *State-owned Multinationals*, New York: IRM/Wiley.

Aujac, Henri (1986), *An Introduction to French Industrial Policy*, in Adams and Stoffaës (1986).

Bain & Company (1989), *France 300*, Rapport pour la Ministère de l'Industrie, Paris.

Bain, J.S. (1956), *Barriers to New Competition*, Cambridge, Mass.: Harvard University Press.

Barsoux, Jean-Louis, and Lawrence, Peter (1990), *Management in France*, London: Cassell.

Bartlett, Christopher, and Ghoshal, Sumantra (1989), *Managing Across Borders: The Transnational Solution*, London: Hutchinson Business Books.

Berle, Adolf (1959), *Power Without Property*, New York: Harcourt, Brace and Co.

Bernholz, Peter (1969), Einige Bemerkungen zur Theorie des Einflusses der Verbände auf die politischen Willensbildung in der Demokratie, *Kyklos*, vol. 22.

Biedenkopf, Kurt, and Miegel, Reinhard (1989), *Investieren in Deutschland*, Stuttgart: Poller.

Boddewyn, Jean J. (1988), Political Aspects of MNE Theory, *Journal of International Business Studies*, vol. 18, no. 3.

Boddewyn, Jean J. and Brewer, Thomas L. (1994), International Business Political Behaviour: New Theoretical Directions, *Academy of Management Review*, vol. 19, no. 1.

233

Boublil, Alain (1990), *Le Soulèvement du Serail*, Paris: Albin Michel.

Braunthal, Gerhard (1965), *The Federation of German Industries in Politics*, Ithaca: Cornell University Press.

Bundesminister für Wirtschaft (1979), 'Grundsatzfragen der Kreditwirtschaft', Bericht der Studienkommission, *Schriftenreihe des Bundesminister für Wirtschaft*, Heft 28, Bonn.

Bundesverband der Deutschen Industrie (1988), *Responsibilities for the Future*, Cologne.

Caves, Richard E. (1982), *Multinational Enterprise and Economic Analysis*, Cambridge: Cambridge University Press.

Cawson, Alan (1989), *The European Consumer Electronics Industry: Corporate Strategies and Public Policy*, in Sharp and Holmes (1989).

Cawson, Alan (ed.) (1985), *Organised Interests and the State*, London: Sage.

Cawson, Alan, Holmes, Peter, and Stevens, Anne (1987), *The Interaction between Firms and the State in France: The Telecommunications and Consumer Electronics Sectors*, in Wilks and Wright (1987).

Cawson, Alan, Morgan, Kevin, Webber, Douglas, Holmes, Peter and Stevens, Anne (1990), *Hostile Brothers: Competition and Closure in the European Electronics Industry*, Oxford: Clarendon Press.

Cecchini, Paolo *et al.* (1988), *1992: The European Challenge*, Aldershot: Wildwood House.

Chandler, Alfred (1990), *Scale and Scope: The Dynamics of Industrial Capital*, Harvard: Belknap Press.

Chandler, Alfred, and Daems, Hermann (eds) (1980), *Managerial Hierarchies: Comparative Perspectives on the Rise of the Industrial Enterprise*, Cambridge, Mass.: Harvard University Press.

Chozel, A., and Payet, H. (1963), *L'Économie Mixte*, Paris: Presses Universitaires.

Coase, Ronald H. (1937), The Nature of the Firm, *Economica*, New Series, 4 November, pp. 386–405.

Cohen, Élie (1989), *L'État Brancardier*, Paris: Calmann Levy.

Cohen, Élie, and Bauer, Michel (1981), *Qui Gouverne les Groupes Industriels?*, Paris: Seuil.

Cohen, Élie, and Bauer, Michel (1985), *Les Grandes Manoeuvres Industrielles*, Paris: Pierre Belfond.

Cox, Andrew (ed.) (1986), *The State, Finance and Industry*, Brighton: Wheatsheaf Press.

Cox, Robert W. (1987), *Power, Production and World Order: Social Forces in the Making of History*, New York: Columbia University Press.

Curzon Price, Victoria (1992), The EEC's Strategic Trade-cum-Industrial Policy: a Public Choice Analysis, in Hilf and Petersmann (1992).

Delapierre, Michel, and Zimmerman, Jean-Benoît (1990), *French Firms in Strategic Partnerships*, in Mytelka (1990).

Dicken, Peter (1987), Global Shift: Industrial Change in a Turbulent World, London: Harper and Row.

Doz, Yves L. (1986), Government Policies and Global Industries, in Porter (1986).

Doz, Yves L. (1987), International Industries: Fragmentation versus Globalisation, in National Academy of Engineering (1987).

DREE/Ministère de l'Industrie (1989), *Où est la Competitivité de la France?*, Paris.

Dunning, John H. (1988), *Explaining International Production*, London: Unwin Hyman.

Dunning, John H. (1992), The Competitive Advantage of Countries and the Activities of Transnational Corporations, *Transnational Corporations* (February), pp. 135–168.

Dunning, John H. (ed.) (1985), *Multinational Enterprises, Economic Structure and International Competitiveness*, New York: IRM/Wiley.

Dyas, Gareth P., and Thanheiser, Hans T. (1976), *The Emerging European Enterprise: Strategy and Structure in French and German Industry*, Boulder, Colorado: Westview Press.

Dyson, Kenneth (1981), The Politics of Economic Management, in Smith and Paterson (1981).

Dyson, Kenneth (1986), The State, Banks and Industry: the West German Case, in Cox (1986).

Dyson, Kenneth (1989), Economic Policy, in Smith, Paterson and Merkl (1989).

Dyson, Kenneth, and Wilks, Stephen (eds) (1983), *Industrial Crisis: A Comparative Study of the State*, Oxford: Robertson.

Economist Advisory Group (1988), *Costs of Non-Europe: Costs of Fragmentation in the EC's Pharmaceutical Industry and Market*, Brussels: European Commission.

Ehrmann, Felix (1957), *Hundert Jahre Verband der Chemischen Industrie*, Frankfurt am Main: Verband der Chemischen Industrie.

Electronics International Corporation (1989), *Electronics in the World: Market–Production–Trade; US–Europe–Japan*, New York.

Ergas, Henry (1984), *Why Do Some Countries Innovate More than Others?*, Brussels: Centre for Policy Studies.

Esser, Josef (1990), Bank Power in West Germany Revised, *West European Politics*, October.

Esser, Josef, and Fach, Wolfgang (1983), 'Social Market' and Modernisation Policy: West Germany, in Dyson and Wilks (1983).

Farnoux, Abel (1982), *Rapport de Synthèse de la Mission Filière Électronique*, Paris: Ministère de l'Industrie.

Fels, Gerhard (1987), Standort Bundesrepublik: die Wettbewerbsfähigkeit der deutschen Wirtschaft, *Volkswirtschaftliche Korrespondenz der Adolf Weber Stiftung*, Nr 7.

Galbraith, John Kenneth (1967), *The New Industrial State*, London: Harmondsworth: Penguin.

Gilpin, Robert (1986), *The Political Economy of International Relations*, Princeton: Princeton University Press.

Green, Diana (1983), Strategic Management and the State: France, in Dyson and Wilks (1983).

Green, Diana (1986), *The State, Finance and Industry in France*, in Cox (1986).

Grosse, Robert and Behrman, Jack (1992), Theory in International Business, *Transnational Corporations*, February, pp. 93–125.

Grou, Pierre (1985), *The Financial Structure of Multinational Capitalism*, Heidelberg: Berg.

Group of Thirty (1984), *Foreign Direct Investment 1973–87*, New York.

Hack, Lothar (1990), Industrieforschung – Vernetzung von globalen und lokalen Formen der Forschungs- und Technologiepolitik, *WSI Mitteilung*, pp. 641–50, October.

Hack, Lothar, and Hack, Irmgard (1985), *Die Wirklichkeit, die Wissenschaft. Zum wechselseitigen Begründungsverhältnis von 'Verwissenschaftlichung der Industrie' und 'Industrialisierung der Wissenschaft'*, Frankfurt am Main: Campus Forschung.

Hall, Peter A. (1986), *Governing the Economy: The Politics of State Intervention in Britain and France*, Cambridge, Mass.: Polity Press.

Hancher, Leigh, and Ruete, Matthias (1987), Legal Culture, Product Licensing and the Drug Industry, in Wilks and Wright (1987).

Hannover, H., and Gremliza, H. (eds) (1980), *Die Linke*, Hamburg: VSA Verlag.

Hayward, Jack (1973), *Governing France: The One and Indivisible Republic*, London: Weidenfeld and Nicolson.

Hayward, Jack (1986), *State and the Market Economy: Industrial Patriotism and Economic Interventionism in France*, Brighton: Wheatsheaf.

Hilf, Meinhard and Petersmann, Ernst-Ulrich (1992), *National Constitutions and International Economic Law*, Amsterdam: Kluwer.

Hilferding, Rudolf (1968), *Das Finanzkapital*, Frankfurt am Main: Europäische Verlagsanstalt.

Hodges, Michael (1989), Making a Reality of the Single European Market: Telecommunications, *Royal Institute of International Affairs*, Discussion Paper 27/6/1989, London.

Hodges, Michael, Woolcock, Stephen, and Schreiber, Kristin (1991), *Britain, Germany and 1992: The Limits of Deregulation*, London: RIIA/Frances Pinter.

Hu, Yao-Su (1984), *Industrial Banking and Specialised Credit Institutions: A Comparative Study*, London: Policy Studies Institute.

Hymer, Stephen H. (1976), *The International Operations of National Firms: A Study of Direct Investment*, Cambridge, Mass.: MIT Press.

Jacquemin, Alexis (ed.) (1984), *European Industry: Public Policy and Corporate Strategies*, Oxford: Oxford University Press.

Juhl, Paulgeorg (1985), The Federal Republic of Germany, in Dunning (1985).

Julius, DeAnne (1990), *Global Companies and Public Policy: the Growing Challenge of Foreign Direct Investment*, London: RIIA/Frances Pinter.

Julius, DeAnne, and Thomsen, Stephen E. (1988), *Foreign Direct Investment among the G 5*, London: RIIA-Chatham House.

Junne, Gerd (1990), Competitiveness and the Impact of Change, in Katzenstein (1990).

Junne, Gerd, and van Tulder, Rob (1988), *European Multinationals in Core Technologies*, New York: IRM/Wiley.

Katzenstein, Peter J. (1984), *Small States in World Markets: Industrial Policy in Europe*, Ithaca: Cornell University Press.

Katzenstein, Peter J. (1987), *Policy and Politics in West Germany: The Growth of a Semi-sovereign State*, Philadelphia: Temple University Press.

Katzenstein, Peter J. (ed.) (1977), Between Power and Plenty: the

Foreign Economic Policies of Advanced Industrial States, *International Organisation*, Special Issue, Autumn.

Katzenstein, Peter J. (ed.) (1990), *Industry and Politics in West Germany: Towards the Third Republic*, Ithaca: Cornell University Press.

Küster, Georg (1974), Germany, in Vernon (1974).

Lecerf, Olivier, Drancourt, Michel *et al.* (1985), *La Dimension Internationale de la Stratégie des Entreprises et la Préparation de l'Avenir*, Paris: Institut de l'Entreprise.

Lesourne, Jacques (1985), *L'Entreprise dans 10 ans*, Paris: Institut de l'Entreprise.

Lindblom, Charles E. (1977), *Politics and Markets: the World's Political-Economic Systems*, New York: Basic Books.

Machin, Howard, and Hall, Peter A. (eds) (1990), *Developments in French Politics*, London: Macmillan.

Machin, Howard, and Wright, Vincent (eds) (1985), *Economic Policymaking under the Mitterrand Presidency, 1981–84*, London: Frances Pinter.

Markovits, Andrei (1986), *The Politics of West German Trades Unions*, Cambridge: Cambridge University Press.

Markovits, Andrei (ed.) (1982), *The Political Economy of West Germany*, New York: Praeger.

Markovits, Andrei, and Allen, Christopher S. (1989), The Trades Unions in West German Politics, in Smith, Paterson and Merkl (1989).

Maurice, M., Sallier, F., and Sylvestre, Jean-Jacques (1982), *Politique d'Education et Organisation Industrielle en France et en Allemagne*, Paris: Presses Universitaires de France.

Michalet, Charles-Albert (1973), *Nationalisation et Internationalisation: Stratégies des Multinationales Françaises*, Paris: La Decouverte.

Michalet, Charles-Albert (1974), France, in Vernon (1974).

Michalet, Charles-Albert (1985), Postface, in Grou (1985).

Michalet, Charles-Albert (1990), Strategic Partnerships and the Changing Internationalisation Process, in Mytelka (1990).

Michalet, Charles-Albert, and Chevallier, Thérèse (1985), France, in Dunning (1985).

Michalet, Charles-Albert, and Delapierre, Michel (1971 and 1981), *La Multinationalisation des Entreprises Françaises*, Paris: CEREM.

Milner, Helen V. (1987), Resisting the Protectionist Temptation: Industry and the Making of Trade Policy in France and the U.S.A. during the 1970s, *International Organization*, Autumn.

Milner, Helen V. (1988), *Resisting Protectionism: Global Industries and the Politics of International Trade*, Princeton: Princeton University Press.

Monopolkommission (1977), Mehr Wettbewerb möglich, *Hauptgutachten der Monopolkommission I*, Baden-Baden: Nomos.

Monopolkommission (1987), *Summaries of the First Five Biennial Reports, 1973–83*, Baden-Baden: Nomos.

Monopolkommission (1988), Die Wettbewerbsordnung erweitern, *Hauptgutachten der Monopolkommission VII*, Baden-Baden: Nomos.

Morgan, Kevin, and Webber, Douglas (1986), Divergent Paths: Political Strategies for Telecommunications in Britain, France and West Germany, *West European Politics*, no. 9, October, pp. 56–79.

Morin, François (1974), *La Structure Financière du Capitalisme Français*, Paris: Calmann-Levy.

Mytelka, Lynn K. (1990 a), Crisis, Technological Change and the Strategic Alliance, in Mytelka (1990).

Mytelka, Lynn K. (1990 b), States, Strategic Alliances and International Oligopolies: the European ESPRIT Project, in Mytelka (1990).

Mytelka, Lynn K. (ed.) (1990), *Strategic Partnerships: States, Firms and International Competition*, London: Frances Pinter.

National Academy of Engineering (1987), *Technology and Global Industry: Companies and Nations in the World Economy,* Washington, D.C.: National Academy Press.

Oberbeck, Herbert, and Baethge, Martin (1990), Computers and Pin-stripes: Financial Institutions, in Katzenstein (1990).

Oesterheld, Werner, and Wortmann, Michael (1987), *Bundesdeutsche Unternehmen im Ausland*, Berlin: The Free University.

Olle, Werner, and Oesterheld, Werner (1985), *Investitionsbelebung, erhöhte Auslandsproduktion und Beschäftigungsstabilisierung in deutschen multinationalen Unternehmen*, Berlin: The Free University.

Organisation of Economic Cooperation and Development (1983), *Positive Adjustment Policies: Managing Structural Change*, Paris.

Organisation of Economic Cooperation and Development (1989), *Review of Industrial Policies 1989*, Paris.

Organisation of Economic Cooperation and Development (1990), *OECD Economic Outlook*, December, Paris.

Organisation of Economic Cooperation and Development (1991), *OECD Economic Outlook*, July, Paris.

Ostry, Sylvia (1992), The Domestic Domain: the New International Policy Arena, *Transnational Corporations*, February, pp. 7–26.

Paterson, William, Grant, Wyn, and Whitston, Colin (1988), *Government and the Chemical Industry: Case Studies from Britain and West Germany,* Oxford: Clarendon Press.

Pelkmans, Jacques, and Winters, Alan (1988), *Europe's Domestic Market*, London: RIIA/Routledge,

Phau-Khac, K., and Pigelet, Jean-Louis (1979), *La Formation et l'Emploi des Docteurs des Sciences*, Paris: Centre d'Etudes et de Recherche sur les Qualifications.

Porter, Michael E. (1986), Competition in Global Industries: a Conceptual Framework, in Porter (ed.) (1986).

Porter, Michael E. (1990), *The Competitive Advantage of Nations*, London: Collier Macmillan.

Porter, Michael E. (ed.) (1986), *Competition in Global Industries*, Cambridge, Mass.: Harvard Business School Press.

Prahalad, C.K., and Doz, Yves L. (1987), *The Multinational Mission: Balancing Local Demands and Global Vision*, New York: The Free Press.

Reich, Robert (1990), Who is Us?, *Harvard Business Review*, January–February.

Reich, Robert (1991), *The Work of Nations: Preparing Ourselves for 21st Century Capitalism*, New York: Alfred A. Knopf.

Réynaud, J.J. (1975), *Les Syndicats en France*, Paris: Seuil.

Robock, S.H., and Simmonds, K. (1989), *International Business and Multinational Enterprises*, Homewood, Illinois: Irwin.

Rugman, Alan, and McIlveen, J. (1985), *Megafirms: Strategies for Canada's Multinationals*, Toronto: Methuen.

Rugman, Alan, Lecraw, Donald, and Booth, Lawrence (1986), *International Business: Firm and Environment*, New York: McGraw Hill.

Sally, Razeen (1993 a), Alcatel's Relations with the French State: the Political Economy of a Multinational Enterprise, *Communications and Strategies*, no. 9 1st quarter, pp. 67–95.

Sally, Razeen (1993 b), The Basle Chemical Multinationals: Corporate Action within Structures of Corporatism in Switzerland, *West European Politics*, vol. 16, no. 4 (October), pp. 561–580.

Sally, Razeen (1994 a), Multinational Enterprises, Political Economy and Institutional Theory: Domestic Embeddedness in the Context of Internationalisation, *Review of International Political Economy*, vol. 1, no. 1, pp. 161–192.

Sally, Razeen (1994 b), The Social Market Economy and Liberal Order: Theory and Policy Implications, *Government and Opposition*, vol. 29, no. 4, pp. 461–476.

Sally, Razeen, and Webber, Douglas (1994 a), *A French Insurance Firm and 'Fortress Germany': The Case of AGF and AMB*, INSEAD case 02/94–4271, Fontainebleau: INSEAD.

Sally, Razeen and Webber, Douglas (1994 b), The German Solidarity Pact: a Case Study in the Politics of the Unified Germany, *German Politics*, vol. 3, no. 1, pp. 18–46.

Savary, Julien (1984), *French Multinationals*, London: IRM/Frances Pinter.

Schiller, Karl (1968), Zukunftsaufgabe der Industriegesellschaft, in Shonfield (1968).

Schneider, Volker (1985), Cooperational and Plurilateral Patterns of Policy-Making for Chemicals Control: a Comparison between West Germany and the U.S.A., in Cawson (1985).

Seitz, Konrad (1990), *Die japanische-amerikanische Herausforderung: die deutsche hoch-technologie Industrie kämpft ums Überleben*, Bonn: Verlag Bonn Aktuell.

Sharp, Margaret (1989), Biotechnology in Britain and France: the Evolution of Policy, in Sharp and Holmes (1989).

Sharp, Margaret, and Holmes, Peter (1989 a), Farewell to the National Champions, in Sharp and Holmes (1989).

Sharp, Margaret, and Holmes, Peter (eds) (1989), *Strategies for New Technologies: Case Studies from Britain and France*, London: Philip Allen.

Shonfield, Andrew (1965), *Modern Capitalism*, London: Royal Institute of International Affairs.

Shonfield, Andrew (ed.) (1968), *Geplanter Kapitalismus*, Cologne: Kiepenhauer und Witch.

Smith, Gordon (1986), *Democracy in Western Germany: Parties and Politics in the Federal Republic*, Aldershot: Gower.

Smith, Gordon, and Paterson, William (eds) (1981), *The West German Model: Perspectives on a Stable State*, London: Frank Cass.

Smith, Gordon, Paterson, William, and Merkl, Peter H. (eds) (1989),

Developments in German Politics, London: Macmillan.

Stoffaës, Christian (1980), *La Grande Ménace Industrielle*, Paris: Livre du Poche, Collections Pluriel.

Stoffaës, Christian (1983), Objectifs Économiques et Critères de Gestion du Secteur Public Industriel, *Revue Économique*, no. 9.

Stoffaës, Christian (1984), French Industrial Strategy in Sunrise Sectors, in Jacquemin (1984).

Stopford, John, and Strange, Susan (1991), *Rival States and Rival Firms: Competition for World Market Shares*, Cambridge: Cambridge University Press.

Stopford, John, and Turner, Louis (1988), *Britain's Multinationals*, New York: IRM/Wiley.

Stopford, John, Dunning, John, and Haberich, Klaus O. (1980), *The World Directory of Multinational Enterprises*, London: Macmillan.

Strange, Susan (1988), *States and Markets: An Introduction to International Political Economy*, London: Frances Pinter.

Strange, Susan (ed.) (1984), *Paths to International Political Economy*, London: George Allen and Unwin.

Streit, Manfred (1993), European Industrial Policy: an Economic and Constitutional Challenge, *Staatswissenschaft und Staatspraxis*, no. 3.

Suleiman, Ezra (1974), *Politics, Power and Bureaucracy in France*, Princeton: Princeton University Press.

Suleiman, Ezra (1978), *Elites in French Society*, Princeton: Princeton University Press.

Thoenig, J.-C. (1973), *L'Ere des Technocrates: Le Cas des Ponts et Chaussées*, Paris: Les Etudes d'Organisation.

Union des Industries Chimiques (1990), *The French Chemical Industry in Figures (1989)*, Paris.

United Nations Centre on the Transnational Corporation (UNCTNC) (1991), *The Triad in Foreign Direct Investment*, New York.

Varain, Heinz-Josef (1977), *Interessenverbände in Deutschland*, Cologne: Kiepenhauer und Witch.

Verband der Chemischen Industrie e.V. (1990), *Chemiewirtschaft in Zahlen 1989*, Frankfurt am Main.

Vernon, Raymond (ed.) (1974), *Big Business and the State*, Cambridge, Mass.: Harvard University Press.

Webber, Douglas (1986), *The Politics of Telecommunications Deregulation in the FRG*, University of Sussex School of Social Sciences Government–Industry Relations Project, Brighton.

Webber, Douglas, Moon, Jeremy, and Richardson, J.J. (1984), State Promotion of Information Technology in France, Britain and West Germany, *Strathclyde Papers on Government and Politics*, no. 33, Glasgow.

Wilkinson, Christopher (1984), Trends in Industrial Policy in the EC: Theory and Practice, in Jacquemin (1984).

Wilks, Stephen, and Wright, Maurice (eds) (1987), *Government–Industry Relations: West Europe, U.S. and Japan*, Oxford: Clarendon Press.

Williams, Roger (1984), The International Political Economy of Technology, in Strange (1984).

Williamson, Oliver E. (1975), *Markets and Hierarchies: Analysis and Antitrust Implications*, New York: The Free Press.

Wright, Vincent (1983), *Government and Politics in France*, London: Hutchinson.

Zysman, John (1977), The French State in the International Economy, in Katzenstein (1977).

Zysman, John (1983), *Governments, Markets, Growth*, Ithaca: Cornell University Press.

Zysman, John, and Sandholtz, Wayne (1989), 1992: Recasting the European Bargain, *World Politics*, October.

NAME INDEX

NAME INDEX

SUBJECT INDEX

244

245